EVERYMAN,
I WILL GO WITH THEE,
AND BE THY GUIDE,
IN THY MOST NEED
TO GO BY THY SIDE

CONFUCIUS

THE
ANALECTS

TRANSLATED BY ARTHUR WALEY

WITH AN INTRODUCTION
BY SARAH ALLAN

EVERYMAN'S LIBRARY

Alfred A. Knopf NewYork London Toronto

184

THIS IS A BORZOI BOOK
PUBLISHED BY ALFRED A. KNOPF

First included in Everyman's Library, 2000
Copyright © the Arthur Waley Estate
The Analects of Confucius, translated by Arthur Waley, first published in
1938 by George Allen & Unwin Ltd., London

Introduction, Bibliography and Chronology © 2000
by Everyman's Library
Typography by Peter B. Willberg and M. J. Tanner
Second printing (US)

US website: www.randomhouse.com/everymans

ISBN: 0-375-41204-2 (US)
1-85715-184-4 (UK)

A CIP catalogue reference for this book is available from the
British Library

Book design by Barbara de Wilde and Carol Devine Carson

Typeset in the UK by AccComputing, North Barrow, Somerset

Printed and bound in Germany by GGP Media GmbH, Pössneck

THE ANALECTS

CONTENTS

Introduction xi

Select Bibliography xxv

Chronology xxix

Translator's Foreword xxxi

Translator's Preface 7

The Analects 73

Additional Notes 223

Textual Notes 241

Index 253

INTRODUCTION

By the middle of the sixth century BC when Confucius was born, China was sliding rapidly towards civil war. It was five centuries since King Wu, continuing the task begun by his father, King Wen, had brought 'all-under-heaven' – that is, most of what we now call China – under the rule of the Chou Dynasty (c. 1100–222 BC). The Chou homeland was in the west (in present-day Shensi Province) and King Wu had enfeoffed his allies and relatives as feudal lords in some seventy states in order to solidify his power. His brother, the Duke of Chou, became lord of the eastern state of Lu (in present-day Shantung Province), and helped to put down the rebellions that still flared up after the establishment of the dynasty.

When King Wu died, his son, King Ch'eng, was still a child, so the Duke of Chou ruled on his behalf, as his regent. When the young king reached maturity, the Duke restored the throne to him, thus ensuring the continuity of the dynasty – and his own reputation throughout Chinese history as the archetype of the virtuous minister. The Chou Dynasty prospered until 771 BC when tribal incursions forced them to move their capital from near present-day Sian eastward along the Yellow River Valley to Loyang. From that time on, Chou power declined and that of the feudal lords increased. Moreover, the larger states began to engulf the smaller ones, so that in Confucius' lifetime, only about ten states remained.

Confucius (551–479 BC) was in many regards a surprising person to have so influenced the course of civilization that the cultures of China, Japan and Korea are, even today, characterized as 'Confucian'. He was not a religious figure – he refused to discuss gods, miraculous events, or life after death, observing that until we know about life, we cannot hope to understand death. His life story was also undramatic. His ambitions were political, but he achieved only minor office. The son of an impoverished branch of a minor aristocratic family, he travelled from state to state hoping to achieve influence. Although he encountered some hostility on his journeys, he was mostly ignored, neglected or mocked, rather than persecuted, and he died of illness in his early seventies.

Moreover, Confucius left no great works of literature. He probably edited a dry year-by-year chronicle of Lu, his native state, known as the *Spring and Autumn Annals* (*Ch'un-ch'iu*), changing the occasional word so that the events described had the appropriate moral implications. He is also associated with the *Book of Changes* (*I Ching*), and may have been interested in it in his old age, perhaps even writing one of the commentaries, but this association remains problematic. He often quoted from the *Book of Songs* (*Shih Ching*) and he may have taken part in the selection of a little more than three hundred verses from a larger corpus. He also liked to quote the *Book of History* (*Shu Ching*), but there is no evidence that he took any direct part in its compilation.

Confucius did, however, teach, and after his death, he left a small group of devoted disciples. The *Analects*, which are translated here by Arthur Waley, were written by those disciples and their own followers. After Confucius died, his students put together their records of things that he had told them, including some of their observations about his behaviour, to make the book that we now have. This process took place over a period of generations, possibly centuries – exactly how long is a matter of dispute. The work that resulted is what we now call the *Analects*.

The Chinese title of this work is *Lun Yü. Lun* means 'selected'. *Yü* means 'words' or 'statements' and the book consists largely of short statements prefaced by the words 'the master said'. The title is often translated as 'Sayings of Confucius'. Because educated Chinese memorized this book for two millennia, many of the passages in it have become sayings. However, they were not sayings when they were first written down, but statements that Confucius made to his disciples on particular occasions, often in answer to their questions. The *Analects* also includes some of the disciples' own statements, as written down by their own followers.

The *Analects* was a book that people studied and meditated on line by line over the course of a lifetime, not one that they simply sat down and read, as we do today. It consists of short passages in an apparently random order. Originally, these passages would have been used by Confucius' disciples when they taught their own students. They would expound upon them orally, explaining their original context and larger meaning as they passed them down to the next generation. In later times, as the distance from the master became greater and the language harder to understand, the text of the *Analects* was accompanied by written commentaries. These traditional commentaries are the primary source of Waley's extensive notes to his translation (see Appendix 1) and they are the basis of all modern understanding of this work.

The language in which the *Analects* is written – classical Chinese – has a relationship to modern Chinese analogous to that of Latin to a modern Romance language, such as Spanish or French, and most literature was written in classical Chinese until the early twentieth century, just as Europeans wrote in Latin in pre-modern times. One advantage of the Chinese writing system over a phonetic system, such as our alphabet, is that the characters in ancient texts can be read with modern pronunciations, so that Chinese today have more ready access to their historical literature than Europeans. Many of the passages in the *Analects* have become proverbs used in daily speech and no one has difficulty understanding them.

Nevertheless, the language has changed. Whereas classical Chinese was largely monosyllabic, with each word represented by a character, modern Chinese is largely polysyllabic, with each syllable of a word represented by a character. Some characters have dropped out of use and others have changed their meaning over time. The *Analects* are also a very laconic text, so there is very little context and that often makes interpretation difficult. For example, the *lun* of *Lun Yü* could be interpreted as 'discussed'. This is its most common meaning, and it would make sense, but the early commentators explain it as a word that had the same pronunciation but is usually written with a slightly different character, meaning 'selected', and this interpretation is generally accepted.

Confucius was the first philosopher of ancient China in the sense that he was the first thinker to form a school of followers who studied with him and passed his ideas down to later generations. Although he was not notably successful during his lifetime, Confucius began to dominate the intellectual life of ancient China soon after his death. His followers split into eight competing groups. Little has passed down to us from the period between Confucius and his most important follower, Mencius (*fl.* fourth century BC), though the discovery in 1993 of a group of philosophical texts written on strips of bamboo from a fourth-century BC tomb near Kuo-tien (Guodian) in Hupei Province includes material that some scholars identify as the lost book of Confucius' grandson Tzu Ssu and other related material. As yet unpublished material from a robbed tomb, thought to be in the same region, now in the collection of the Shanghai Museum, promises to shed further light on this early period in the development of Confucianism.

By the fourth century, Confucius' status among his followers was such that Mencius declared, 'Ever since people came into this world, there has never been anyone greater than Confucius' (*Mencius* IIA.2). However, the best evidence for Confucius' stature in this period comes from the vehemence with which the competing philosophical schools criticized him. The period of civil war, which ensued when the feudal lords began to refuse to recognize Chou suzerainty in the centuries following Confucius' death, was traditionally called the Warring States Period (480–222 BC). During this period, 'one hundred schools' of philosophy also contended for supremacy, and the thinkers travelled from state to state, each offering his own key to peace, political power, or, at least, survival.

All of these schools took Confucius and his followers as their primary target. For example, Mo Tzu, who advocated love for all, without discrimination according to kinship, and promotion according to merit, blamed the Confucians for elaborate rites and expensive funerals that depleted the public purse. The Taoist Chuang Tzu (or his disciples) mockingly put his own words praising Lao Tzu into the mouth of Confucius and derided the Confucians for wearing ridiculous antiquated clothing. The Legalist Han Fei Tzu, who wanted to bolster the power of the ruler with a strict code of reward and punishment, warned against the Confucian tendency to place their own moral judgments above the statutory edicts of the ruler.

Historically, Confucius' most influential followers were Mencius and Hsün Tzu (310–219 BC). Mencius' own words were collected by his disciples shortly after his death in a book that bears his name. The passages in the *Mencius* are longer, with more indication of their context, than those in the *Analects*. Hsün Tzu, fifty years or so later, authored his own work and developed his themes in an ordered manner, sometimes disagreeing explicitly with the earlier philosopher. Mencius, however, was ultimately the most influential of the two. Indeed, with its longer, more easily understood passages and more developed arguments, the *Mencius* was almost as influential as the *Analects*.

Although Confucius clearly believed that people could perfect themselves and that people with greater moral force could influence others, the question of whether human nature was good or bad does not seem to have arisen in his time. He remarked only that people are by nature similar, but far apart in actual practice (XVII.2). By the fourth century BC, however, this had become one of the most hotly debated questions among early Chinese philosophers and the various Confucian schools took different stands. Mencius argued that human nature is good. By this he meant not that people are good, but that they have the inherent tendency to be so. Thus, for example, anyone, seeing a child about to fall in a well, will instinctively act to save him or her. If people are not good, it is because of the depravity of society and they would become good if there were a good king whose government fostered this natural tendency.

Hsün Tzu, on the other hand, argued that human nature is bad. If people are good, it is because the ancient sage kings created cultural forms, such as literature and ritual, which taught them how to be good. Human appetites are the same as those of the animals, and left to themselves, they would behave in the same manner. In other words, goodness is learned behaviour, not natural. Although Hsün Tzu's understanding of ritual – as a means of inculcating values and teaching people to behave in a socially beneficial manner – is based upon the *Analects*, his emphasis on external behaviour led directly to the Legalist idea that people could be manipulated by codes of reward and punishment to the benefit of the ruler, rather than trained to act morally.

The Legalists won the battle, but only briefly. In 221 BC, the far western state of Ch'in united the land under the rule of the 'First Emperor', Ch'in Shih Huang Ti. The First Emperor was a militaristic autocrat who standardized the measurements, reformed the script and built the Great Wall. Today, he is also well known because archaeologists have excavated pits surrounding his tomb that contain an entire army of life-size terracotta soldiers, meant to protect him from his enemies after death. In an attempt to eradicate any challenge to his authority, he ordered the burning of the Confucian books, and all other works that had no practical function, and the live burial of the Confucian scholars. Nevertheless, the rule of Ch'in collapsed soon after the First Emperor died in 209 BC, probably from ingesting an elixir of immortality made of cinnabar.

To Confucianists, the story of the rebellion that led to the fall of the Ch'in and the establishment of the Han Dynasty (206 BC–AD 220) was an exemplary tale that demonstrated the superiority of moral training over coercion. According to the Ch'in legal code, an officer who was late in performing his duties was executed. Thus, when an officer who was moving a group of convicts from one place to another found that he was late, he released them and started a rebellion that led to the collapse of the Ch'in Dynasty. If the emperor had inculcated loyalty by humaneness, rather than attempting to control his people with draconian punishments, the Ch'in Dynasty might not have been so short-lived.

The new Han emperor was an uncouth man who conquered with military force, not the moral suasion recommended by Confucius, and he was initially no more Confucian than the Ch'in rulers. Once in power, however, like the emperors who founded the successive dynasties throughout Chinese history, he found that he needed to give his court ritual authority and an aura of legitimacy. Advised that, although the Confucians were not good at warfare, they were useful in maintaining and developing a state, he appointed specialists in the rites from Confucius' native state of Lu.

During the Han Dynasty, Confucianism became the orthodox philosophy of the state and the Confucian canon – the *Book of Songs, Book of History, Record of the Rites, Spring and Autumn Annals, Book of Changes*, and the no longer extant *Book of Music* – were designated classics, the core texts in the training of all aspiring officials. During the Confucian renaissance that took place during the Sung Dynasty (AD 960–1279), the neo-Confucian philosopher Chu Hsi (AD 1130–1200) expanded the list, giving the *Analects* prime importance, with a new commentary that he wrote himself. These then became the basis of all education.

As Arthur Waley observes, there were three versions of the *Analects* in circulation at the end of the Han Dynasty. In 1973, a version of the *Analects*, written with a brush on slips of bamboo, as was the custom at that time, was excavated from a tomb that was closed in 55 BC at Ting-chou in Hopei Province. The tomb had been robbed, probably in ancient times, and the text was badly damaged. Only about half remained, but many scholars believe that this bamboo slip text is the lost Lu version, the major source for the version of the text that became the standard edition (known as the Marquis Chang edition). Although there are many minor differences between this text and the standard edition, this discovery demonstrates that by the first century BC, the *Analects* had already reached a form much like the one that we read today.

Confucius claimed that he only transmitted what had been taught to him and that he did not make anything up (VII.1). This is undoubtedly true in the sense that his terms and ideas all find their sources in an earlier tradition. Nevertheless, he transformed the religious tradition that he had inherited into an ethical system, giving the ritual structures of ancient times an entirely new meaning. In so doing, he established the concerns of Chinese philosophical discourse that persisted throughout Chinese history. In this, he resembled Plato or Aristotle. The world-view from which he began, however, was very different from that of the ancient Greeks.

The essence of native Chinese religion, often called

'ancestor worship', was that people continued to need food after death and to exercise power over the living. These beliefs are already found in the earliest extant Chinese texts, divination inscriptions on bone and shell, usually called 'oracle bone inscriptions', from the Shang-Yin (or Shang) Dynasty (c.1700–1100 BC). These record divinations made by the Shang-Yin kings about the schedule and content of elaborate ritual sacrifices which they made to their ancestors. The Shang-Yin ancestors could not only curse their descendants personally, they could also affect the entire realm which they ruled by cursing the weather and harvest. There were also nature spirits, such as those of the mountains and rivers, to which the Shang-Yin kings made offerings.

At the top of this scheme was a shadowy figure known as Shang Ti, or simply Ti. The Shang-Yin kings did not make offerings directly to Shang Ti, and he does not appear to have been an ancestor of their own, but their own ancestors were able to intercede with him on their behalf. Arthur Waley makes the plausible suggestion that Shang Ti was probably the Supreme Ancestor and that T'ien, 'Sky' or 'Heaven', which is used interchangeably with Shang Ti in the Chou Dynasty, was a collective term referring to the ancestors who dwelt there. Here, it is important to remember that, in spite of Waley's use of 'God' in his translation of the text, Shang Ti was not a creator God or a transcendent deity in the manner of the great monotheistic religions, but an impersonal force equated with the sky. Moreover, there were no heavens and hells before the introduction of Buddhism in the Han Dynasty, which could serve to reward or punish people after death.

Religion in ancient China had very little to do with morality. Nor was there a sphere of absolute transcendence that could be contrasted with the temporal world. The ancestors were the progenitors of living persons and still tied to them through kinship and ritual. In the Shang-Yin Dynasty, the primary role of the court was to perform the rites of exchange with the ancestors that would appease their anger and ensure the prosperity of the land. In the early Chou period, these rites were extended further with the exchange of ritual offering vessels in a court setting. Confucius, however, gave the rites a new meaning, as cultural forms which expressed the appropriate relationships between all people within society.

Human society, in Confucius' view, was based on the instinctive love between children and their parents. Filial piety thus became more than the offering of ancestral sacrifices, though it continued to encompass these offerings and the rites that accompanied them. It was also the offering of love and respect to one's parents, and by extension to all elders and superiors. Conversely, parents also love and nurture their children and this relationship was the model for good government. Confucius hoped that if one of the feudal rulers could be persuaded to govern in a humane manner, as the kings of ancient times had done, he would receive the mandate of Heaven, and bring society back to its natural, ordered state. An important aspect of this model, which is hierarchical rather than egalitarian, is that there is no divine right. Only the humane ruler who nurtures his people is a legitimate king.

Confucius also expanded the idea of nobility from its hereditary foundation to nobility of behaviour. Thus, he used the term *chün-tzu*, which originally meant 'son of a lord', to refer to anyone who behaved according to the way of a gentleman, that is, in a manner appropriate to noble status, regardless of his family origin. Moreover, he argued that names must be used 'correctly'. Even if a person was the son of a lord, he was not a *chün-tzu* unless he behaved as such. In this apparently linguistic reform lay the suggestion for a radical restructuring of society. The rites, and the attitudes of respect and consideration that ritual fostered, were the means by which one became such a gentleman.

Ritual was thus transformed from prescribed rules appropriate within a ceremonial or religious context into the means by which a person learned how to be human in the fullest sense. Confucius offered an ethic for the organization of human society. More precisely, he offered an explanation of how and why the rulers of ancient times had governed so perfectly that all society was at peace, and the individuals within it were able to fulfil their personal potential without resentment. That Confucius took the ancient rulers as the source of his moral code is a further reflection of the importance of native Chinese religion, in which ancestors served the role of gods, to his thought.

The past in the *Analects*, as in other texts of the period, began not with a creation myth, but with an era of perfect rulers. The first of these was the sage, Yao, who was as sublime as the sky (VIII.19), but had an evil son; so he appointed his minister, Shun, to succeed him. Shun's moral force (*tê*) was so great that he had only to 'place himself gravely and reverently with his face due south' (XV.4) for the empire to be well governed, but he too rejected his son(s) as inadequate, and appointed his minister Yü, who was 'flawless' (VIII.21).

Yü, who is mentioned only briefly in the *Analects* as 'draining and ditching' (VIII.21), is described in other texts as a mythical figure who drained the riverbeds and built up the mountains, ridding the world of its excess water. According to Chou tradition, Yü was the founder of the first hereditary dynasty, the Hsia. The Hsia kings passed down the rule until the last Hsia ruler so oppressed the people that he was overthrown by T'ang, the founder of the next dynasty, the Shang-Yin, assisted by his wise minister Yi Yin. The Shang-Yin (or Shang) Dynasty was also hereditary until its rulers became tyrannical and the last Shang-Yin king was overthrown by the Chou.

Archaeological excavation has yielded a rich mosaic of Neolithic and early bronze age finds throughout China, but the earliest excavated texts are divination inscriptions from the middle of the Shang-Yin Dynasty. These inscriptions and extensive archaeological excavations have confirmed the history of the Shang-Yin, though how the historical records concerning the period before the Shang-Yin relate to the material evidence from archaeological excavation is still a matter of dispute. One reason for this dispute is that the historical records have a clear ideological bias. To Confucius, history had a pattern. He assumed that the cosmos has an inherent moral order – that is, the Way (*tao*) of Heaven (*t'ien*) is a moral one and Heaven responds to virtue or 'moral force', as Waley aptly translates the Chinese term *tê* – but that it was also subject to change.

The idea of a changing mandate of Heaven in which

degenerate hereditary rulers are replaced by kings who accord with the will of Heaven – that is, rule humanely for the benefit of the people – is commonly attributed to Confucius' hero, the Duke of Chou. According to this theory, in the pre-dynastic period, sage rulers appointed virtuous ministers as their successors; in the dynastic period, hereditary rule was founded by a good king with the assistance of a virtuous minister and faltered when the kings oppressed the people and lost the mandate of Heaven. The more ancient the period, the more perfect the model, but Confucius despaired of ever knowing enough about any period earlier than the Chou.

According to Confucius, 'Heaven does not speak, yet the four seasons run their course thereby' (XVII.19). History too had its seasons and dynasties ran their course, to be replaced by other dynasties. In Confucius' time, it had already been five hundred years since the founding of the Chou Dynasty, and so he could reasonably hope to find a ruler whom he could assist in founding a new dynasty. It is possible that Confucius hoped to become a king himself, as some have suggested, but the tone of the *Analects* suggests that his aim was to play the role of virtuous minister rather than that of founding king. He cultivated himself as a gentleman and trained his disciples to act with ritual correctness as subjects. There is no evidence that he aspired to be more than the virtuous minister who enabled a hereditary lord to found a new dynasty.

If the time is not right, then there is little that even a sage can do. The omens that might portend a new dynasty – the river map or the phoenix – never appeared in Confucius' lifetime. This was the tragedy of Confucius' life – being born at the wrong time – and a sense of poignancy pervades the *Analects*. This is not the tragedy of the Greek hero who was predestined to fail. Nor is it that of Job, whose faith was tested by a wilful God. It is simply the recognition that our lives all depend upon the time in which we are born, even that of a man like Confucius, and if the season is wrong, no matter how hard we try, we cannot succeed.

For more than two millennia, from the beginning of the Han Dynasty until the end of the Ch'ing in 1911, Confucianism served virtually unchallenged as the foundation for the moral principles that governed Chinese society and the Chinese state. In recent years, as the ideological influence of communism has diminished, many Chinese have once again begun to look to Confucianism as a means of revitalizing their culture. Which aspects of Confucianism are essential, which worth preserving, and which to be discarded as archaisms, inherent in a traditional society but no longer applicable in a modern context, are questions that remain to be resolved, not only in China, but in all of the East Asian cultures within the sinitic sphere of influence.

To the Westerner who wishes to understand China or, indeed, Japan, Korea or Vietnam, an understanding of Confucian philosophy is a necessary key. But Confucius and his *Analects* offer more than a key to understanding East Asian cultures. They have something more to teach us, simply as people living in the world, about how a person may conduct his life, something that is not particular to time or place, nor dependent upon any fixed set of beliefs. This is simply that to be good is to fulfil our potential as humans. It takes effort – we must not only learn from those who came before us, but also think for ourselves – and there may be no rewards for that effort in this world or the next, but it is a pleasure in and of itself and all society is the beneficiary.

*

Arthur Waley (1890–1966), whose translation of the *Analects* follows here, was the most influential translator of Chinese and Japanese literature in the twentieth century. He is best known for his translations of Chinese poetry and for his magnificent translation of the *Tale of Genji* from the Japanese. His Chinese and Japanese were both self-taught and although he worked for many years in the British Museum, he was not a trained scholar. His milieu was Bloomsbury – Edith Sitwell included him among *Some English Eccentrics* – not the academy, and he took pride that his translations were always written for a general rather than a specialist audience. One reason for the success of his translations is that he attempted to re-create the sense of the original work, not simply render its literal meaning.

The *Analects* is the most scholarly of Waley's translations, extensively footnoted, with an excellent Introduction, Appendices and Textual Notes, all of which have been included here. Like most sinologists who began their studies in the 1960s, I was introduced to Chinese literature by Waley's translations, which have been one of my inspirations. I read almost everything that he had translated, including the *Analects*. Nowadays, the study of early Chinese philosophy is a much more sophisticated field than it was when Waley translated the *Analects* in 1934 and, because of extensive archaeological excavations, we know much more about the history of ancient China than anyone did almost seventy years ago. Having found that some of Waley's translations, such as those of early *yüeh-fu* poetry, beautiful as they remain, include significant misreadings, I was surprised and delighted, on rereading the *Analects*, to discover that the fresh intelligence and simple good sense with which he approached the text is combined with a profound erudition and impeccable scholarship. This is not only a work of historical importance, but one that still accomplishes what it set out to do when it was first written.

Sarah Allan

SELECT BIBLIOGRAPHY

OTHER TRANSLATIONS OF THE 'ANALECTS'

AMES, ROGER T. and HENRY ROSEMONT, JR., *The Analects of Confucius: A Philosophical Translation. A New Translation based on the Dingzhou fragments and other recent archaeological finds*, Ballantine, New York, 1994. Based upon a manuscript found in a first-century BC tomb in Shantung Province.

BROOKS, E. BRUCE and TAEKO BROOKS, *The Original Analects: Sayings of Confucius and his Successors*, Columbia University Press, New York, 1998. Attempts to establish a chronological sequence for all the chapters of the *Analects*.

DAWSON, RAYMOND, *Confucius: The Analects*, Oxford University Press, Oxford, 1993.

HINTON, DAVID, *The Analects of Confucius*, Counterpoint, Washington, D.C., 1998. Highly readable translation.

LAU, D. C., *Confucius: The Analects*, Penguin, Harmondsworth, 1979. Often cited as a standard translation. A revised edition with accompanying Chinese text, was published by the Chinese University of Hong Kong Press, 1992.

LEGGE, JAMES, *The Chinese Classics*, v. 1 (*Confucian Analects, Great Learning and The Doctrine of the Mean*), 2nd rev. ed., Clarendon Press, Oxford, 1893. Over one hundred years old, but still frequently cited.

LEYS, SIMON, *The Analects of Confucius*, W. W. Norton & Co., New York, 1997, Very readable translation.

POUND, EZRA, *Confucius*, New Directions, New York, 1951. Interesting, but Pound could not read Chinese.

TRANSLATIONS OF RELATED TEXTS

AMES, ROGER T., *Sun-tzu: The Art of Warfare. The First English Translation Incorporating the Recently Discovered Yin-ch'ueh-shan Texts*, Ballantine, New York, 1995. Classic of military philosophy.

GRAHAM, A. C., *Chuang Tzu: The Inner Chapters*, George Allen & Unwin, London, 1981. Excellent translation of this enjoyable Taoist classic.

HENRICKS, ROBERT G., *Lao-tzu's Tao-te Ching: A Translation of the Startling New Documents Found at Guodian*, Columbia University Press, New York, 2000. The first translation of an early version of the text found in a fourth-century BC tomb.

KNOBLOCK, JOHN, *Xunzi: A Translation and Study of the Complete Works*, Stanford University Press, Stanford, 1988 (volume 1), 1990 (volume 2),

1992 (volume 3). Scholarly translation of the important Confucian work by Hsün Tzu.

LAU, D. C., *Lao Tzu: Tao Te Ching*, Everyman's Library, New York, 1994. Introduction by Sarah Allan. Tranlation based upon the manuscripts found in a second-century BC tomb at Changsha Ma-wang-tui.

LAU, D. C., *Chinese Classics: Tao Te Ching*, Chinese University of Hong Kong Press, 1982. This edition includes translations of both the traditional Wang Pi and excavated Ma-wang-tui editions with accompanying Chinese text.

LAU, D. C., *Mencius*. Penguin, 1970. Excellent, scholarly translation, with a fine introduction. Revised edition, with acompanying Chinese text, published by the Chinese University of Hong Kong Press, 1984.

LAU, D.C. and ROGER T. AMES, *Sun Pin: The Art of Warfare. A comprehensive translation of the fourth-century BC Chinese military philosopher and strategist*, Ballantine, New York, 1996. Newly discovered text by a fourth-century BC descendant of Sun Tzu.

LYNN, RICHARD JOHN, *The Classic of Changes: A New Translation of the I Ching as Interpreted by Wang Bi*, Columbia University Press, New York, 1994. Reliable translation of the *I Ching* as understood by the Han Dynasty commentator.

NIENHAUSER, WILLIAM H. JR., *The Grand Scribe's Records*, Indiana University Press, Bloomington, 1994. Scholarly translation of the great historical work, Ssu-ma Ch'ien's *Shi-chi*.

WALEY, ARTHUR, *The Book of Songs*, Grove Press, London, 1937.

FURTHER READING

ALLAN, SARAH, *The Heir and the Sage: Dynastic Legend in Ancient China*, Chinese Materials Center, San Francisco, 1981. Analysis of the conflicting themes of rule by heredity and rule by virtue in early philosophical texts.

ALLAN, SARAH, *The Shape of the Turtle: Myth, Art and Cosmos in Early China*, State University of New York Press, Albany, 1991. Reconstruction of various aspects of Shang Dynasty thought.

ALLAN, SARAH, *The Way of Water and Sprouts of Virtue*, State University of New York Press, Albany, 1991. On the root metaphors of early Chinese philosophical concepts.

ALLAN, SARAH and CRISPIN WILIAMS, ed., *The Guodian Laozi: Proceedings of the International Conference, Dartmouth College, May, 1998*, Institute for East Asian Studies, Berkeley, 2000. Discussion of the *Lao Tzu* and other early texts found in a fourth-century BC tomb.

FINGARETTE, HERBERT, *Confucius: The Secular as Sacred*, Harper Torchbooks, New York, 1972. Influential analysis of the *Analects*.

SELECT BIBLIOGRAPHY

FUNG YU-LAN, *A Short History of Chinese Philosophy*, trans. Derk Bodde, Macmillan, New York, 1958. Straightforward history of early Chinese philosophy. Dated, but still useful.

GRAHAM, A. C., *Disputers of the Tao: Philosophy and Philosophical Argument in Ancient China*, Open Court, La Salle, Illinois, 1989. The most important work on early Chinese philosophy in the last fifty years.

HALL, DAVID and ROGER T. AMES, *Thinking Through Confucius*. State University of New York Press, Albany, 1987. Important study of the *Analects* in the context of comparative philosophy.

HALL, DAVID and ROGER T. AMES, *Anticipating China: Thinking Through the Narratives of Chinese and Western Culture*, State University of New York Press, Albany, 1995. Compares philosophical underpinnings of Chinese and European culture.

JENSEN, LIONEL, *Manufacturing Confucianism*, Duke University Press, Durham, North Carolina, 1998. On the encounter between the Jesuits and the Chinese tradition.

MOTE, FREDERICK W., *Intellectual Foundations of China*, Alfred A. Knopf, New York, 1989. Good introduction to early Chinese philosophy.

RICHARDS, I. A., *Mencius on the Mind*, Kegan Paul, London, 1932.

SCHWARTZ, BENJAMIN I., *The World of Thought in Ancient China*, Harvard University Press, Cambridge, Mass., 1985. Good introduction to early Chinese philosophy.

WALEY, ARTHUR, *Three Ways of Thought in Ancient China*, George Allen and Unwin, London, 1939. Very readable work on three very different ways of thought (Chuang Tzu, Mencius and the Realists).

CHRONOLOGY

Yao, traditionally reigned 2356–2256 BC
Shun, traditionally reigned 2255–2206 BC
Yu, traditionally reigned 2255–2198 BC
Hsia Dynasty, traditionally 2255–1766 BC
Shang Dynasty: *c.* 1700–1100 BC
Chou Dynasty: *c.* 1100–222 BC
   Western Chou: *c.* 1100–771 BC
   Eastern Chou: *c.* 770–256 BC
      The Spring and Autumn Period: 722–481 BC
         Confucius (551–479 BC)
         Lao Tzu, traditionally sixth century BC
      The Warring States Period: 480–222 BC
         Mo Tzu, *fl.* fifth century BC
         Mencius, *fl.* fourth century BC
         Chuang Tzu, middle of the fourth to beginning of the
         third century BC
         Han Fei Tzu, died 233 BC
Ch'in Dynasty, 221–207 BC
Han Dynasty, 206 BC–AD 220

T R A N S L A T O R ' S
F O R E W O R D

———

This book, begun years ago, has been several times rewritten and laid aside. My difficulties were due to the fact that the *Analects* really consist of two parts: Books III to IX, which form a perfectly consistent whole and apparently belong together; and Books I and II and X to XX, which are extremely miscellaneous in content and character. I thought at one time of dividing the translation into two parts, and writing a separate introduction to each. But this would have involved altering the order of the chapters, and such a re-arrangement, with its obvious inconveniences, is only worth while in cases (like that of the *Book of Songs*) where a text is impossible to study satisfactorily in its existing order. The Translator's Preface as it stands refers to both sections of the work; but it will be seen that the account of early Confucian ideas is based chiefly on Books III to IX.

The present book is somewhat dry and technical in character. But I would not have it supposed that I have definitely abandoned literature for learning, or forgotten the claims of the ordinary reader. My next book, *Three Ways of Thought in Ancient China*, is wholly devoid of technicalities and indeed in most ways is a contrast to this work on the *Analects*.

I wish to thank in particular Dr Walter Simon, of the School of Oriental Studies, who supplied many valuable suggestions and corrections. Some Chinese characters have more than one reading, and where such characters occur in proper names there is often a doubt as to which reading should be followed. In several instances (e.g. Ch'ü Po Yü, P'i Ch'ên, Prince Ch'ao of Sung), Dr Simon indicated to me which reading was followed by the seventeenth-century Manchu translation, and I have thought it best to follow the Manchu readings, which are authoritative in such a case. I wish also to thank Professor Pelliot for lending me a reproduction of the Tun-huang MS., Professor Haloun for many valuable hints when the book was in its earlier stages, and Mr R. C. Trevelyan for the great trouble he took in detecting misprints.   A.W. 1938

THE

ANALECTS

OF CONFUCIUS

TO C. G. SELIGMAN

True philosophy lies in being Humpty Dumpty without a great fall.
MAY CHESSHIRE

CONTENTS

TRANSLATOR'S PREFACE   7

Introduction   7
Terms   21
Appendix I: The Interpretations   ..   63
Appendix II: Biographical Dates   ..   70

THE ANALECTS   73

Book I   75
Book II   80
Book III   86
Book IV   94
Book V   99
Book VI   107
Book VII   115
Book VIII   124
Book IX   130
Book X   138
Book XI   144
Book XII   153
Book XIII   161
Book XIV   169
Book XV   182
Book XVI   191
Book XVII   198
Book XVIII   206
Book XIX   212
Book XX   219

TRANSLATOR'S PREFACE

Thought grows out of environment. Ideally speaking the translator of such a book as the *Analects* ought to furnish a complete analysis of early Chinese society, of the processes which were at work within it and of the outside forces to which it reacted. Unfortunately our knowledge of the period is far too incomplete for any such synthesis to be possible. The literary documents are scanty and of uncertain date; scientific archaeology in China has suffered constant setbacks and is still in its infancy. All that I have attempted in the following pages is to arrange such information as is accessible under a series of disconnected headings, in a convenient order, but without pretence of unity or logical sequence.

CONFUCIUS

The Confucius of whom I shall speak here is the Confucius of the *Analects*.[1] One could construct half a dozen other Confuciuses by tapping the legend at different stages of its evolution. We should see the Master becoming no longer a moral teacher but a 'wise man' according to the popular conception of wisdom that existed in non-Confucian circles in China and in our own Middle Ages, an answerer of grotesque conundrums, a prophet, a magician even. We should see the disappointed itinerant tutor of the *Analects* turning into

1 I omit the obviously legendary material in Book XVIII, and the ritual portrait in Book X, for reasons explained below, p. 48. Also a few passages akin to Book XVIII (such as XIV, 34, 41, 42, and XVII, 1) in that they clearly emanate from circles hostile to Confucius.

7

a successful statesman and diplomatist, employed not only in his own country but in neighbouring States as well.[1]

But I shall act here on the principle recently advocated by that great scholar Ku Chieh-kang, the principle of 'one Confucius at a time'. Not that we can regard the Confucius of the *Analects* as wholly historical; still less, that we must dismiss as fiction all data about the Master that do not happen to occur in this book. But in the first place the biographical facts deducible from the *Analects* are those which are most relevant to an understanding of the book itself; and secondly, the picture of Confucius given in the *Analects*, besides being the earliest that we possess, differs from that of all other books in that it contains no elements that bear patently and obviously the stamp of folk-lore or hagiography. What then was Confucius? It appears from the *Analects* that he was a private person who trained the sons of gentlemen in the virtues proper to a member of the ruling classes. It is clear, however, that he was not content with this position and longed for a more public one, either in his own State or in some other, which would give him the opportunity to put into practice the Way which he regarded as that of the Former Kings, the Way of Goodness, long ago discarded by the rulers of the world in favour of a Way of violence and aggression. There is not the slightest indication that he ever obtained such a position. Twice, however, he speaks of himself as 'following after' the Great Officers of Court. Those who ranked next to the Great Officers (*Ta Fu*) were the Knights (*shih*) and if Confucius ranked immediately after the Great Officers (as he seems to suggest)

---

1 The legend of Confucius's worldly success, transferred to the West, has continued its growth on European soil. Meyer's *Konversationslexicon* (1896) goes so far as to say that he was 'received with the highest honours at every Court' in China.

he must at the time have been *Shih-shih*,[1] Leader of the
Knights, which was not politically speaking a position
of any importance. Discontented with the slow progress
of his doctrines in the land of Lu, Confucius travelled
from State to State,[2] seeking for a ruler who would
give the Way its chance. The only disciples actually
mentioned as accompanying him are Jan Ch'iu, Tzu-lu,
and his favourite disciple Yen Hui. The States and towns
which they visited (Ch'i, Wei, Ch'ên, Ts'ai and K'uang)
all lay within the modern provinces of Shan-tung and
Honan. The strangers evidently met with a hostile
reception, and had occasionally to endure severe priva-
tion. Several of the disciples were in the service of Chi
K'ang-tzu, the dictator of Lu; and it may have been
owing to their good offices that Confucius was at last
encouraged to return to his native State.

Concerning his private life, we learn from the *Analects*
that he had been brought up in humble circumstances.[3]
Of his marriage nothing is said; but two children are
mentioned, a daughter[4] and a son whom the Master
outlived.[5] An older brother is mentioned, but Confucius
seems to have acted as head of the family, and this is
explained by later tradition as due to the fact that the
elder brother was a cripple.

Confucius speaks of himself in one place (II, 4) as

1 The original function of the *shih-shih* was to 'keep the Knights in
order'; Cf. *Mencius* I, 2, VI, 2. In practice he acted under the orders of the
Minister of Justice and functioned as a sort of police-magistrate. In
the second stage of its development the Confucian legend represents the
Master as achieving the position of Minister of Justice, an idea which may
well have grown out of his having in fact been Leader of the Knights.

2 This mobility was typical of Chinese society. Not only moralists, but
warriors, craftsmen and even peasants moved from State to State, if they
thought that by doing so they could improve their chances of success.

3 IX, 6. But the saying from which we learn this was a disputed one,
and an alternative version of it is given immediately afterwards, 'But Lao
says the Master said . . .' etc. This alternative version refers to lack of official
employment, but not to poverty.   4 V, 1.   5 XI, 7.

being over seventy. As to the exact dates of his birth and death the *Analects* tell us nothing. It can be inferred, however, from references to contemporary persons and events, that the time of his main activity was the end of the sixth and the first twenty years or so of the fifth century.[1]

After his apotheosis in the Han dynasty Confucius was credited with the omniscience and moral infallibility of the Divine Sage. This view of him appears, indeed, to have been current even during his lifetime; for we find him at pains to disclaim any such attributes.[2] Nor would he allow himself to be regarded as Good,[3] a disclaimer that is natural enough, seeing that he accords this title only to a few legendary heroes of the remote past. Even in the social virtues which formed the basis of his teaching he claimed no pre-eminence. There was not, he said, a hamlet of ten houses but could produce men as loyal and dependable as himself. He denied (though one disciple at least seems to have had the opposite impression) that he possessed any unusual stock of knowledge;[4] still less would he admit that such knowledge as he possessed was innate or inspired.[5] What he regarded as exceptional in himself was his love of 'learning', that is to say, of self-improvement, and his unflagging patience in insisting upon the moral principles that had (in his view) guided the godlike rulers of the remote past. His task, then, like that of the English trainer of *chün-tzu* (gentlemen's sons) in the great Public Schools, was not so much to impart knowledge as to inculcate moral principles, form character, hand down unaltered and intact a great tradition of the past.[6] He speaks of himself as a veritable P'êng Tsu (i.e. Nestor)

1 I will not here enter into the difficult question of how the dates (551–479 B.C.) later accepted as official were first arrived at. Cf. Maspero, *La Chine Antique*, p. 455, and below, p. 70.
2 VII, 33.   3 *Ibid.*   4 XV, 2.   5 VII, 19.   6 VII, 1.

in his devoted reliance upon 'antiquity'; and if we want further to define what he meant by this reliance on the past, we find it, I think, in Mencius's saying: Follow the rules of the Former Kings, and it is impossible that you should go wrong.[1]

What then was this antiquity, who were the great figures of the past whom Confucius regarded as the sole source of wisdom?

THE ANCIENTS

Were we to take them in the order of their importance to him, I think we should have to begin with the founders and expanders of the Chou dynasty; for in his eyes the cultures of the two preceding dynasties found their climax and fulfilment in that of the early Chou sovereigns.[2] Above all, we should have to deal first with Tan, Duke of Chou, who had not only a particular importance in the Lu State, but also a peculiar significance for Confucius himself.[3] But it is more convenient to take them in their 'chronological' order, that is to say, in the order in which the mythology of Confucius's day arranged them. We must begin then with the *Shêng*, the Divine Sages.[4] These were mythological figures, historicized as rulers of human 'dynasties'; but still endowed with divine characteristics and powers. The *Analects* mention three of them, Yao, Shun and Yü the Great; but they occupy a very restricted place in the book.[5] Yao and Shun are twice[6] mentioned in the stock phrase (if a man were to do this), then 'even Yao and

1 *Mencius*, IV, 1, I.   2 III, 14.   3 VII, 5.

4 See *The Way and Its Power*, p. 91. Mencius and later writers use the term *shêng* in a much wider sense, applying it even to a comparatively recent person such as Liu-hsia Hui.

5 I except Book XX, which has not necessarily anything to do with the beliefs of Confucius. Yü is legendary; but the Hsia dynasty is probably not wholly mythological.

6 VI, 28; XIV, 45.

Shun could not criticize him'; meaning that such a man would himself be to all intents and purposes a *shêng*. Yao appears otherwise only in the eulogy of VIII, 19, where he is exalted as the equal of God.[1] The eulogy of Shun which follows tells us that with only five servants to help him he kept order 'everywhere under Heaven'. Elsewhere[2] he is said to have ruled by *wu-wei* (non-activity), through the mere fact of sitting in a majestic attitude 'with his face turned to the South'. We have here the conception, familiar to us in Africa and elsewhere, of the divine king whose magic power regulates everything in the land. It is one which is common to all early Chinese thought, particularly in the various branches of Quietism that developed in the fourth century B.C. The *shêng*, however, only 'rules by non-activity' in the sense that his divine essence (*ling*) assures the fecundity of his people and the fertility of the soil. We find Shun assisted in his task by 'five servants',[3] who are clearly conceived of as performing the active functions of government.

Yao and Shun are not mentioned in the *Book of Songs*, and there is reason to suppose that their cult did not form part of the Chou tradition. The third Divine Sage, Yü the Great, generally[4] associated in Chinese legend with a Deluge Myth akin to that of the Near East, figures in the *Analects* not as the subduer of the Flood but as patron of agriculture. He drains and ditches the land[5] and tills the fields,[6] his name being coupled with that of the harvest-god Hou Chi. Yü the Great is 'historicized' as founder of the Hsia dynasty, whose 'times' (i.e. calendar of agricultural operations) Confucius

---

1 *T'ien*; literally, 'Heaven'.   2 XV, 4.

3 VIII, 20. One of them was presumably Kao Yao, mentioned in XII, 22.

4 But not in the *Songs*, where he generally appears as a Creator connected indeed with irrigation, only once as a flood-subduer.

5 VIII, 21.   6 XIV, 6.

recommends, in answer to a question about the ideal State.[1]

T'ang, the founder of the Shang-Yin dynasty which preceded the Chou, is only once mentioned. It was supposed in Confucius's day that the remnants of the Shang-Yin people had settled in Sung and that the Sung State perpetuated the traditions of the fallen dynasty. But Confucius himself doubted whether Yin culture could really be reconstructed by evidence supplied from Sung.[2]

THE DISCIPLES

Later tradition credits Confucius with seventy-two[3] disciples; but the compilers are hard put to it to bring the number up to anything like so imposing a total. In the *Analects* some twenty people figure, who might possibly be regarded as disciples, in so far as they are represented as addressing questions to Confucius. But far fewer appear as definite 'frequenters of his gate'. The most important of them, in the history of Confucianism, is Master Tsêng, who is credited in the *Analects* with twelve sayings of his own. The Master Tsêng of Book VIII is, however, a very different person from the Master Tsêng of Book I, the latter resembling far more closely the Tsêng of later tradition, and of the *Tsêng Tzu* fragments.[4] Humanly the most distinctive of the disciples are Yen Hui and Tzu-lu, who are perfect examples of the contrasted types of character that psychologists call introvert and extravert. Both of them died before Confucius, and were thus unable to influence the subsequent

1 XV, 10.

2 III, 9. Systematic excavation at An-yang, the site of one of the Yin capitals, has put us in possession of far more information about Yin culture than Confucius was able to obtain.

3 Seventy-two is a sacred number, connected with the quintuple division of the year of 360 days. Cf. XI, 25.

4 Collected by Yüan Yüan, *Huang Ch'ing Ching Chieh*, 803–806.

development of the school. Tzu-lu played a considerable part in contemporary history and is mentioned in the chronicles from 498 down to the time of his death in 480. Two other disciples are well known to history, Jan Ch'iu appears as a lieutenant of the usurping Chi Family from 484 till 472; and Tzu-kung figures largely in inter-State diplomacy from 495 till 468.

The name of Master Yu, who figures so prominently in Book I, only to disappear almost completely in the remaining Books, happens by chance to occur in the *Tso Chuan* Chronicle under the year 487. But he was evidently not a person of high social status; for he served as a foot-soldier.

It is clear that after the Master's death, Tzu-hsia, like Master Tsêng, founded a school of his own; for his disciples are spoken of in Book XIX. To him, too, are attributed about a dozen sayings. Two other disciples, Tzu-chang and Tzu-yu, are also obviously regarded by the compilers of the *Analects* as being of special importance; for they, too, are credited with sayings of their own.

THE ANALECTS[1]

There is not much doubt that *Lun Yü* (*Analects*, to use the English equivalent that Legge's translation has made so familiar) means 'Selected Sayings'. *Lun*, as a term connected with the editing of documents, occurs indeed in *Analects*, XIV, 9. The contents of the book itself make it clear that the compilation took place long after the Master's death. Several of the disciples already have schools of their own, and the death of Master Tsêng, which certainly happened well into the second half of the fifth century, is recorded in Book VIII. It is

1 This section might well be omitted by readers without special knowledge of Chinese literature.

clear, too, that the different Books are of very different date and proceed from very different sources. I should hazard the guess that Books III–IX represent the oldest stratum. Books X and XX (first part) certainly have no intrinsic connection with the rest. The former is a compilation of maxims from works on ritual; the latter consists of stray sentences from works of the *Shu Ching* type. Book XIX consists entirely of sayings by disciples. The contents of XVIII and of parts of XIV and XVII are not Confucian in their origin, but have filtered into the book from the outside world, and from a world hostile to Confucius. Book XVI is generally and rightly regarded as late. It contains nothing characteristic of the milieu that produced Books III–IX, and it would not be difficult to compile a much longer book of just the same character by stringing together precepts from works such as the *Tso Chuan* and *Kuo Yü*. Only in one passage of the *Analects* do we find any reference to ideas the development of which we should be inclined to place later than the ordinarily accepted[1] date of the book, namely the middle of the fourth century. I refer to the disquisition on 'correcting names' in XIII, 3. In *Mencius* (early third century B.C.) there is not a trace of the 'language crisis',[2] and we have no reason to suppose that the whole sequence of ideas embodied in this passage could possibly be earlier in date than the end of the fourth century. That the writer of the passage realized its incompatibility with the doctrines of Confucius – the insistence on punishments is wholly un-Confucian – is naïvely betrayed in the introductory paragraphs. Tzu-lu is made to express the greatest astonishment that Confucius should regard the reform of

1 I mean accepted by scholars as the date of the material contained in the book. The date of its compilation may well be later.

2 See *The Way and Its Power*, p. 59. *Mencius*, VI, 2. VI, is unintelligible, and has in any case never been interpreted as relevant.

language as the first duty of a ruler and tells him impatiently that his remark is quite beside the point.

We may, of course, be wrong in thinking that the whole complex of ideas connected with 'reforming language in order to adjust penalties' dates from as late as the end of the fourth century. There may be special reasons why we find no echo of such ideas in *Mencius*. Or again, the compilation of the *Analects* may be much later than we suppose; but this alternative involves linguistic difficulties. It may, on the other hand, be a better solution to regard this passage as an interpolation on the part of Hsün Tzu or his school, for whom the absence of any reference in the sayings of Confucius to what they themselves taught as a fundamental doctrine must certainly have been inconvenient.

It is curious that only one pre-Han text shows definite evidence of familiarity with the *Analects*. The *Fang Chi* (part of the *Li Chi*; supposed to be an extract from the *Tzu Ssu Tzu*) quotes *Analects*, II, 11, and names the *Lun Yü* as its source. The *Fang Chi* also quotes books of the *Shu Ching* which were unknown in Han times, not being found either in the official collection or among the books rediscovered but uninterpreted. It is therefore certainly a pre-Han work. There are, apart from this, many cases in which pre-Han authors, such as Hsün Tzu, Lü Pu-wei, Han Fei Tzu, use maxims or anecdotes that are also used in the *Analects*. But there is nothing to show that the writer is quoting the book as we know it now. Mencius, it is clear, used a quite different collection of sayings, which contained, indeed, a certain number of those which occur in the *Analects*, often differently worded and allotted to quite different contexts; but he quotes at least three times as many sayings that do not occur in the *Analects* at all.

It would be rash, however, to conclude that the *Analects* were not known or did not exist in the days of

Mencius and Hsün Tzu. We possess only a very small fragment of early Confucian literature. Could we read all the works that are listed in the *Han Shu* bibliography, we should very likely discover that some particular school of Confucianism based its teaching on the *Analects*, just as Mencius based his on another collection of sayings. The *Doctrine of the Mean* and the *Great Learning*, works of very uncertain date but certainly pre-Han, both use sayings from the *Analects*, which may well be actual quotations.

The history of the text from *c.* 150 B.C.[1] till the time (second century A.D.) when at the hands of Chêng Hsüan the book received something like its present form I must leave to others to write. The task is one which involves great difficulties. The data are supplied not by scientific bibliographers but by careless repeaters of legend and anecdote. Some of the relevant texts (e.g. *Lun Hêng*, P'ien 81) are hopelessly corrupt; the real dates of supposedly early Han works which show knowledge of the *Analects* are impossible to ascertain. At every turn, in such studies, we are forced to rely, without any means of checking their statements, upon writers who clearly took no pains to control their facts.

This much, however, is certain: during the period 100 B.C. to A.D. 100 two versions were currently used, the Lu version (upon which our modern version is chiefly based) and the Ch'i version,[2] which had two extra chapters. Much later (second century A.D.?)[3] a third version came into general use. This was the Ku Wên (ancient script) text collated by Chêng Hsüan when he made his famous edition, of which fragments

1 It is quoted by name in the *Han Shih Wai Chuan*, which presumably dates from the middle of the second century.

2 Now lost, save for a few fragments.

3 Legge's suggestion that Chang Yü (died 5 B.C.) used the Ku version is not borne out by the texts.

have been recovered from Tun-huang. We know[1] some twenty-seven instances in which the Ku version differed from the Lu, and in all but two of these instances the version we use to-day follows Ku not Lu. I state these facts merely that the reader may know roughly what is meant when in the course of this book I mention Ku and Lu readings. The real origin of the Ku version[2] remains very uncertain and a discussion of the question, bound up as it is with the history of the other Ku Wên texts, would lead us too far afield.

A last question remains to be answered. How far can we regard any of the sayings in the *Analects* as actual words of Confucius? In searching for such authentic sayings we must use certain precautions. Obviously, we shall not find them in Book X,[3] nor in Book XX.[4] Books XVI–XVII clearly do not emanate from a source at all near to the earliest Confucianism. Book XVIII is, indeed, full of anti-Confucian stories, of just the same sort that we find in Taoist works, naïvely accepted by the compilers; Book XIV has a considerable element of the same description (34, 41, 42). The story of the meeting with Yang Huo (XVII, 1) is of just the same kind. We shall have to remember that in ancient Chinese

1 Through the *Shih Wên* and the fragments from Tun-huang. The *Hsin-lun* of Huan T'an (*c.* A.D. 1) says that Ku had four hundred characters different from Lu.

2 Alleged to have been found, (1) during the Emperor Ching's reign (156–141 B.C.); (2) at the beginning of the Han Emperor Wu's reign (140 B.C.); (3) at the end of his reign (87 B.C.); by (1) Prince Kung of Lu (in Lu from 154–127 B.C.; (2) the Emperor Wu himself; (1) during the demolition of Confucius's house; (2) before the demolition, which was at once suspended; (1) according to some accounts without supernatural manifestations; (2) according to others, to the accompaniment of supernatural music.

The accounts also differ considerably as to what books were found and as to who hid them there.

3 Which is simply a collection of traditional ritual maxims.

4 Which, apart from the few sayings appended at the end, is a collection of sentences from texts of the *Shu Ching* type.

literature sayings are often attributed to a variety of people; (indifferently, for example, to Master Tsêng and Confucius, or to Confucius and Yen Tzu) and bear in mind that such sayings were probably more or less proverbial. We certainly must not forget that Confucius describes himself as a transmitter, not an originator, and that the presence of rhyme or archaic formulae, or of proverbial shape in the sayings often definitely stamps them as inherited from the past. Bearing all these facts in mind I think we are justified in supposing that the book does not contain many authentic sayings, and may possibly contain none at all. As I have already pointed out, I use the term 'Confucius' throughout this book in a conventional sense, simply meaning the particular early Confucians whose ideas are embodied in the sayings.

Supposing, however, someone should succeed in proving that some particular saying was really uttered by the Master, it would still remain to be proved that the context in which the remark occurred in the *Analects* was really the original one; and the context of a remark profoundly affects its meaning. In later literature, particularly the *Li Chi* (Book of Rites) and *Shih Chi* (Historical Records), we find a good many of Confucius's more cryptic remarks given contexts, put into settings of an explanatory description, and it has been suggested that in such cases we have the original form and intention of the sayings, which in the *Analects* have for some reason become divorced from their proper surroundings. That this should be so is against all the canons of textual history. Always, in similar cases, we find that the contexts have been invented as glosses upon the original *logia*. In the oldest strata of the Synoptic Gospels isolated sayings occur which in the more recent strata are furnished, often very arbitrarily, with an explanatory setting. It is a process that we can see at work over and over again in Buddhist hagiography. I have therefore seldom called attention to these manipulations of the text by the later Confucian schools, and have been content to leave the isolated *logia* as I found them.

TERMS

JÊN[1]

This word in the earliest Chinese means freemen, men of the tribe, as opposed to *min*, 'subjects', 'the common people'.[2] The same word, written with a slight modification,[3] means 'good' in the most general sense of the word, that is to say, 'possessing the qualities of one's tribe'. For no more sweeping form of praise can be given by the men of a tribe than to say that someone is a 'true member' of that tribe. The same is true of modern nations; an Englishman can give no higher praise than to say that another is a true Englishman. In the *Book of Songs* the phrase 'handsome and good' (*jên*) occurs more than once as a description of a perfectly satisfactory lover. *Jên*, 'members of the tribe' show a forbearance towards one another that they do not show to aliens, and just as the Latin *gens*, 'clan', gave rise to our own word 'gentle', so *jên* in Chinese came to mean 'kind', 'gentle', 'humane'. Finally, when the old distinction between *jên* and *min*, freemen and subjects, was forgotten and *jên* became a general word for 'human being', the adjective *jên* came to be understood in the sense of 'human' as opposed to 'animal', and to be applied to conduct worthy of a man, as distinct from the behaviour of mere beasts.

Of this last sense (human, not brutal) there is not a trace in the *Analects*. Of the sense 'kind', 'tender-

1 See textual notes.
2 See *The Way and Its Power*, p. 148.
3 See textual notes.

hearted' there are only two examples,[1] out of some sixty instances in which the word occurs. Confucius's use of the term, a use peculiar to this one book, stands in close relation to the primitive meaning. *Jên*, in the *Analects*, means 'good' in an extremely wide and general sense. 'In its direction'[2] lie unselfishness and an ability to measure other people's feelings by one's own. The good man is 'in private life, courteous; in public life, diligent; in relationships, loyal'.[3] Goodness (on the part of a ruler) is complete submission to ritual.[4] The Good do not grieve[5] and will necessarily be brave.[6] At the same time, it cannot be said that *jên* in the *Analects* simply means 'good' in a wide and general sense. It is, on the contrary, the name of a quality so rare and peculiar that one 'cannot but be chary in speaking of it'.[7] It is a sublime moral attitude, a transcendental perfection attained to by legendary heroes such as Po I, but not by any living or historic person. This, however, is far from being understood by the disciples, who suggest as examples of goodness not only Tzu-wên (seventh century B.C.), Ch'ên Wên-tzu (sixth century), Kuan Tzu (seventh century), but even contemporaries and associates such as Tzu-lu, Jan Ch'iu, Kung-hsi Hua, Jan Yung. All such claims the Master abruptly dismisses. Indeed so unwilling is he to accord the title *jên* that he will not even allow it to a hypothetical person who 'compassed the salvation of the whole State'.[8] Such a one would be a Divine Sage (*shêng*), a demi-god; whereas *jên* is the display of human qualities at their highest. It appears indeed that *jên* is a mystic entity not merely analogous to but in certain sayings practically identical with the Tao of the Quietists. Like Tao, it is contrasted with 'knowledge'. Knowledge is active and frets itself away;

1 XII, 22 and XVII, 21.   2 VI, 28.   3 XIII, 19.
4 XII, 1.   5 IX, 28.   6 XIV, 5.   7 XII, 3.   8 VI, 28.

Goodness is passive and therefore eternal as the hills.[1] Confucius can point the way to Goodness, can tell 'the workman how to sharpen his tools',[2] can speak even of things 'that are near to Goodness'. But it is only once, in a chapter bearing every sign of lateness,[3] that anything approaching a definition of Goodness is given.

In view of this repeated refusal to accept any but remote[4] mythological figures as examples of *jên*, to accept[5] or give a definition of Goodness, there is surely nothing surprising in the statement of Book IX (opening sentence) that 'the Master rarely discoursed upon Goodness'.[6]

It seems to me that 'good' is the only possible translation of the term *jên* as it occurs in the *Analects*. No other word is sufficiently general to cover the whole range of meaning; indeed terms such as 'humane', 'altruistic', 'benevolent' are in almost every instance inappropriate, often ludicrously so. But there is another word, *shan*, which though it wholly lacks the mystical and transcendental implications of *jên*, cannot conveniently be translated by any other word but 'good'. For that reason I shall henceforward translate *jên* by Good (Goodness, etc.) with a capital; and *shan* by good, with a small g.

TAO

Unlike *jên*, *tao* has not in the *Analects* a technical or peculiar meaning, but is used there in just the same sense as in early Chinese works in general. *Tao* means literally a road, a path, a way. Hence, the way in which

1 VI, 21. For the capital G, see below.   2 XV, 9.   3 XVII.

4 Po I, Shu Ch'i, Pi Kan, Wei Tzu and Chi Tzu is the complete list. All of them belonged, according to legend, to the end of the Yin dynasty. The last three occur in Book XVIII, which emanated from non-Confucian circles.

5 Cf. XIV, 2.

6 A vast mass of discussion has centred round this passage. Cf. *Journal of the American Oriental Society*, December 1933 and March 1934.

anything is done, the way in which, for example, a kingdom is ruled; a method, a principle, a doctrine. It usually has a good meaning. Thus 'when *tao* (the Way) prevails under Heaven' means when a good method of government prevails in the world; or rather 'when *the* good method prevails', for Confucius 'believed in the ancients', that is to say, he believed that the one infallible method of rule had been practised by certain rulers of old, and that statecraft consisted in rediscovering this method. But there seem to have been other 'Ways'; for Confucius[1] speaks of 'this Way' and 'my Way'. Moreover, in one passage[2] he is asked about *shan-jên chih Tao*, 'the Way of the good people', and replies (according to my interpretation) disapprovingly that 'those who do not tread in the tracks (of the ancients)' cannot hope to 'enter into the sanctum'. 'Good people' is a term often applied in Chinese to those who share one's views. Thus Quietists called other Quietists 'good people'. The 'good people' here intended evidently sought guidance from some source other than the example of the ancients, and they may well have been Quietists.

But we are also told that Confucius did not discourse about the Will of Heaven[3] or about 'prodigies' and 'disorders' (of Nature).[4] We have only to read other early books to see that the world at large attached extreme importance to the Will of Heaven as manifested by portents such as rainbows, comets, eclipses; and to monstrosities such as two-headed calves and the like. It may be that the doctrine of those who sought guidance from such signs rather than from the records of the Former Kings came to be known as the 'Way of the good people'. In general, however, the word *Tao* in the

1 It would be pedantic always to say 'the early Confucians' or the compilers of the *Analects*; though that is, strictly speaking, what I mean when I say 'Confucius'.
2 XI, 19.   3 V, 12.   4 VII, 20.

Analects means one thing only, the Way of the ancients as it could be reconstructed from the stories told about the founders of the Chou dynasty and the demi-gods who had preceded them.

The aspect of Confucius's Way upon which Western writers have chiefly insisted is his attitude towards the supernatural. It has been rightly emphasized that he was concerned above all with the duties of man to man and that he 'did not talk about spirits'.[1] From a false interpretation of two passages (VI, 20 and XI, 11) the quite wrong inference has, however, been drawn that his attitude towards the spirit-world was, if not sceptical, at least agnostic. In the first passage a disciple asks about wisdom. The wisdom here meant is, of course, that of the ruler or member of the ruling classes, and the point at issue is one frequently debated in early Chinese literature: which should come first, the claims of the people or those of the spirit-world? In concrete terms, should the security of the whole State, which depends ultimately on the goodwill of the Spirits of grain, soil, rivers and hills, be first assured by lavish offerings and sacrifices, even if such a course involves such heavy taxation as to impose great hardship on the common people? Or should the claims of the people to what it is 'right and proper' (*i*) for them to have be satisfied before public expenditure is lavished upon the protecting spirits? The reply of Confucius is that the claims of the people should come first; but that the spirits must be accorded an attention sufficient to 'keep them at a distance', that is to say, prevent them from manifesting their ill-will by attacking human beings; for just as we regard sickness as due to the onslaught of microbes, the Chinese regarded it as due to demoniacal 'possession'.

1 VII, 20.

The same question concerning the priority in budget-making of human and ghostly claims is discussed in the second passage. Tzu-lu asks about 'the service of spirits', meaning, as has generally been recognized, the outlay of public expenditure on sacrifice and other ceremonies of placation. The Master's reply is, 'How can there be any proper service of spirits until living men have been properly served?' Tzu-lu then 'asked about the dead'. A much debated question was whether the dead are conscious; and it was suggested that if they are not, it must clearly be useless to sacrifice at any rate to that portion of the spirit-world which consists of the spirits of the dead, as opposed to those of hills, streams, the soil, etc. Confucius does not wish to commit himself to any statement about, for example, the consciousness or unconsciousness of the dead, and adroitly turns the question by replying, 'Until a man knows about the living,[1] how can he know the dead?' All that is meant by the reply (which is a rhetorical one and must not be analysed too logically) is that for the *chün-tzu*[2] questions about the existence led by the dead are of secondary importance as compared to those connected with the handling of living men.

There is not, as Western writers have often supposed, any allusion to an abstract metaphysical problem concerning the ultimate nature of Life. Nor are the two passages discussed above in any way isolated or exceptional. They are, on the contrary, characteristic of the general diversion of interest from the dead to the living, from the spirit-world to that of everyday life, which marks the break-up of the old Chou culture, founded upon divination and sacrifice.[3]

1 Or 'knows about life'.
2 See below, p. 28.
3 Cf. *The Way and Its Power*, pp. 24 seq.

TÊ[1]

This word corresponds closely to the Latin *virtus*. It means, just as *virtus* often does, the specific quality or 'virtue' latent in anything. It never (except by some accident of context) has in early Chinese the meaning of virtue as opposed to vice, but rather the meaning of 'virtue' in such expressions as 'in virtue of' or 'the virtue of this drug'. In individuals it is a force or power closely akin to what we call character and frequently contrasted with *li*, 'physical force'. To translate it by 'virtue', as has often been done, can only end by misleading the reader, who even if forewarned will be certain to interpret the word in its ordinary sense (virtue as opposed to vice) and not in the much rarer sense corresponding to the Latin *virtus*. For this reason I have generally rendered *tê* by the term 'moral force', particularly where it is contrasted with *li*, 'physical force'. We cannot, however, speak of a horse's *tê* as its 'moral force'. Here 'character' is the only possible equivalent; and in the case of human beings the term 'prestige' often comes close to what is meant by *tê*.

SHIH[2]

This word is often translated 'scholar'; but this is only a derived, metaphorical sense and the whole force of many passages in the *Analects* is lost if we do not understand that the term is a military one and means 'knight'. A *shih* was a person entitled to go to battle in a war-chariot, in contrast with the common soldiers who followed on foot. Confucius, by a metaphor similar to those embodied in the phraseology of the Salvation Army, calls the stout-hearted defenders of his Way 'Knights'; and hence in later Chinese the term came to be applied to upholders of Confucianism and finally to

1 Cf. *The Book of Songs*, p. 346. See below p. 45.
2 See textual notes.

scholars and literary people in general. The burden of most of the references to *shih* in the *Analects* is that the Knight of the Way needs just the same qualities of endurance and resolution as the Soldier Knight. A saying such as 'A knight whose thoughts are set on home is not worthy of the name of knight'[1] refers in the first instance to real knights, and is only applied by metaphor to the spiritual warriors of Confucius's 'army'. If like Legge we translate 'the scholar who cherishes his love of comfort . . .', we lose the whole point. As we shall see later, Confucius was himself a knight in the literal sense, and it is probable, as we have seen, that in his later years he was senior knight, 'leader of the knights', responsible for their discipline.

CHÜN-TZU

Chün is the most general term for 'ruler', and a *chüntzu* is a 'son of a ruler'. The term was applied to descendants of the ruling house in any State, and so came to mean 'gentleman', 'member of the upper classes'. But the gentleman is bound by a particular code of morals and manners; so that the word *chün-tzu* implies not merely superiority of birth but also superiority of character and behaviour. Finally the requisite of birth is waived. If an ox is of one colour and thus fit for sacrifice, what does it matter that its sire was brindled?[2] He who follows the Way of the *chün-tzu* is a *chün-tzu*; he who follows the way of 'small' (i.e. common) people is common. And what is the Way of the Gentleman? With the detailed code of his manners I shall deal presently, when discussing Book X. As to his deportment in general, it is defined for us by the disciple Tsêng[3] in terms that exactly correspond to the traditional Western conception of a gentleman: we recognize him by the fact that his movements are free from any brusqueness or viol-

1 XIV, 3.   2 VI, 4.   3 VIII, 4.

28

ence, that his expression is one of complete openness and sincerity, that his speech is free from any low and vulgar or as we should say 'Cockney' tinge.

As regards his conduct, he must be extremely careful to make friends only with people of his own sort.[1] But he need never be lonely; for so long as he behaves as a gentleman should, he will be welcomed by his 'brothers' (i.e. by other gentlemen) 'everywhere within the Four Seas'.[2] The whole world is his club. The alliances of 'small people' are directed against others, are hostile and destructive in intent; but those of the gentlemen exist only for mutual satisfaction. He has no politics, but sides with the Right wherever he finds it.[3]

He must not lay himself open to the accusation of 'talking too much';[4] still less must he boast[5] or push himself forward or in any way display his superiority, except in matters of sport,[6] and even here he is restrained by the complicated dictates of fair play, by the elaborate etiquette which constitutes the 'rules of the game'. Nor must he exalt himself by the indirect method of denigrating other people, a method characteristic of 'small men'.[7]

His education, like that given till recently at gentlemen's schools in England, consists chiefly of moral training; he learns in order to build up his *tê* (character). To learn anything of actual utility, to have practical accomplishments, is contrary to the Way of the *chüntzu*[8] and will lead to his merely becoming a 'tool',[9] an instrument dedicated to one humdrum purpose. Such a general, moral education will produce a Knight of the

---

1 I, 8.   2 XII, 5.   3 IV, 10.   4 XVII, 17.

5 XIV, 29. Here, as in other points, the Chinese code has a particular affinity with ours. 'Swank' in all its forms is far more severely condemned by the English gentleman than by the patrician, for example, of Latin countries.

6 III, 7.   7 XII, 16.   8 IX, 6.   9 II, 12.

Way ready to face all emergencies 'without fret or fear'. [1]
His head will not be turned by success, nor his temper
soured by adversity.[2] Success, however, is a theme seldom dealt with in the *Analects*; for it is well known that
the Way 'does not prevail in the world', and the merits
of the true *chün-tzu* are not such as the world is likely
to recognize or reward. 'Lack of recognition' is, indeed,
one of Confucius's most frequent topics, and to feel no
resentment (*yüan*) when repeatedly cashiered or neglected is the *chün-tzu*'s highest virtue.

Moderation in conduct and opinion is a well-known
hallmark of the true gentleman: 'The *chün-tzu* avoids
the absolute, avoids the extreme.'[3] Mencius tells us that
'Confucius was one who abstained from extremes.'[4] 'To
exceed is as bad as not to reach.'[5] This conception of
virtue as a middle way between two extremes is one
which we have no difficulty in understanding; for it is
familiar to us as part of our popular heritage from Greek
philosophy. It is, however, one which rapidly disappears
so soon as purely magical, non-social virtues are held in
esteem. The reputation of an Indian ascetic, for
example, is in proportion to the 'excessiveness' of his
behaviour; and a society which admired St. Simeon on
his pillar would not easily have understood either the
μηδὲν ἄγαν of the Classical Greeks or the 'middle
conduct' (*chung hsing*) inculcated by Confucius.

That good lies between two extremes has been very
generally accepted by those who have tried to view
the world rationally. As a political principle it was the
foundation of nineteenth-century Liberalism and in
particular of English Liberalism. In many cases the

1 XII, 4.   2 I, 1.

3 *Han Fei Tzu*, 33. (Roll XII); adapted in *Tao Tê Ching*, XXIX.

4 *Mencius*, IV, 2. X.

5 *Analects*, XI, 15. Cf. XIII, 21. I leave out of account the famous dictum
(VI, 27) about the Golden Mean (*chung-yung*); for the original meaning of
the passage is far from clear. See additional notes.

doctrine is one which can hardly be disputed. Thus 'softness' (unwillingness to inflict pain or take life) carried to its logical conclusion involves extinction; and so, with equal sureness, does 'hardness' (indifference to the infliction of death and suffering). Unfortunately it is extremes and not compromises that most easily become associated with strong emotional impulse. The downfall of Liberalism has been due to the failure to associate the Middle Way with any strong trend of emotion. The success of Confucianism, its triumph over 'all the hundred schools' from the second century B.C. onwards, was due in a large measure to the fact that it contrived to endow compromise with an emotional glamour.

As regards the translation of the term *chün-tzu* I see no alternative but to use the word 'gentleman', though the effect is occasionally somewhat absurd in English. One needs a word which primarily signifies superiority of birth, but also implies moral superiority. Neither Legge's 'superior man', nor Soothill's various equivalents ('man of the higher type', 'wise man', etc.) fulfil this condition. The late Sir Reginald Johnston proposed 'the princely man'; but this seems to me (I may be peculiar in my interpretation) to suggest lavish expenditure rather than superiority of birth or morals.[1]

HSIAO

This word seems originally to have meant piety towards the spirits of ancestors or dead parents.[2] In the *Analects* it still frequently has this meaning; but it is also applied to filial conduct towards living parents, and this is its

1 This was written before Sir Reginald Johnston in his *Confucianism and Modern China* adopted 'gentleman' as the most exact equivalent to *Chün-tzu*.

2 In the *Book of Songs hsiao* refers almost exclusively to piety towards the dead. Out of twelve instances nine can only be taken in this sense; the other three are non-committal.

usual meaning in current Chinese. In this change of meaning we may see, I think, another example of that general transference of interest from the dead to the living which marked the break-up of the old Chou civilization. There is, however, reason to believe that filial piety played a relatively small part in the teaching of the earliest Confucians. By far the larger number of references to it in the *Analects* occur in Books I and II which do not, I think, belong to the earliest strata of the work. But it seems clear that during the fourth century B.C. a place of extreme importance had already been allotted by the Confucians to *hsiao* in its extended sense of piety towards living parents. For it was with reference to this virtue that the followers of Confucius came into conflict with those of Mo Tzu, who taught that affection and solicitude ought to be equally extended to all mankind and not reserved in a special degree for parents or relations. Towards the end of the third century B.C. *hsiao* became, at any rate in certain Confucian schools, the summit of all virtues, and in the *Canon of Filial Piety* which may have existed[1] in some form in the third century, but did not, I think, reach its present form till at least a century later, *hsiao* is surrounded by the mysterious halo that attends the term *jên* in the *Analects*.

But it seems that the compilers of the *Canon of Filial Piety* were hard put to it to get their material. For in one place[2] they have reproduced a panegyric upon the potency of ritual observance, preserved in the *Tso Chuan* chronicle,[3] and by altering the word *li* ('ritual') to *hsiao* they have turned it into a eulogy of filial piety.

1 The allusion to the *Canon of Filial Piety* in *Lü Shih Ch'un Ch'iu* is probably an intrusion of commentary into text.
2 Paragraph 7.
3 Chao Kung, 25th year.

WÊN[1]

The original meaning of the word *wên* is criss-cross lines, markings, pattern. It also means a written character, an ideogram. This, however, is scarcely a separate meaning from that of pattern, for in early China certain patterns served equally as ideograms, both being conventionalizations of pictures. Thus the character for 'eye' also figures as a decoration on Chou bronzes. *Wên*, again, means what is decorated as opposed to what is plain, ornament as opposed to structure, and hence the things that vary and beautify human life, as opposed to life's concrete needs. In particular, *wên* denotes the arts of peace (music, dancing, literature) as opposed to those of war. The arts of peace, however, everything that we should call culture, have a *tê* that is useful for offensive purposes. They attract the inhabitants of neighbouring countries; and it must be remembered the States of ancient China were just as anxious to attract immigration as modern European States are to repel it. For vast areas still remained to be opened up for agriculture; there was room for everyone, and fresh inhabitants meant fresh recruits for the army. 'If the distant do not submit, cultivate the power of *wên* to bring them to you.'[2] It is clear then that *wên* means something very like our own word culture and served many of the same purposes. The prestige (*tê*) of culture is to-day used by us for military purposes. During the War, for example, efforts were made by both sides to win over neutrals by displays of culture,[3] such as the sending of theatrical companies, pictures and the like. The power of *wên* is also used, as in ancient China, to attract immigrants, but only those of the temporary kind called tourists.

For Confucius the *wên* (culture) *par excellence* was that

1 Cf. *The Book of Songs*, p. 346.   2 XVI, 1.

3 'Just as military preparations must not be revealed, so too culture must not be concealed'. *Kuo Yü*, ch. 2.

established by the founders of the Chou dynasty. To gather up the fragments of this culture and pass them on to posterity was the sacred mission entrusted to him by Heaven.[1] His native State, Lu, was generally regarded as the main depository of Chou culture;[2] but we find him, on a visit to Ch'i, ready to admit the superiority of a musical performance there to anything of the kind he had known in Lu,[3] and it was only 'after his return from Wei'[4] that the correct ritual use of the ancestral hymns and Court songs was properly established.

The term *wên* is, however, often used in the *Analects* in a narrower sense than that of civilization or culture. We have seen that one of its primary senses is that of 'a written character', and it occurs once[5] in the *Analects* with this meaning. *Wên-hsüeh* (letter–study) is the ordinary Chinese term for literature or literary pursuits, and it already has this meaning in the *Analects*. Moreover, when we are told that one in whom 'substance preponderates over ornament' (*wên*) will degenerate into a mere savage; while one in whom ornament prevails over substance degenerates into a mere scribe, it is obvious that the *wên* in question is literature and not culture in general.

The earlier English translators were embarrassed by the term *wên*, because although they knew that it corresponded in a general way to our word 'culture', they were entirely unfamiliar with the practical efficacies (*tê*) with which the Chinese associated the word. Legge, indeed, in one passage translates *wên* 'the Cause of truth', not being able to convince himself that Confucius could have been interested in transmitting anything so frivolous as a mere 'culture'.

1 IX, 5.
2 Cf. *Tso Chuan*, Chao Kung, 2nd year.
3 VII, 13.   4 IX, 14.   5 XV, 25.

T'IEN

Apart from cases where Heaven (*t'ien*) merely means 'the sky' (for example in the common phrase *t'ien-hsia*, 'that which is under heaven', i.e. the whole world),[1] it clearly corresponds to our word Heaven and to the German *Himmel* in the sense of Providence, Nature, God. Heaven is the dispenser of life and death, wealth and rank (XII, 5). The *chün-tzu* must learn to know the will (*ming*) of Heaven and submit to it patiently, a hard lesson that Confucius himself did not master till the age of fifty (II, 4). Concerning 'the ways of Heaven' he was unwilling to discourse (V, 12); but its name lingered on his lips in certain ancient formulae, such as those of oath-taking and of submission to fate in times of affliction. His 'Heaven has bereft me!' at the time of Yen Hui's death and his 'It is (Heaven's) will that we should lose him,' at the death-bed of Po Niu, correspond to the Moslem *kismet* and to our own 'God's will be done'. Confucius is made sometimes to speak as though he regarded himself as under the special protection of Providence, just as he certainly regarded himself as charged with a peculiar mission as transmitter of the rapidly disappearing Chou culture.[2] But I fancy that phrases such as 'Heaven implanted *tê* in me; what can such a one as Huan T'ui do to me?' (VII, 22) are, like 'Heaven has bereft me', etc., pious formulae, signifying confidence in God's protection.

T'ien then corresponds for the most part to our Heaven and, as with us, occurs chiefly in pious, traditional formulae. There is, however, at any rate one passage where the translation 'Nature' would not be out of place: 'Does Nature (*t'ien*) speak? No; but the four seasons are regulated by it; the crops grow by it' (XVII, 19). The Chinese conception of Heaven is, then, a very

1 Or again in the 'climbing to the sky' of XIX, 25.
2 IX, 5.

familiar one. The only question that arises is why a word meaning 'sky' should also have the connotations God, Providence, etc.? The problem is clearly one which cannot be attacked from the Chinese side alone.

The Sanskrit *deva*, the Greek θεός, the Latin *deus* – indeed the words for 'God' in most Indo-European languages – are sometimes alleged to be connected with roots meaning 'sky'. This is far from certain. It is only between Chinese and Germanic that we get a complete parallel in the use of *t'ien* and Heaven (*Himmel*). Is the original meaning of *t'ien* 'sky' and hence God, because God lives in the sky; or was it the other way round? To the term Heaven as used in the average early Chinese text exactly corresponds the term *Shang Ti* used constantly in the *Book of Songs*, and occasionally elsewhere. *Shang* means upper, top-most, supreme; *Ti* means[1] 'ancestor' in the sense in which the Ancestors sometimes figure in the religions of the South Seas or Africa. A *Ti* is not simply an ancestor, i.e. a grandfather, great-grandfather or the like. It is not a word of relationship, but means a royal ancestor, the deified spirit of a former king. The *Ti* dwell in the Court of Heaven; and it seems to me that *t'ien*, 'Heaven', is used in Chinese as a collective term meaning 'those who dwell in Heaven', just as the 'House of Lords' frequently means those who sit in that House.[2] The older term *Shang Ti*, found side by side with *t'ien* in the *Book of Songs* and used apparently in exactly the same sense, originally meant, I think, the Supreme Ancestor, in the sense of the first of the line of Royal Ancestors. But it is commonly taken in the sense 'The *Ti* that is above', i.e. in the sky, and alternates with *T'ien Ti*, 'Heavenly *Ti*'. The fuller expressions 'Supreme *Ti*' and 'Heavenly *Ti*' do not occur in the

1 i.e. in actual use. I am not concerned with the philosophic glosses of the early dictionaries and commentaries.
2 Cf. *The Way and Its Power*, p. 21.

36

Analects; but in the collection of ancient fragments which constitutes Book XX, the word *Ti* is used by itself in the sense of Heaven or God, in a very personal sense, for *Ti* is spoken of as having servants and a heart.

HSIN

This character is written *jên* ('man') at the side of *yen* ('word'), and is generally translated 'good faith', 'faithfulness', 'truth', etc. In early Chinese it almost always refers to keeping promises, fulfilling undertakings. It does not mean telling the truth; nor do all early peoples regard telling the truth as good in itself. What early Chinese literature, as also that of the Hebrews, condemns is 'bearing false witness', i.e. telling lies that lead to harm. Other sorts of lie are ritually enjoined; for example, that of saying one is ill instead of bluntly refusing an invitation or declining to see a visitor. The necessity of this sort of lie is recognized by 'society' in Europe; but not by the Church. Confucius once (XVII, 20) told a lie of this kind, and Soothill wrote (in 1910) concerning it, 'That such laxity on the part of China's noblest Exemplar has fostered that disregard for truth for which this nation is so notorious, can hardly be denied.' In this instance a man of the world would have understood Confucius better than a clergyman has done. In the passage concerned Confucius shows not 'laxity', but on the contrary a strict attention to manners.

SSU

The mere fact that the physical sensations connected by the Chinese with 'thinking' were evidently very different from our own, should warn us against believing that what they meant by *ssu* (the word ordinarily translated 'think') was identical with what we mean by 'to think'. The Chinese located thought as going on in the middle of the body. We locate it in the head, and though this may be due to self-suggestion, we definitely connect it with sensations in the head and not in the belly.

There is evidence that in its origin the word *ssu* meant to observe outside things. A *ssu-t'ing* was an observation-post in the market, from which the overseer could observe which stall-holders were cheating.[1] So it came to mean to fix the attention not only on something exterior but also on a mental image, as for example, that of a person from whom one is separated; hence 'to be in love'. This use occurs once in the *Analects* (IX, 30): 'It is not that I do not think of you. . .'. There are nine other passages where *ssu* occurs, and in all but two the meaning implied is that of 'directing one's attention', or something very close to it. When one sees people who are better than oneself, one should turn one's attention to equalling them (IV, 17). One should not act till one has looked into the matter three times (V, 19). When one sees a chance of gain, one should divert one's attention to whether it can be pursued without violation of what is right (XIV, 13).[2] One should occupy one's attention with what belongs to one's own rank in society (XIV, 28). There are 'nine points' which should occupy a gentleman's attention (XVI, 10). One should question searchingly and pay close attention to what one is told (XIX, 6).

It may be rather forced to use the word 'attention' in some of these cases; but what I want to emphasize is that in each case we are dealing with a process that is only at a short remove from concrete observation. Never is there any suggestion of a long interior process of cogitation or ratiocination, in which a whole series of thoughts are evolved one out of the other, producing

1 There is, of course, the possibility that *ssu* is here merely a phonetic substitute for some other character.
2 XIX, 1, is practically a repetition of this.

on the physical plane a headache and on the intellectual, an abstract theory. We must think of *ssu* rather as a fixing of the attention (located in the middle of the belly) on an impression recently imbibed from without and destined to be immediately re-exteriorized in action.

These considerations will help us to understand the two remaining passages in which *ssu*, 'to think', is used. 'If one learns but does not think, one is lost; if one thinks but does not learn, one is in danger' (II, 15). 'I once ate nothing all day and did not go to bed all night in order to think. It was no use. Far better, to learn' (XV, 30).

'Learning', as I clearly show in my note on the passage (see below, p. 188), means copying the ancients. It may be objected that the meaning of both passages is evident, and that I am making a great fuss about nothing. They are, however, certainly open to misunderstanding. Chu Hsi (died A.D. 1200) paraphrases *ssu* as 'seeking within the heart', evoking a whole complex of ideas – the 'good knowledge' of Mencius, the 'inward power' of Lao Tzu, the *bodhi* of the Zen Buddhists – which are entirely foreign to the *Analects*. Mencius, the Quietists, the Buddhists all believed that a well of wisdom lay buried deep in the human breast. But Confucius believed nothing of the kind, and all suggestions that *ssu* in these passages means some kind of *yoga*, seem to me utterly unfounded. Moreover, I think that the average European reader of the current translations, coming across the maxim 'Learning without thought is useless' (Legge, Soothill), might easily imagine that 'thought' meant a process of logical reasoning, a sustained interior argumentation, full of 'therefores' and 'becauses'. There is, as a matter of fact, hardly a single example of these conjunctions in the *Analects*. The 'all day and all night' of XV, 30, is simply a way of saying 'you may think (i.e. survey the matter in hand as the overseer surveys the market) till you are blue in the face. You are wasting time. It is much better to find out what the ancients did under similar circumstances.' The theme of II, 15 is slightly different: Learning and turning over in your mind what you have learnt are equally important. Here again, however, the sort of 'thought' that we write with a capital, contrast with Action, and associate with a wrinkled brow, is not in the least what is meant.

WANG

Chou legend centres round its two first kings (*wang*), Wên and Wu. *Wên* in this name probably meant 'mighty';[1] Wu means 'warrior'. But in Confucius's time *wên*, as we have seen, meant the arts of peace as opposed to those of war, and a theory had grown up that every great armed conquest was preceded by a period of cultural preparation, a building up of *tê* (moral force) as distinct from the *li* (physical force) of the warrior, which unless backed by *wên* (culture) cannot prevail. King Wên, the first Chou monarch, was naturally credited with the initial, cultural achievements and King Wu (the Warrior) with the military triumphs which established the Chou hegemony.

To Confucius, however, it was neither Wên nor Wu, but Wu's brother Tan, Duke of Chou, who was the real hero of the Chou conquest. This point of view was a purely local one. The Duke of Chou is barely mentioned in the *Book of Songs*.[2] But legend regarded him as the founder of the Ducal House in Lu; and Confucius, as a professed Conservative and Legitimist, dwelt fondly on the memory of this local Ancestor and felt a

1 As it presumably does when it occurs as a stock epithet of 'ancestor'. *Wên*, 'pattern' is probably quite a different word.
2 There are only two *Songs* (232 and 251) which mention him.

profound discouragement when the Duke of Chou no longer appeared to him in his dreams.[1]

The coming of Divine Sages and World Monarchs, in China as elsewhere, was heralded by portents. Confucius watched in vain for the appearance of such signs: 'the phoenix does not arrive and the river gives forth no chart'.[2] Birds have everywhere been regarded as intermediaries between Heaven and Earth. The sudden appearances and movements of birds were interpreted as ominous, in China as in the West. The sacred *fêng* (phoenix), half-bird, half-snake, acclaimed the holy kingship of Shun; it was a winged messenger, part man, part bird that heralded the coming of the western Saviour.

The legend of the river-omen existed in two forms, which were merely local variants of the same belief. The portent referred to in the *Analects* is the 'River Chart',[3] which is brought out of the river (usually understood to mean the Yellow River) by an animal that is a mixture of horse and dragon. The variant legend concerns the 'Writings from the Lo River', which are brought out of the Lo river (in Honan) by a Divine Tortoise. But the 'River Chart' is also sometimes spoken of as being brought by the Tortoise; indeed, the confusion between the two legends lasts till the thirteenth century.

There are two explanations as to what the Chart and the Writings consisted of. One is, that they contained the divinatory diagrams of the *Book of Changes*, that is to say the eight trigrams arrived at by arranging two symbols in every possible group of three. The other is, that they were magic arrangements of numbers. The

---

1 VII, 5.

2 IX, 8.

3 *T'u* means 'plan', 'plot', 'scheme'; it may be cognate to *t'u*, 'land', and mean originally 'to plot out land'.

two theories are closely related; for the process[1] of shuffling the forty-nine stalks in order to discover which divinatory diagram concerned one, was bound up both with ideas of numerical symbolism and with the natural properties of numbers. At the beginning of the Sung dynasty the theory was that the River Chart was the 'magic square'

$$4 \quad 9 \quad 2$$
$$3 \quad 5 \quad 7$$
$$8 \quad 1 \quad 6$$

in which the columns, whether added horizontally, vertically or diagonally always come to fifteen. Many Sung writers[2] are quite definite on this point. The River Chart with its nine chambers, they say, 'has five for its centre, carries nine on its head, treads on one, has three at the left, and seven at the right, has two and four on top, and six and eight below'.

But the magic square had behind it a long history. It was believed, certainly in the second century B.C. and probably much earlier, that the Nine chambers of the Ming T'ang (the ruler's audience-hall) had in ancient times been an architectural embodiment of the magic square.[3] It would then, I think, be fairly safe to assume that Confucius regarded the River Chart as a magic arrangement of symbols or numbers, and that he very likely identified it with the 'magic square' (492, 357, etc.) alluded to above.

WANG AND PO

In the *Analects* and in subsequent Chinese literature we find the term *wang* (king) used in a very special sense,

1 Well described in Richard Wilhelm's book on the *I Ching*.

2 See *T'u Shu* encyclopaedia, XXI, 51, and charts on fols. III, 12 and IV, 12.

3 *Ta Tai Li Chi*, 67.

that of a Saviour King who, unlike the monarchs of the world around us, rules by *tê*, by magico-moral force alone. The coming of such a Saviour was looked forward to with Messianic fervour. Were a True King to come, says Confucius, in the space of a single generation Goodness would become universal.[1] With the Saviour King is always contrasted the *Po* (verb, *pa*, 'to be a *po*'). The word originally means 'elder', 'senior', and in the early days of the Chou dynasty when the various conquered domains were ruled by descendants of the conquering House it was applied to the senior among the feudal barons. After the central authority of the Chou declined it was applied to any local ruler who succeeded in acquiring an ascendancy over the rest, with a view (in theory at any rate) to re-establishing the pontifical authority of the Chou monarch. The greatest of the *Po* were Huan of Ch'i (middle of the seventh century) and Wên of Chin (second half of the seventh century). A *Po* acts by *li* (physical force) and not by *tê*. His achievements cannot lead to the reign of universal Goodness. The material consequences of such a hegemony may be immense. The two great *Po* saved China from complete immersion by the barbarians: but for the efforts of Huan 'we should be wearing our hair loose and folding our garments to the left'.[2] But the *Po* is guided by opportunism alone, his Way is not that of the Former Kings, his achievements are in the political not in the moral sphere. His fellow barons may reluctantly yield to his superior strength; but he cannot inspire 'everywhere under Heaven' that longing for spontaneous submission which overcame even the wild tribes of the west and north when the Saviour King T'ang appeared: 'when he advanced towards the East, the savages of the West were jealous; when he advanced towards the South, the

1 XIII, 12.   2 XIV, 18.

barbarians of the North were jealous, saying "Why did he not advance upon us first?" Everywhere the people turned their gaze towards him, as men gaze towards a rainbow in days of drought.'[1]

WRITTEN TRADITION[2]

No doubt what Confucius knew of the Former Kings and of the 'antiquity' which he loved so well was derived partly from oral, partly from written sources. We must not, however, in dealing with societies where both sorts of tradition exist, attempt to make too sharp a distinction between the two. Wherever texts exist at all, even if they are accessible only to a small minority, the two sorts of tradition are bound to infiltrate one another. A Mongol peasant who tells the story of Buddha's life may have learnt most of the episodes orally from other members of the tribe, who also learnt most of them orally. But he may very well have learnt other episodes from a Lama who has read them in a book. And the same Lama, should he write a book, would be likely enough to incorporate in his story folk-lore elements belonging to an oral tradition. A Majorcan peasant who tells one stories about the Moors has probably never read a book about the Moors or, indeed, any book at all. But much of what he tells could ultimately be traced to printed texts.

Knowledge, in ancient Chinese phraseology, consists in 'hearing much'. In the chronicles, when the judgments of a famous man upon episodes of the past (events, say, of the seventh and sixth centuries) are recorded, he is invariably spoken of as 'hearing about' the event, even if it occurred centuries before his time; seldom, as reading about it. Confucius continually quotes ancient sayings, many of them in the form of

1 *Mencius*, I, 2. XI.
2 This section too may be omitted by the general reader.

didactic verse. How many of these are drawn from written collections we have no means of knowing. The one written work which almost certainly existed in his time and to which we may reasonably suppose he had at least occasional access was the *Book of Songs*. Concerning this most important of all Chou texts I will say no more here, but refer the reader to my recently published *The Book of Songs*.[1] A far more thorny and complicated problem is presented by another book to which the *Analects* sometimes refer. This is the collection of documents known as *Shu Ching*. The European reader is familiar, through the translations of Legge and Couvreur, with a version of this text containing fifty-six books or chapters. Of these all but twenty-eight were strung together from very miscellaneous sources in the third century A.D. The sources used were mainly though not exclusively pre-Han, and the view is sometimes taken that even though the compilation of these forged books was late, their matter is early and therefore relevant to the study of Chou tradition. This is not really so; for isolated sentences have been detached from their context and strung together in such a way as completely to falsify the meaning. It may be convenient to the reader if I here give a list of the books which are not the work of a third-century forger:

(1) Yao Tien (second half now printed as Shun Tien)
(2) Kao Yao Mo (second half now printed as I Chi)
(3) Yü Kung
(4) Kan Shih
(5) T'ang Shih
(6) P'an Kêng
(7) Kao Tsung Yung Jih
(8) Hsi Po K'an Li

1 Allen and Unwin, 1937. Vol. I. Translations, Vol. II. Textual Notes.

(9) Wei Tzu
(10) Mu Shih
(11) Hung Fan
(12) Chin T'êng
(13) Ta Kao
(14) K'ang Kao
(15) Chiu Kao
(16) Tzu Ts'ai
(17) Shao Kao
(18) Lo Kao
(19) To Shih
(20) Wu I
(21) Chün Shih
(22) To Fang
(23) Li Chêng
(24) Ku Ming (second half now printed as K'ang Wang Chih Kao)
(25) Pi Shih
(26) Lü Hsing
(27) Wên Hou Chih Ming
(28) Ch'in Shih

Those which have any chance of being contemporary documents are (13) to (28), excluding (26). (13), (15) and (21) are put in a class apart by Ho Ting-shêng,[1] as according most completely with the language and ideas of the inscriptions. In no document of the *Shu Ching*, however, does the use of pronouns (*wo*, 'I', *êrh*, 'you', etc.) concord with Western Chou inscriptions. P'an Kêng (6) is linguistically very close to (13)–(23) and was probably written as propaganda in favour of the transference of the Capital to the East at the close of the Western Chou period (*c.* 770 B.C.?). The rest are later texts which were dressed up in superficial resemblance

1 National Sun Yat-sen University: *Linguistic and Historical Review* (in Chinese). V, 49 (1928).

46

to the style of the Books, in order to gain credence and authority. The *Analects* quote exclusively from Books that are now lost (only the third–century A.D. forgeries of them exist); save in the one instance of XIV, 43 which is practically a quotation from Wu I (20). In general, however, the genuinely archaic books, being merely archival documents, are less quoted in Confucian literature than the later more moralistic compilations, intended at the outset for edification.

Confucius has been represented by some European writers as a bookish man. Soothill even went so far as to suggest that he had 'the scholar's indifferent digestion'. We have, however, no reason to suppose that his reading went beyond the *Songs* and *Shu Ching*, possibly some ritual texts and collections of moral sayings, and perhaps the Court annals of his own State.[1] His youth (of which we know little) was certainly not spent in poring over books, but presumably in hunting and fighting, the occupations common to his class. In the chronicles we find his disciples (for example, Jan Ch'iu and Fan Ch'ih) riding out to battle together; and again we have no reason to suppose that the Master's active years were spent differently from theirs.

RITUAL

It is very unlikely that any ritual texts existed until the decline of Chou civilization. So long as the rites were practised, it was unnecessary to fix them in writing. Probably the first books of ritual were composed for the benefit of such offshoots of the Chou ruling caste as were settled in the remoter conquered territories, and were in danger of becoming out of contact with the central culture. Whether Confucius knew any such texts or derived his knowledge of ritual solely from oral

1 This is very doubtful. Official annals were only accessible to high officers of state.

maxims is uncertain. All of the ritual books that we possess contain ancient material; but all[1] of them were certainly composed long after the time of Confucius.

The Confucius of the *Analects* is not much concerned with the details of ritual, either public or domestic. Correct observance of small social rites, what we call 'good manners', belongs, of course, equally to the Chinese and to our conception of the gentleman, as does also the insistence upon 'giving a fair chance' both to one's competitors in sport[2] and to one's victims in the chase.[3] But the actual text of the *Analects* is concerned with the general principles of conduct, with morality rather than manners; and so little guidance on the details of behaviour could the composers of the work find in the traditional sayings of the Master that they were obliged to insert in it, in order to meet the demands of a later Confucianism that was preoccupied above all with the details of ritual, a long ritual text, dealing in reality with the behaviour of gentlemen in general, but adapted and amplified in such a way as to read as though it were a description of Confucius's own behaviour. This text (Book X), though we cannot (as many Western writers have done) use it as biographical material, throws so much light on early Confucian ideas that it will be worth while to consider its contents in detail. The first characteristic about it that strikes us is the profusion of reduplicative words (similar to such English formations as 'sing-song', 'hurly-burly' and the like). In fulfilling religious rites it is not sufficient merely to say the correct words or perform the correct actions. Each rite requires also an appropriate 'attitude', one of

1 Some Western scholars make an exception of the *I Li*, which is mainly concerned with the domestic ritual of everyday life. But this book, too, shows, for example, in the sections on mourning, the same tendency to build up theoretical schematizations rather than to describe actual practices, which marks the other ritual works.

2 III, 7.   3 For fishing and shooting, see VII, 26.

reverence, eagerness, reluctance, joy, gloom and so on.[1] It is these attitudes (*jung*) that are defined by the expressive reduplicatives mentioned above. Such definitions are not confined to behaviour on ritual occasions. In VII, 4, we find the Master's attitude when sitting quietly at home described by a pair of typical 'expressive reduplicatives'. There was, in fact, no circumstance in life for which a particular attitude was not seemly and appropriate. In this respect we do not differ substantially from the Chinese. Anyone who knows how to behave adopts a special attitude when in church, one of reverence and constraint; he listens to the observations of his superiors in a special attitude of alert attention, his tenderly admirative attitude when taking the hand of an influential hostess is as different as possible from that which he adopts when shaking hands with a tennis opponent. A gentleman who adopted the wrong attitude on any one of these or a hundred other occasions would show grave ill-breeding. The assumption, for example, of a playful attitude when handing round the collecting-box in church or of the 'tenderly admirative' attitude when interviewing a male superior would be sufficient to close the most promising social or public career.

It might be objected that our 'attitudes' are of a spontaneous, instinctive kind – that they arise 'naturally' out of the situations to which they belong. But in point of fact they only seem to us natural and inevitable because we are used to them. The English church-going attitude, so far from arising naturally from the feelings connected with a place of worship, is peculiar to Anglicanism. It is far more extreme, in its contrast with the attitudes of everyday life, far more stylized and artificial than that practised in other Protestant countries (the

1 See *The Way and Its Power*, p. 160.

'off-hand' attitude of the Dutch when in church has often impressed English travellers); in a southern Catholic church the contrast is even less noticeable, with the Moslem (whose religion functions equally inside and outside the Mosque) it hardly exists at all.

The difference, in respect of 'attitudes', between us and the ancient Chinese is that we learn them and practise them unconsciously; whereas with the Chinese they were a subject of conscious interest and attention. A high standard was set, gentility implied a fastidious *expertise* in the niceties of bearing, a whole armoury of gesture and attitude was developed, beside which our humble stock (hat-raising, hand-shaking and the like) seems meagre indeed.

The commonest method of symbolizing one's own 'smallness' as contrasted with the 'greatness' of another is to shrink oneself. Even we, with our impoverished vocabulary of attitude, maintain various forms of ceremonial 'shrinking', such as bowing, nodding, kneeling. The Chinese *chün-tzu* knew a far wider range of bendings and contractions, many of which (but by no means all) are mentioned in Book X of the *Analects*. He 'made himself small' now by, as we should say, grogging at the knees, now by squeezing himself as though creeping through a hole, now by stooping across the bar of his chariot, now by bending at the waist.

Anthropologists are or were in the habit of trying to discover the 'real reason' why particular injunctions or prohibitions were imposed among primitives. If the reason given by the people themselves seemed to them trivial or unintelligible they set it down as a rationalization or, alternatively, attributed it to secretiveness regarding the 'real reason'.

The truth, however, is that there is no 'real reason' for ritual acts. In any community where the performance of such acts is linked to a general system of thought, they will be explained in terms of that system. If the system changes, as frequently happens, without disturbing these ritual acts, they will be reinterpreted in terms of the new system. Where such acts or some of them have not been linked, at any rate in the mind of the person questioned, to any system of thought, they sink to the role of mere etiquette and will be explained as 'customary', as being 'good manners', 'the thing to do', or the like. The ultimate origin of the act or abstentions concerned is a matter for the psychologist, who is at present only able to furnish very speculative and provisional answers.

If, however, we find among people in many parts of the world a prohibition against treading on[1] or lying across thresholds, we can at least say that some of the reasons given for this prohibition belong to ways of thought that are older than others. Huai-nan Tzu,[2] in the second century B.C., gives two alternative reasons for not lying with the head across a threshold, (1) because ghosts inhabit the threshold; (2) because one will catch cold from the draught. It is not difficult to decide which of these two reasons belongs to the earlier way of thinking; and it might seem at first sight as though in this case we had tracked down the prohibition to its source; had found not only an initial but a 'real' reason. For it is well known that in primitive societies the dead were often buried under the threshold, and this practice seems to give an adequate explanation of the threshold 'taboo'.[3] But we are still confronted with the question, why were ghosts believed in and why were they feared? Once more we are in the realm not of anthropology but of psychological speculation.

The *Analects* simply record that on entering the ruler's

1 Book X, 4.
2 P'ien 13, 2 fols. from end.
3 See Frazer, *Folklore in the Old Testament*, Vol. III, p. 11.

palace a gentleman does not step on the threshold and the commentators can tell us no more than that it was not ritually correct to do so. It seems not unreasonable to suppose that in this case an old religious 'taboo' (i.e. a prohibition formally connected with a set of obligatory beliefs) has passed into the domain of etiquette, of things that are done because they are done. It was the task of the ritual theorists in the third century B.C. to detrivialize ritual, to arrest its lapse into the domain of mere etiquette or good manners, by reintegrating it into the current system of thought. The Jews have made similar efforts to reinterpret religious taboos in terms of scientific hygiene.

Matter very like parts of the *Analects* is contained in the *Āpastamba Dharma Sūtra*, a Sanskrit work probably contemporary with the *Analects*, and in the *Mārkandeya Purāna*, which is certainly subsequent to the Christian era. In Chapter XXXIV of the latter work we read that the 'master of a household' must not sleep with his head to the north or the west; compare *Analects*, X, 16. He must not eat stale rice (*Analects*, X, 8, 2) and must not converse 'while impure owing to the fact that he is taking food' (*Analects*, X, 8, 8). The injunction against eating food bought in the market (*Analects*, X, 8, 5) is, of course, inevitable in the case of anyone whose eating is subject to strict taboos, and applied also to Brahmins and Buddhist monks. We also read in the *Purāna* that the 'householder' must not sit with his feet stretched out (XXXIV, 44), which reminds us of *Analects*, XIV, 46, where a disciple is chastised for sitting in a sprawling position.

DRESS

It would be surprising if any code of upper-class behaviour did not deal with the subject of dress, and equally surprising if the dress-regulations contained in the

Analects[1] meant much more to us than our own upper-class dress-regulations (with a white stiff shirt a gentleman wears a white tie if his waistcoat is white, a black tie if his waistcoat is black; with a white waistcoat he wears a long coat, with a black waistcoat he wears a short coat, etc.) would mean to a resurrected Confucius. To understand early Chinese dress-ritual would demand a detailed knowledge of early Chinese social history, such as we are far indeed from possessing. There are, however, certain general analogies to the dress-rules that we are bound by; and I have tried to point out some of these analogies in my notes on the relevant passages. It is my impression that the 'knightly' origin of some regulations had been forgotten. I would hazard the guess that the shortness of the right sleeve was not (as the commentators tell us) intended (originally, at any rate) to facilitate the use of the right hand in general, but in particular to leave it free to defend the *chün-tzu*'s honour with the sword.[2] It is possible that the regulation about bed-coverings has a similar origin. They are to be one and a half times (and not twice) as long as the sleeper, lest trapped in a complete bag of bed-clothes, he may be unable if attacked to defend himself with alacrity. But this is only a speculation.

THE DEAD

No practices have been subject to a more constant re-interpretation than those connected with mourning and burial. In some places,[3] for example, the plugging of all the orifices of the corpse is regarded as a device for preventing the soul escaping and doing harm to the community. In China mortuary jades, used in just the same way, were looked upon as a means of fortifying

1 X, 6.
2 Or dagger. Swords do not seem to belong to Western Chou culture.
3 See Sir James Frazer, *Fear of the Dead*, Vol. II, p. 109.

the 'life' of the departed in his new abode. We find among mankind in general, indeed, two sharply contrasted attitudes towards the dead. In some societies they are feared; in others they are reverenced. The first attitude can exist without any admixture of the second. But the attitude of reverence and love seldom exists without some admixture of fear. Those, for example, who honour and love the dead by day walk none too boldly through a graveyard by night.

Now it is perfectly possible that both these attitudes are expressions of the same fundamental feeling. Certain psychologists call this feeling a 'sense of guilt', and imply that somewhere at the bottom of our hearts we feel that it was we who slew those whom we profess to love. Be that as it may, we find among men as we know them these two sharply contrasted conscious attitudes, and there is not I think the slightest doubt that the attitude of fear is the more primitive. For example, in societies where the two attitudes exist side by side, it is always the less developed members of the community who fear the dead – who refuse, for example, to cross the cemetery by night.

In China the attitude towards the dead was, among the upper classes, at any rate, one solely of love and reverence; and all the rites of burial, mourning and sacrifice to immediate forefathers were interpreted in this sense. It does not, however, by any means follow that these rites and practices had always been so interpreted or that any of them had their origin in the attitude of tenderness and regret. The personal name of the dead was not allowed to be mentioned.[1] If his fame had not spread beyond the family circle he was known as 'the departed father', 'the late uncle', or the like; if he were

1 The evidence of the inscriptions is that the Chou conquerors themselves did not practise this taboo. It had, however, become general long before Confucius's time.

a person of public importance, destined to become as we say, 'known to history', he received a 'posthumous name', descriptive of his virtues:[1] the Steadfast, the Cultured, the Pious. This avoidance of the personal name was interpreted as due to 'respect' for the dead. But it is difficult not to regard it merely as a particular example of the general rule that to name a spirit is to compel its presence; and we may be fairly sure that there was once a time in China when, if the dead were not named, it was through fear lest they should suddenly appear.

As with us, an important feature of funeral rites was the eulogy (*lei*) pronounced over the dead. Later *lei* are, like ours, for the most part merely laudatory, but in that quoted by Tzu-lu in the *Analects* is manifest the desire not merely to placate the dead but to disclaim responsibility, to remind him that the living 'did everything they could': 'we prayed for you (i.e. during your illness) upwards and downwards, to the spirits of Heaven and to the spirits of earth below'.[2]

MOURNING

The mourner leads a life apart, wears special clothes, eats special food, abstains from physical pleasures, retires from public life, and so on. One explanation of why he does these things is that he has been contaminated by contact with death; he has become a sinister person and must be segregated in order to go through a process of 'disinfection'. A quite different interpretation of the mourner's behaviour is given in ancient China. If he leads an abnormal life it is not because he is ritually unclean and must, so to speak, be cured. It is because he would not 'feel at

1 Or of his vices? It is a disputed question whether certain 'posthumous names' are to be taken in a bad sense. Was Li Wang (died 828 B.C.) the Cruel King or the Dignified King? Many Western sovereigns are, of course, 'known to history' by bad names, e.g. Bloody Mary and Theophylact the Unbearable.   2 VII, 34.

ease'[1] in his ordinary clothes, on his ordinary mat, eating his usual food, doing his habitual work. And if someone brought into contact with a mourner must behave towards him in a propitiatory fashion, and even for the time being follow the mourner's regime,[2] it is not (as in some communities) because the mourner may well try to transfer some of his uncleanness to those with whom he comes in contact, and this secondary taint requires to be removed by the same means as the original one; on the contrary, these precautions are due in Chinese theory to respect for the mourner's feelings. But there are practices which fit in badly with this explanation; for example, the prohibition, mentioned in other books besides the *Analects*,[3] against singing on the same day that one has wailed at a funeral.

Preparation for sacrifice, to which Book X devotes a long section, bears a strong resemblance to mourning. The sacrificer segregates himself, alters all his habits, denies himself every indulgence; this time certainly not in order to rid himself of a taint caused by contact with the dead, but to purify himself, to spiritualize himself in such a way as to be fit for contact with the spirit world and at the same time to impress the spirits with the earnestness of the appeals he is about to make.

Spirits are fastidious; it cannot be expected that they will accept the sacrifice and come in person to partake of it, if the sacrificer is in a condition which even his earthly wives or concubines would object to, if he smells of wine or garlic. This idea, I think, underlies the prohibitions against eating onions, garlic, ginger[4] and so

1 XVII, 21.   2 VII, 9; IX, 9; X, 16.   3 VII, 9.

4 The 'He does not eschew ginger-food' (i.e. food sprinkled with ginger), of Book X, takes for granted that the mourner does eschew the eating of ginger as a separate dish. It follows that if pungent herbs, etc., are avoided when we wish to attract spirits they will be used when we wish to repel spirits. It is therefore not surprising that peasants in many parts of Europe hang garlic at their doors to drive away evil spirits.

on, that we find not only in the regime of the sacrificer, who is a temporary priest; but also in that of the permanent priests of Buddhism.

THE MAGIC EFFICACY OF RITUAL

The word *li* ('ritual') is expressed in writing by a picture of a ritual vessel. The original meaning is said to be 'arranging ritual vessels'; and this may very well be true, for it appears to be cognate to a number of words meaning 'to arrange in proper order', 'to put in sequence', etc. But as used in early China *li* would cover everything from the opening of the great doors of St. Peter's down to saying 'Bless you!' when someone sneezes.[1] Modern writers have said that Confucius, in common with the early Chinese in general, attributed a magic influence to ritual. In a sense this is true. The influence of saying 'God bless you!' can hardly be considered otherwise than a magic one; and no doubt Confucius attributed a like influence to all the small prescriptions and conventions that we should put under the heading of good manners. But the rites to which Confucius attributed a true magic efficacy in the fullest sense were, naturally enough, not those that he saw practised around him in everyday life, nor the usurped rites illicitly carried on by the dictators of Lu;[2] but those enacted by the ideal monarchs of the legendary past, by Yao and Shun, by Yü the Great, by Wên and Wu of Chou, and above all by the Duke of Chou, patron saint of Lu.

Wherever the idea of divine kingship prevails we find coupled with it the conviction that upon the correct performance of kingly ritual depends the whole welfare of the State, the fertility of its lands, the fruitfulness of its trees, the fecundity both of its women and of its herds and flocks. The Divine King (*T'ien wang*) in

1 There are other words for 'deportment', 'seemliness', and so on. But *li* is the generic word which covers them all.   2 III, 1 and 2.

ancient China was the Emperor (the 'Son of Heaven')
and the State rulers merely inherited a fraction of his
divinity. In Confucius's time there was no longer a Son
of Heaven. The King of Chou still used this title, but
the mere fact that the local rulers no longer deferred to
him showed that he had lost his heavenly 'appointment'.
The Imperial rites, too, had long ago fallen into abey-
ance; with the parody of them that was enacted in his
native State Confucius had no patience: 'At the Ancestral Sacrifice, as for all that comes after the libation –
I had rather not witness it!'[1]

Not only were the rites incorrectly performed, but
their *shuo* (explanation) was lost,[2] and with it the magic
power that enabled Divine Kings to 'deal with all things
under Heaven as easily as I lay my finger here'.[3]

That countries could really adopt with success a
home policy of government by the magic of ritual (as
opposed to government by penalties) and a foreign
policy of 'giving way' (*jang*) as opposed to one of push
and grab (*chin-ch'ü*) is a fundamental part of Confucius's
Way. If a king could for a single day fully and completely
carry out the kingly ritual, the whole country would
'surrender' to his Goodness. 'Keep order among them
by chastisement and they will flee from you; keep order
among them by ritual and they will come to you of
their own accord.'[4]

I do not think Confucius attributed this magic power
to any rites save those practised by the divinely
appointed ruler. It is true that the correct practice of
ritual by 'those above' (as opposed to 'those below', i.e.
the *min*, 'masses') also exercises a profound influence

1 III, 10.
2 i.e. They had become divorced from the circle of ideas to which they
originally belonged, and had not been successfully reinterpreted. A rite
divorced from its *Shuo* has as little efficacy as a scripture apart from its
traditional interpretation (also called *Shuo*).
3 III, 11.   4 II, 3.

upon the populace. In a country where the *chün-tzu* are punctilious in their ritual observances[1] the small people will be punctilious in the discharge of their duties towards their superiors,[2] and will be easy to rule.[3] It is for the upper classes to 'set a good example', as we say; to exert a good influence. In regard to this function of the *chün-tzu* I do not think that the Confucian conception was very different from ours. The idea that human institutions should be harmonized (*ho*) with the operations of Nature, should for example be arranged in categories, corresponding to the seasons, the planets, the points of the compass, though it is referred to by Master Yu in one entirely isolated passage,[4] does not belong to the teaching of Confucius in the *Analects*.

The Chinese have a special word for things done 'after a fashion', in a hugger-mugger way, but not according to the proper ritual.[5] Such things are said to be fluked (*kou*). What is done in this way may seem for the moment to 'work', just as a hastily patched tyre may carry us for a mile or two as comfortably as a properly mended one. But the *chün-tzu*'s code, like that of the old-fashioned artisan, compels him to 'make a good job' of whatever he undertakes. A temporary success secured by irregular means gives him no satisfaction; it is stolen (*t'ou*), not honestly come by.[6] True, the social virtues (loyalty, promise-keeping, respect for elders, courage in the cause of right) come first, are the groundwork upon which *li* (ritual) must be built.[7] 'A man that is not good, what can he have to do with ritual?'[8] But right conduct does not proceed automatically from right feelings. It is virtuous to respect Heaven; but if (to take a Western

1 Including, of course, etiquette and manners.
2 XIII, 4.   3 XIV, 44.   4 I, 12.
5 See additional note on XIII, 3.
6 The word 'steal' is often coupled with or substituted for *kou*.
7 *Li hou yeh*, 'Ritual is secondary.' III, 8.
8 III, 3.

equivalent) one took off one's shoes in church instead of one's hat as a sign of respect, *pu hsing*: 'it would not work'. The domain of Chinese ritual, of obligatory acts and abstentions was a vast one. Three hundred rules of major ritual and three thousand minor observances had, according to the usual computation,[1] to be mastered. The expression 'to know', used by itself, means 'to know the rites', and he who lacked this *savoir faire* could not be regarded as a gentleman. It might, indeed, seem to us that the *chün-tzu*, faced with the necessity of learning 3,300 injunctions,[2] was in some danger of turning into precisely what is everywhere held to be inconsistent with his status – was in danger, that is to say, of turning into a qualified specialist. But it was with the relation of ritual as a whole to morality and not with the details of etiquette and precedence that the early Confucians were chiefly concerned. Master Tsêng, indeed, even goes so far as to say that the ordering of ritual vessels is a matter for the special officers put in charge of them, and does not fall within the *chün-tzu*'s proper sphere.[3]

MUSIC AND DANCING (YO)

Our view of music as an agreeable arrangement of sounds,[4] listened to solely for enjoyment, and of dancing as a means of social distraction combined with mild bodily exercise, is a very abnormal one. Everywhere

1 e.g. *Chung-yung*, XXVII, 3 and *Li Chi*, X.

2 Some of them seem to us superfluous: 'If when you are calling on another gentleman, he begins to yawn and stretch himself, twiddles his hair-pins, fiddles with the knob of his sword, shuffles his feet and asks how the time is going, you will not be at fault in proposing to retire.' (*Li Chi*, XVII.) This is less absurd than it sounds; for the wording implies that the visitor is inferior in age or status, and in such cases (as in our own Court etiquette) it was for the host and not the guest to terminate the interview.

3 VIII, 4.

4 Obviously there are in our use of music some remnants of an earlier conception; particularly its use in connection with war.

during the greater part of man's history and by a large portion of the world's inhabitants even to-day these related arts are regarded in a way wholly different from the way in which we regard them. Music, in the view not only of primitives, but in that of almost all non-European peoples, exercises a magic power not only over the heart of man (as we in Europe would to some extent admit), but also over the forces of nature. Everyone familiar with early Chinese books knows the story, existing in countless variants, of Duke P'ing of Chin[1] and the baleful music – how drawn by the magic of an evil tune eight huge black birds swooped from the south and danced on his terrace, black clouds blotted out the sky, a tempest tore down the hangings of his palace, broke the ritual vessels, hurled down the tiles from the roof; the king fell sick, and for three years no blade of grass grew in Chin, no tree bore fruit.

A similar view of the magic power of music over the forces of nature still prevails in India; it is by music and dancing that rain is produced all over Africa, just as it was in ancient China. I do not think that Confucius would have questioned the possibility of music possessing such power; but it was to the music of the Divine Sages and not to the 'songs of Wei and Chêng' that he attributed it; and this 'music of the ancients' had all but disappeared. The music of the Succession Dance (*Shao*), which Confucius characterizes as 'perfectly beautiful' apparently did not exist in Lu. Later legend regarded it as the accession music of the Divine Sage Shun; but it also figures as a Chou dance, and we do not know whether Confucius regarded any of the magical music of the Sages as surviving in his time.

When he heard the Succession music, he 'did not notice what he was eating' for three months afterwards. This gives the impression that Confucius's whole being

1 The incident is placed by legend in about 533 B.C.

was profoundly stirred by the performance, much in the same way as the young Bach was moved by the organ-playing of Buxtehude. And, indeed, if we could register the exact physiological reactions in the two cases, we might well find that they were very much the same. But we should be mistaken if we supposed that Confucius's conscious attitude towards music, his 'interpretation' of its place in life, concorded in the least with that of a European musician. To him, as to the ancient Greeks, it was important above all as an instrument of education.[1] It promotes virtue; it is an intrinsic part of the Way that causes gentlemen to love other gentlemen and makes small men easy to rule.

1 VIII, 8.

APPENDIX I

There are two main interpretations of the *Analects*, the 'old' and the 'new'. The old interpretation is that of the *Lun Yü Chi Chieh*, 'Collected Explanations of the *Lun Yü*', presented to the throne by a committee of scholars about A.D. 240. The chief commentators whose explanations were here collected are Pao Hsien (6 B.C.–A.D. 65), Ma Jung, Chêng Hsüan, Wang Su, the noted literary forger (A.D. 195–256) and Chou-shêng Lieh, who is interesting to us from the fact that he was a native of Tun-huang, the scene of Sir Aurel Stein's and Professor Pelliot's epoch-making archaeological discoveries. A commentary falsely attributed to K'ung An-kuo (*c.* 130–90 B.C.) was also used. It seems likely that the editors did not originally indicate which explanations were extracted from which commentaries. Possessors of the book added the names as best they could, and there was subsequently a good deal of confusion as to which commentary any particular gloss really came from; for the commentaries themselves fell out of use and disappeared. It seemed, indeed, in the highest degree unlikely that any of them would be recovered. But as has already been mentioned, a considerable part of Chêng Hsüan's commentary was found at Tun-huang. Many of the glosses that the current *Lun Yü Chi Chieh* attributes to him occur *verbatim* in the Tun-huang fragments; but there are also many discrepancies.

The main object of the old interpreters was to make

the text easily comprehensible to current readers.[1] They do not use it as a peg either for pure philology or for moral edification. To this end they explain allusions to persons and events by reference to the annals and to the much-expanded legend of Confucius and his disciples, as it existed in their time. For the rest, they confine themselves to translating archaisms into the language of their own day, and to bringing allusions to rituals and usages into line with current ritual theories. Almost all the information they supply is such as anyone familiar with extant early literature could even to-day easily supply for himself. They are valuable in that they show the new interpretation to have had no ancient authority. But they seldom help anyone with a complete knowledge of early Chinese literature a step further towards understanding the real difficulties of the text.

The old interpretation, in all its essentials at any rate, held the field until the second half of the twelfth century. Hitherto the *Analects* had been a scripture among other scriptures, studied by those who were adept in ancient literature. But in the Sung dynasty it became a school-book, and finally not merely *a* school-book, but *the* school-book, basis of all education. This transformation was due almost entirely to the efforts of one very remarkable man, Chu Hsi (A.D. 1130–1200). Chu Hsi was occupied with the *Analects* during the greater part of his life. His labours were embodied in a series of books, culminating in the *Lun Yü Chi Chu* of 1177. But we possess very minute records of his

1 What follows, refers in the main to the *Chi Chieh*; Huang K'an (died A.D. 545) is already considerably more expatiatory; his sub-commentary on the *Chi Chieh* was lost in China, but rediscovered in Japan in 1720 by Nemoto Hakushu, who published it at Yedo in 1750, with a preface by the well-known scholar Fukube Genkyo. It was reprinted in China in the nineteenth century. Fragments have also been recovered at Tun-huang, and these show that the current text is a contamination of the Huang K'an commentary with later commentaries.

conversations,[1] and we see him down till his last years still wrestling with the problems that the *Chi Chu* had provisionally disposed of; meeting criticisms of that work and constantly modifying his published opinions.

Chu Hsi, like Confucius, was a 'transmitter rather than an originator'. His main object was to popularize the new approach to the Confucian Classics taught by the brothers Ch'êng.[2]

Neo-Confucianism, as we call the school to which the Ch'êng brothers belonged, had its origins in the ninth century.[3] If it seems to us to spring into the world unheralded upon the rise of the Sung, it is only because of the hiatus due to the disturbed state of China in the long period of anarchy between T'ang and Sung. The method of this school, as applied to the Classics, was a complete reinterpretation in terms of the syncretist philosophy (deeply influenced by Taoism and Zen Buddhism) which had gradually grown up since the ninth century.

Chu Hsi has been called a great scholar, but no one would call him so who had any experience of the difference between scholarship and theology. For though Chu Hsi was not a theologian in the literal sense of the term, though he is concerned with a Truth rather than with a God, his methods are at every point those of the theologian, not those of the scholar. It was not his aim to discover, as a scholar would have done, what the Classics meant when they were written. He assumed that there was one Truth, embodied equally in the teachings of the brothers Ch'êng and in the sayings of Confucius. In the teachings of the brothers this Truth

1 Those referring to the *Analects* are conveniently collected in chapters 10 to 19 of the *Chu Tzu Ch'üan Shu*.

2 Ch'êng Hao (A.D. 1032–1085), Ch'êng I (1033–1107).

3 The mental furniture of the average chün-tzu in the ninth century was derived impartially from Confucianism, Taoism and Buddhism.

lay on the surface; in the *Analects* it lay hidden behind the words, and was not easily accessible even to those who had fully embraced it in its more exoteric manifestations. Chu Hsi's task was to make this hidden Truth, ensconced in the Classical books, accessible to everybody. To him every sentence vibrated with this Truth. The old interpreters allowed the reader to go his own way, only coming to his assistance occasionally where an archaism or allusion was likely to hold him up. Chu Hsi is always at our elbow, ready to save us from the 'obfuscation' of thinking that the text really means what it says. Again and again Confucius confesses to ignorance and imperfection. Chu Hsi is at hand to tell us that this is only ritual modesty; 'How could a Sage really err, how could a Sage truly not know?'; or to construe the sentence differently, so that 'You and I are not equal to him' (V, 8) becomes 'I grant you are not equal to him'; or to make a Sage figure as a Sage should, so that 'sent on a mission' becomes 'sent on a mission by Confucius' (VI, 3). He is there to save us from supposing that a Sage ever spoke the dialect of his native State (VII, 17); and all the time, by perpetual paraphrase and adaptation, he brings the recalcitrant text into line with Truth, so that in the end the *Analects* become as orthodox a Neo-Confucian treatise as any that proceeded from the classroom of the brothers Ch'êng. Chu Hsi was a great popular educator, a great evangelist; but in no sense was he a scholar.

The following discourse of Yu Tso (flourished *c.* A.D. 1100) on *Analects*, XII, 1, contained in his *Lun Yü Tsa Chieh*, is a good example of the mixed Taoist-Buddhist interpretation of the *Analects*, which prevailed in Sung times:

Goodness is the heart of man. All that the word Goodness means is 'getting access to one's real heart'. In its true and original state the heart did not experience pleasure, anger, grief or delight. But once a man begins to pursue his own private ends, harassed by rage and desire, he ceases to be in any proper sense a man. If on the other hand, he can overcome the personal cravings of his human heart and return to the impersonal state that belongs to the heart of Tao, then he will regard others just as he regards himself; will regard things just as he regards men, and the true original state of this man's nature will be manifested. Henceforward he will be seen to treat his parents as parents should be treated, to show consideration to his inferiors and affection towards all creatures, all of which will follow spontaneously from workings of his real, unspoiled heart. That is what is meant by the saying 'Goodness is overcoming one's personal self and returning to *li*.'[1] For *li* simply means the natural state of the heart. It is a question of getting the heart back to its original state; that one thing and no more. It is not a question of recognizing a duty as a duty, and doing it; or of recognizing a creature as a creature, and loving it. Nor is it a matter of piling day on day or month on month before one can attain to the end desired. If a man can for a single day return to the original state, go back to the always-so,[2] then the ten thousand things will be for him all of like form and condition, and wherever he goes there will be Goodness. That is why the Master said, 'If for a single day a man can overcome his personal self and return to *li*, everything under Heaven for that man turns into Goodness.'

Chu Hsi himself is, as a rule, careful to avoid interpretations too markedly Buddhist or Taoist in character. He does not, however, refrain from using expositions

1 Literally 'ritual'; but in the language of the Sung philosophers it had come to mean 'the natural'.
2 The vocabulary belongs to Taoism; the conception, to the Sudden Illumination branch of Zen Buddhism.

wholly bound up with Sung scholasticism and having no connection whatever with doctrines which could possibly have existed in the time of Confucius. For example, on *Analects*, 1, 2, he reproduces a passage from Ch'êng Hao which insists that while Goodness is inborn, family piety is not; for it is well known that 'nature' consists 'solely of four constituents, Goodness, Conscience, Reverence and Knowledge'. All this is not merely alien to but directly contradicts the teaching of the *Analects*. Confucius would, for example, have been surprised indeed to learn that Goodness, the quality he so persistently refused to accord even to his most favoured disciples, was common to all men; and that inborn knowledge, which he himself expressly disclaimed,[1] was to be reckoned as an inevitable part of human equipment.

The methods of critical philology were first applied to the text by scholars such as Yüan Yüan (1764–1849), Wang Nien-sun (1744–1832),[2] Wang Yin-chih (1766–1834), Yü Yüeh (1821–1906). The only European writer who has used these native studies to any purpose is Chavannes, in dealing with the biography of Confucius in *Mémoires Historiques*, Vol. V. All existing translations of the *Analects* rely entirely on the 'scriptural' interpretation of Chu Hsi. It is the Chu Hsi interpretation which, except in small academic circles, is still accepted unquestioningly everywhere in the Far East and which, in so far as Confucius has not been replaced by Sun Yat-sen, still forms the basis of moral education. Translations such as those of Legge, Soothill, Couvreur

1 VII, 19.

2 Valuable commentaries on passages in the *Analects* will be found scattered about his *Tu Shu Tsa Chih*, and in the *Ching I Shu Wen* of his son Wang Yin-chih. Much of the best work of the eighteenth- and nineteenth-century scholars is collected in the *Huang Ch'ing Ching Chieh* ('Classical Commentaries of the Ch'ing Dynasty') and its continuation *Huang Ch'ing Chieh Hsü Pien*, referred to henceforward as H.C.C.C. and H.P.

and Richard Wilhelm have therefore by no means lost their value; at the same time, there is room for a version such as mine, which attempts to tell the European reader not what the book means to the Far East of to-day, but what it meant to those who compiled it. I have used the work of the eighteenth-century and nineteenth-century native scholars, and appreciated it. But in many ways, especially as regards phonology, it is completely out of date; and my chief guide throughout has been a knowledge of the rest of early Chinese literature.

The references to *Chou Li* are to the *Chou Li Chêng I* of Sun I-jang. The transliteration used throughout is that of Wade, save for the omission of the short mark over *u* following *ss* and *tz*, and the occasional use of *Yi* for *I* where confusion with the English first person singular was likely. The substitution of an apostrophe for the 'rough breathing', to mark aspirated consonants, is a concession to the preferences of the printer.

APPENDIX II

Interest tends to centre upon certain kinds of biographical data to the exclusion of others. Western scholars think it extremely important to discover exactly when people were born and exactly when they died. About various other kinds of biographical data we have no curiosity at all. Chinese legend finds it consequent to record the exact height of its heroes,[1] and the American writer, Ella Wheeler Wilcox, reflecting presumably a fairly general interest in the subject, records[2] that one of her characters 'did not weigh over 110 pounds at most'. A European biographer is not expected to give exact data about height or weight; but he is prepared to spend months in discovering whether his subject was born on the first or the second of July, and no one would consider that he was wasting his time.

The Chinese were not lacking in a sense of chronology. But they applied it exclusively to public events and persons connected with public events. If you take up an ordinary Chinese biographical dictionary, such as the fat green one published by the Commercial Press, you will find that exact dates are given only in the case of persons who held high official positions and whose lives were intertwined with high affairs of State. Otherwise we are generally only told to what dynasty a person belonged, which is fairly vague, considering that

1 See Granet, *La Pensée Chinoise*, pp. 202 seq.
2 *The Worlds and I*, p. 273.

dynasties often lasted for several hundred years. At the most, we are told during what period (and the Ch'ien Lung period, for example, lasted sixty years) he passed his official examinations.

The Confucius of the *Analects* did not hold any high official rank. That his real dates should really have been handed down is against all probability. We do not, for example, know the dates of other great teachers, such as Mo Tzu, Chuang Tzu, Mencius. I do not personally doubt that the currently accepted dates (551–479 B.C.) and the slight variants upon them still current in the Han dynasty were supplied at a time when legend had turned Confucius into a great statesman, a person of public importance, the dates of whose birth and death were matters that concerned the State. What his family must in any case have known is the day of the year upon which his anniversary was kept. If it was known that he died on the twenty-sixth day of the sixty-day cycle, in the fourth month, it could be discovered which years had a day answering to this description, and of the possible years one could be fastened upon as the official date. M. Maspero has suggested that the actual date may quite likely have been a quarter of a century later than the accepted one.

THE ANALECTS

THE ANALECTS – *Lun Yü*

BOOK I

1 The Master said, To learn and at due times to repeat what one has learnt, is that not after all[1] a pleasure? That friends should come to one from afar,[2] is this not after all delightful? To remain unsoured even though one's merits are unrecognized by others, is that not after all what is expected of a gentleman?

2 Master Yu[3] said, Those who in private life behave well towards their parents and elder brothers, in public life seldom show a disposition to resist the authority of their superiors. And as for such men starting a revolution, no instance of it has ever occurred. It is upon the trunk[4] that a gentleman works. When that is firmly set up, the Way grows. And surely proper behaviour towards parents and elder brothers is the trunk of Goodness?

3 The Master said, 'Clever talk and a pretentious manner'[5] are seldom found in the Good.

4 Master Tsêng[6] said, Every day I examine myself on

1 See textual notes. The 'after all' implies 'even though one does not hold office'.

2 Several of the disciples belonged to other States (e.g. Wei and Ch'i); but there is no evidence that they came to Lu on account of Confucius. Unless, however, there is here some allusion that escapes us, the phrase must refer to the visits of admirers from abroad, perhaps friends made during the Master's journeys in Honan.   3 See p. 14.

4 i.e. upon what is fundamental, as opposed to 'the twigs', i.e. small arts and accomplishments, which the gentleman leaves to his inferiors.

5 Traditional phrase. Cf. *Shu Ching*, Kao Yao Mo.   6 See p. 14.

these three points: in acting on behalf of others, have I always been loyal to their interests? In intercourse with my friends, have I always been true to my word? Have I failed to repeat[1] the precepts that have been handed down to me?

5 The Master said, A country of a thousand war-chariots cannot be administered unless the ruler attends strictly to business, punctually observes his promises, is economical in expenditure, shows affection towards his subjects in general, and uses the labour of the peasantry only at the proper times of year.[2]

6 The Master said, A young man's duty is to behave well to his parents at home and to his elders abroad, to be cautious in giving promises and punctual in keeping them, to have kindly feelings towards everyone, but seek the intimacy of the Good. If, when all that is done, he has any energy to spare, then let him study the polite arts.[3]

7 Tzu-hsia said, A man who

Treats his betters as betters,
Wears an air of respect,
Who into serving father and mother
Knows how to put his whole strength,
Who in the service of his prince will lay down
  his life,
Who in intercourse with friends is true to his
  word—

1 And so keep in memory.
2 i.e. not when they ought to be working in the fields. Bad rulers, on the contrary, listen to music or go hunting when they ought to be attending to business, continually employ labour on ostentatious building schemes, etc.
3 i.e. learn to recite the *Songs*, practise archery, deportment, and the like.

others may say of him that he still lacks education,[1] but I for my part should certainly call him an educated man.

8 The Master said, If a gentleman is frivolous,[2] he will lose the respect of his inferiors and lack firm ground[3] upon which to build up his education. First and foremost he must learn to be faithful to his superiors, to keep promises, to refuse the friendship of all who are not like him.[4] And if he finds he has made a mistake, then he must not be afraid of admitting the fact and amending his ways.

9 Master Tsêng said, When proper respect towards the dead is shown at the End and continued after they are far away the moral force (tê)[5] of a people has reached its highest point.

10 Tzu-Ch'in[6] said to Tzu-kung,[7] When our Master arrives in a fresh country he always manages to find out about its policy.[8] Does he do this by asking questions, or do people tell him of their own accord? Tzu-kung said, Our Master gets things by being cordial, frank, courteous, temperate, deferential. That is our Master's way of enquiring – a very different matter,[9] certainly, from the way in which enquiries are generally made.

1 i.e. knowledge of ritual, precedents, the correct use on social occasions of verses from the *Songs*, etc.

2 i.e. irresponsible and unreliable in his dealings with others.

3 The sentence runs awkwardly and is probably corrupt.

4 i.e. of those who still reckon in terms of 'profit and loss', and have not taken *jên* (Goodness) as their standard.

5 Cf. Translator's Preface, p. 27.

6 Disciple of Confucius. See XVI, 13 and XIX, 25

7 See Translator's Preface, p. 14.

8 Not, of course, about the details of administration, but about the secret, general maxims which inspire the ruler.

9 The double particle *ch'i-chu*, peculiar to the *Analects* and *Kung-yang Chuan*, does not seem to differ in meaning from the ordinary modal *ch'i*.

11 The Master said, While a man's father is alive, you can only see his intentions; it is when his father dies that you discover whether or not he is capable of carrying them out. If for the whole three years of mourning he manages to carry on the household exactly as in his father's day, then he is a good son indeed.[1]

12 Master Yu said, In the usages of ritual it is harmony[2] that is prized; the Way of the Former Kings from this[3] got its beauty. Both small matters and great depend upon it. If things go amiss, he who knows the harmony[4] will be able to attune them. But if harmony itself is not modulated by ritual, things will still go amiss.[5]

13 Master Yu said,

> In your promises cleave to what is right,
> And you will be able to fulfil your word.
> In your obeisances cleave to ritual,
> And you will keep dishonour at bay.
> Marry one who has not betrayed her own kin,
> And you may safely present her to your
>   Ancestors.[6]

14 The Master said, A gentleman who never goes on eating till he is sated, who does not demand comfort in his home, who is diligent in business and cautious in speech, who associates with those that possess the Way

1 See Translator's Preface, p. 31.

2 Harmony between man and nature; playing the musical mode that harmonizes with the season, wearing seasonable clothes, eating seasonable food, and the like.

3 i.e. from harmony.

4 i.e. the act that harmonizes with the moment.

5 See Translator's Preface, p. 59.

6 Lines 2, 4, and 6 rhyme. For the last rhyme, which belongs to a well-established type, see Karlgren, *The Rimes in the Sung section of the Shi King*. For the presentation of the bride to the husband's ancestors, see *The Book of Songs*, p. 90.

and thereby corrects his own faults – such a one may indeed be said to have a taste for learning.

15 Tzu-kung said, 'Poor without cadging, rich without swagger.' What of that?[1] The Master said, Not bad. But better still, 'Poor, yet delighting in the Way;[2] rich, yet a student of ritual.' Tzu-kung said, The saying of the *Songs*,[3]

>As thing cut, as thing filed,
>As thing chiselled, as thing polished

refers, I suppose, to what you have just said? The Master said, Ssu, now I can really begin to talk to you about the *Songs*, for when I allude to sayings of the past, you see what bearing they have on what was to come after.

16 The Master said, (the good man) does not grieve that other people do not recognize his merits. His only anxiety is lest he should fail to recognize theirs.

---

1 i.e. what of it as a motto?
2 See textual notes.
3 *The Book of Songs* p. 46, which describes the elegance of a lover. Tzu-kung interprets it as describing the pains the gentleman has taken to improve his character, and suggests that Confucius prefers the second maxim ('Poor, yet delighting . . .') because it implies a greater effort of self-improvement.

BOOK II

1 The Master said, He who rules by moral force (*tê*) is like the pole-star, which remains in its place while all the lesser stars do homage to it.

2 The Master said, If out of the three hundred *Songs* I had to take one phrase to cover all my teaching, I would say 'Let there be no evil in your thoughts.'[1]

3 The Master said, Govern the people by regulations, keep order among them by chastisements, and they will flee from you, and lose all self-respect. Govern them by moral force, keep order among them by ritual[2] and they will keep their self-respect and come to you of their own accord.[3]

4 The Master said, At fifteen I set my heart upon learning. At thirty, I had planted my feet firm upon the ground. At forty, I no longer suffered from perplexities. At fifty, I knew what were the biddings of Heaven. At sixty, I heard them with docile ear. At seventy, I could follow the dictates of my own heart; for what I desired no longer overstepped the boundaries of right.

---

1 *The Book of Songs*, p. 275, l. 7, where however *ssu* does not mean 'thoughts', but is an exclamation, 'oh', 'ah', or the like; but in applying ancient texts it is the words themselves that matter, not the context; and these words can be reapplied in any sense which they are conceivably capable of bearing.

2 See Translator's Preface, p. 59.

3 See textual notes.

5 Mêng I Tzu[1] asked about the treatment of parents.
The Master said, Never disobey! When Fan Ch'ih[2] was
driving his carriage for him, the Master said, Mêng
asked me about the treatment of parents and I said,
Never disobey! Fan Ch'ih said, In what sense did you
mean it? The Master said, While they are alive, serve
them according to ritual. When they die, bury them
according to ritual and sacrifice to them according to
ritual.[3]

6 Mêng Wu Po[4] asked about the treatment of parents.
The Master said, Behave in such a way that your father
and mother have no anxiety about you, except concerning your health.

7 Tzu-yu[5] asked about the treatment of parents. The
Master said, 'Filial sons' nowadays are people who see
to it that their parents get enough to eat. But even dogs
and horses are cared for to that extent. If there is no
feeling of respect, wherein lies the difference?

8 Tzu-hsia[6] asked about the treatment of parents. The
Master said, It is the demeanour[7] that is difficult. Filial
piety does not consist merely in young people undertaking the hard work, when anything has to be done,

1 A young grandee of Lu, whose father sent him to study with Confucius. He died in 481 B.C.
2 A disciple.
3 Evidently by 'disobey' Confucius meant 'disobey the rituals'. The
reply was intended to puzzle the enquirer and make him think. In *Mencius*,
III, 1, II, 2, 'While they are alive ...', etc., is given as a saying of Master
Tsêng. Here and elsewhere 'sacrifice' means offerings in general and not
only animal-sacrifice.
4 Son of Mêng I Tzu.
5 A disciple; see Translator's Preface, p. 14.
6 See Translator's Preface, p. 14.
7 This is Chêng Hsüan's interpretation. Pao Hsien (6 B.C.–65 A.D.) takes
sê to mean the expression of one's parents, which must be watched for
hints of approval or disapproval.

or serving their elders first with wine and food. It is something much more than that.

9 The Master said, I can talk to Yen Hui[1] a whole day without his ever differing from me. One would think he was stupid. But if I enquire into his private conduct when he is not with me I find that it fully demonstrates what I have taught him. No, Hui is by no means stupid.

10 The Master said, Look closely into his aims, observe the means by which he pursues them, discover what brings him content – and can the man's real worth[2] remain hidden from you, can it remain hidden from you?

11 The Master said, He who by reanimating[3] the Old can gain knowledge of the New is fit to be a teacher.

12 The Master said, A gentleman is not an implement.[4]

13 Tzu-kung asked about the true gentleman. The Master said, He does not preach what he practises till he has practised what he preaches.

---

1 The favourite disciple. His early death is several times referred to in this book. It would be possible to put this passage in the past and suppose it to have been spoken after Yen Hui's death; but I see no reason to do so.

2 i.e. whether he is fit to be entrusted with office. There is no need to have seen him actually handling practical issues. Cf. *Mencius*, IV, I, XV.

3 Literally, 'warming up'. The business of the teacher is to give fresh life to the Scriptures by reinterpreting them so that they apply to the problems of modern life. All scriptures (Homer, the *Koran*, our own Bible) have been used in this way. I have seen 'The poor ye have always with you' used as an argument against slum-clearance. We have read above how Tzu-kung showed himself to be a true teacher by 'reanimating' a passage from the *Songs*.

4 i.e. a specialist, a tool used for a special purpose. He need only have general, moral qualifications.

14 The Master said, A gentleman can see a question from all sides without bias. The small man[1] is biased and can see a question only from one side.

15 The Master said, 'He who learns but does not think,[2] is lost.' He who thinks but does not learn is in great danger.[3]

16 The Master said, He who sets to work upon a different strand destroys the whole fabric.[4]

17 The Master said, Yu,[5] shall I teach you what knowledge is? When you know a thing, to recognize that you know it, and when you do not know a thing, to recognize that you do not know it. That is knowledge.[6]

18 Tzu-chang was studying the *Song* Han-lu.[7] The Master said, Hear much, but maintain silence[8] as regards doubtful points and be cautious in speaking of the rest; then you will seldom get into trouble. See much, but ignore what it is dangerous to have seen, and be cautious in acting upon the rest; then you will seldom want to

1 Cf. Translator's Preface, p. 29. For the maxim, Cf. *Kuo Yü*, 8.

2 For 'thinking', see Translator's Preface, p. 37.

3 I imagine that the first clause is a proverbial saying, and that Confucius meets it with the second clause. The proverb says: 'To learn without thinking is fatal.' Confucius says: To think but not to learn (i.e. study the Way of the ancients) is equally dangerous.

4 The metaphor is one of weaving or netting. 'Strand' (*tuan*) is a sprout, something that sticks out, and so 'the loose end of a thread'. The moral Way as opposed to the opportunist Way of the World must be followed consistently. It is no use working at it in disconnected patches.

5 Familiar name of the disciple Tzu-lu, see Translator's Preface, p. 14.

6 That knowledge consists in knowing that one does not know is a frequent theme in early Chinese texts. Cf. *Tao Tê Ching*, ch. LXXI.

7 *The Book of Songs*, p. 213. It puns on Han-lu, the name of a mountain, and *han-lu* 'seeking princely rewards, preferment'.

8 Literally, 'leave a gap', a metaphor derived from the language of copyists and scribes. Cf. XV, 25.

undo your acts. He who seldom gets into trouble about what he has said and seldom does anything that he afterwards wishes he had not done, will be sure incidentally[1] to get his reward.

19 Duke Ai[2] asked, What can I do in order to get the support of the common people? Master K'ung[3] replied, If you 'raise up the straight and set them on top of the crooked', the commoners will support you. But if you raise the crooked and set them on top of the straight, the commoners will not support you.

20 Chi K'ang-tzu[4] asked whether there were any form of encouragement by which he could induce the common people to be respectful and loyal. The Master said, Approach them with dignity, and they will respect you. Show piety towards your parents and kindness towards your children, and they will be loyal to you. Promote those who are worthy, train those who are incompetent; that is the best form of encouragement.

21 Someone, when talking to Master K'ung, said, How is it that you are not in the public service? The Master said, The Book[5] says: 'Be filial, only be filial and friendly towards your brothers, and you will be contributing to government.' There are other sorts of service quite different from what you[6] mean by 'service'.

1 See additional notes. From 'Hear much' to 'acts' is in rhyme, but would be awkward to print as verse.

2 Duke of Lu from 494–468.   3 i.e. Confucius.

4 Head of the three families who were *de facto* rulers of Lu. Died 469 B.C.

5 i.e. what Europeans call the *Book of History*. The passage does not occur in the genuine books (see Translator's Preface, p. 46). What it meant in its original context no doubt was 'Be pious to your ancestors ... be generous in rewarding your officers of State.' Confucius 'reanimates' the ancient text, in order to prove that a virtuous private life makes a real contribution towards the public welfare.

6 *Ch'i* corresponds to the Latin *iste*.

22 The Master said, I do not see what use a man can be put to, whose word cannot be trusted. How can a waggon be made to go if it has no yoke-bar or a carriage, if it has no collar-bar?

23 Tzu-chang[1] asked whether the state of things[2] ten generations hence could be foretold. The Master said, We know in what ways the Yin modified ritual when they followed upon the Hsia.[3] We know in what ways the Chou[4] modified ritual when they followed upon the Yin.[5] And hence we can foretell what the successors of Chou will be like, even supposing they do not appear till a hundred generations from now.

24 The Master said, Just as to sacrifice to ancestors other than one's own is presumption, so to see what is right and not do it is cowardice.

---

1 See Translator's Preface, p. 14.

2 As regards ritual.

3 Supposed to have ruled in the 3rd and 2nd millennia B.C.

4 The dynasty which still had a nominal hegemony in the time of Confucius.

5 The fall of Yin took place in the eleventh century B.C. It was on the site of one of their capitals that the famous 'Honan oracle-bones' were found.

BOOK III

1 Master K'ung said of the head of the Chi family[1] when he had eight teams[2] of dancers performing in his courtyard, If this man can be endured, who cannot be endured!

2 The Three Families used the *Yung Song*[3] during the removal of the sacrificial vessels. The Master said,

> *By rulers and lords attended,*
> *The Son of Heaven, mysterious—*

What possible application can such words have in the hall of the Three Families?

3 The Master said, A man who is not Good, what can he have to do with ritual? A man who is not Good, what can he have to do with music?

4 Lin Fang asked for some main principles in connection with ritual. The Master said, A very big question. In ritual at large it is a safe rule always to be too sparing rather than too lavish; and in the particular case of mourning-rites, they should be dictated by grief rather than by fear.[4]

1 One of the Three Families that had usurped most of the powers of the Duke of Lu.   2 See additional notes.
3 'He comes in solemn state ...' *The Book of Songs*, p. 231. Its use was obviously only appropriate at the Emperor's Court. It would have been out of place at the Duke's palace, and was still more so in the hall of the Three Families.   4 See textual notes.

5 The Master said, The barbarians of the East and North have retained their princes. They are not in such a state of decay as we in China.[1]

6 The head of the Chi family was going to make the offerings on Mount T'ai.[2] The Master said to Jan Ch'iu,[3] Cannot you save him from this? Jan Ch'iu replied, I cannot. The Master said, Alas, we can hardly suppose Mount T'ai to be ignorant of matters that even Lin Fang enquires into![4]

7 The Master said, Gentlemen never compete. You will say that in archery they do so. But even then they bow and make way for one another when they are going up to the archery-ground, when they are coming down and at the subsequent drinking-bout. Thus even when competing, they still remain gentlemen.

8 Tzu-hsia asked, saying, What is the meaning of

Oh the sweet smile dimpling,
The lovely eyes so black and white!
Plain silk that you would take for coloured stuff.[5]

The Master said, The painting comes after the plain groundwork.[6] Tzu-hsia said, Then ritual comes

1 Where in several States the ruling families had been ousted by usurpers.

2 To the spirit of the mountain, a thing which the Duke alone had the right to do. The offering is said to have consisted of jade objects.

3 Who was in the service of the Chi family.

4 The mountain must surely know enough of ritual to be aware that no sacrifice but the Duke's could be accepted. The sense is carried on from IV, 4.

5 So dazzling is the contrast that the effect is that of painted stuff rather than of a design in black and white. The first two lines occur in *Song* 86, where however they are not followed by the third line.

6 Confucius reinterprets the third line of verse in the sense 'It is on plain silk that one makes coloured designs,' or the like. In scriptural reinterpretation the fact that the new meaning does not fit in with the original context is of no consequence.

afterwards?[1] The Master said, Shang[2] it is who bears me up. At last I have someone with whom I can discuss the Songs!

9 The Master said, How can we talk about the ritual of the Hsia? The State of Ch'i[3] supplies no adequate evidence. How can we talk about the ritual of Yin? The State of Sung supplies no adequate evidence. For there is a lack both of documents and of learned men. But for this lack we should be able to obtain evidence from these two States.

10 The Master said, At the Ancestral Sacrifice, as for all that comes after the libation, I had far rather not witness it![4]

11 Someone asked for an explanation of the Ancestral Sacrifice. The Master said, I do not know. Anyone who knew the explanation could deal with all things under Heaven as easily as I lay[5] this here; and he laid his finger upon the palm of his hand.[6]

1 Can only be built upon Goodness.

2 Familiar names of Tzu-hsia. For a further discussion of this passage, see additional notes.

3 In Honan, where descendants of the Hsia still carried on the sacrifices. Confucius laments that these States had not preserved the documents and rites of their ancestors. The interrogative particles seem to have been accidentally omitted.

4 In interpreting such passages as this we have to be careful not to read them in the light of later and to a large extent Utopian, theoretical books of ritual. Confucius was obviously displeased by the way in which the *Ti* (Ancestor-sacrifice) was carried out in Lu; presumably because it was too closely modelled on Imperial ritual; more than that we cannot say. See above p. 57.

5 See textual notes.

6 For the magical effect of ritual in controlling men and things, see Translator's Preface, p. 57. For the anecdote, cf. *Chung Yung*, XIX, 6, and *K'ung Tzu Chia Yü*, 27. (Lun Li).

12 Of the saying, 'The word "sacrifice" is like[1] the word "present"; one should sacrifice to a spirit as though[2] that spirit was present,' the Master said, If I am not present at the sacrifice, it is as though there were no sacrifice.[3]

13 Wang-sun Chia[4] asked about the meaning of the saying,

> Better pay court to the stove
> Than pay court to the Shrine.[5]

The Master said, It is not true. He who has put himself in the wrong with Heaven has no means of expiation left.

14 The Master said, Chou could survey the two preceding dynasties. How great a wealth of culture! And we follow upon Chou.[6]

15 When the Master entered the Grand Temple[7] he asked questions about everything there. Someone said, Do not tell me that this son of a villager from Tsou[8] is

1 See textual notes.

2 i.e. with the same demeanor and expression. Cf. *Li Chi*, XIII, end, 'In general, in sacrifice demeanour and expression should be as though one were in the presence of the person who is being sacrificed to.'

3 i.e. do not worry about 'spirits being present' and the like. What matters is the state of mind of the sacrificer. If he is not heart and soul 'there', the sacrifice is useless. On the purely subjective value of sacrifice, see *Hsün Tzu*, P'ien XIX, end.

4 Commander-in-chief in the State of Wei, mentioned under the year 502 B.C. in the *Tso Chuan*.

5 This rhymed saying means that it is better to be on good terms with the hearth-god and have a full belly than waste one's food on the Ancestors, who cannot enjoy it. Confucius, who is usually able to reinterpret old maxims in a new, moral sense, finds himself obliged to reject this cynical piece of peasant-lore *in toto*.

6 i.e. we in Lu have all three dynasties, Hsia, Yin, and Chou to look back upon and imitate.

7 Erected in honour of the first Duke of Chou.

8 A village with which Confucius's family had been connected.

expert in matters of ritual. When he went to the Grand Temple, he had to ask about everything. The Master hearing of this said, Just so! such is the ritual.[1]

16 The Master said, the saying

> *In archery it is not the hide that counts,*
> *For some men have more strength than others,*

is the way of the Ancients.[2]

17 Tzu-kung wanted to do away with the presentation[3] of a sacrificial sheep at the announcement[4] of each new moon. The Master said, Ssu! You grudge sheep, but I grudge ritual.

18 The Master said, Were anyone to-day to serve his prince according to the full prescriptions of ritual, he would be thought a sycophant.

19 Duke Ting (died 495 B.C.) asked for a precept concerning a ruler's use of his ministers and a minister's service to his ruler. Master K'ung replied saying, A ruler in employing his ministers should be guided solely by the prescriptions of ritual. Ministers in serving their ruler, solely by devotion to his cause.

1 i.e. precisely by doing so I showed my knowledge of ritual; for the asking of such questions is prescribed by ritual. For questions of this sort, see additional notes.

2 i.e. it is not piercing the hide stretched as a target that counts. In this ancient rhymed saying Confucius saw a maxim which metaphorically resumed the whole way of the Ancient Sages, who ruled by Goodness, not by force. For the first of the two lines, cf. *I Li*, Couvreur's translation, p. 173. Cf. also *Chou Li*, where *chu p'i* seems merely to mean 'hitting the target'. See additional notes.

3 By the Duke to his State officers. This is the explanation of Liu T'ai-kung (1751–1805). See H.C.C.C. 798.

4 To the Ancestors, who are kept informed of everything that goes on below.

20 The Master said, The Ospreys![1] Pleasure not carried to the point of debauch; grief not carried to the point of self-injury.

21 Duke Ai asked Tsai Yü[2] about the Holy Ground. Tsai Yü replied, The Hsia sovereigns marked theirs with a pine, the men of Yin used a cypress, the men of Chou used a chestnut-tree, saying, 'This will cause the common people to be in fear and trembling.'[3] The Master hearing of it said, What is over and done with, one does not discuss. What has already taken its course, one does not criticize; what already belongs to the past, one does not censure.[4]

22 The Master said, Kuan Chung[5] was in reality a man of very narrow capacities. Someone said, Surely he displayed an example of frugality? The Master said, Kuan had three lots of wives,[6] his State officers performed no double duties. How can he be cited as an example of frugality? That may be, the other said; but surely he had

1 *The Book of Songs*, No. 87, which begins by describing a lover's grief at being separated from his lady and ends by describing their joyful union. Confucius sees in it a general guide to conduct, whether in joy or affliction. The opening words are: '*Kuan, kuan* cry the ospreys.'

2 A disciple in whom Confucius was much disappointed.

3 Pun on *li* a chestnut-tree and *li* 'to be in awe'.

4 The usual explanation of this passage makes Confucius's comment refer to Tsai Yü's pun 'which might lead the Duke to severe measures' in dealing with his people (Legge, p. 26). The comment, however, is phrased in such a way that it must be taken as referring to the remote and not to the immediate past. It is perhaps unfortunate, Confucius suggests, that the founders of the Chou dynasty chose a tree with so inauspicious a name; but it was ill-bred of Tsai Yü to criticize them in conversation with Duke Ai of Lu, who were their direct descendant.

5 Kuan Tzu, seventh century B.C., the statesman who built up the power of the Ch'i kingdom. Confucius regarded him as having merely increased the political prestige of his country without raising its moral status. See Introduction, p. 43.

6 Each consisting of a wife and two 'understudies' (bridesmaids); only a feudal lord was entitled to such an establishment.

a great knowledge of ritual? The Master said, Only the ruler of a State may build a screen to mask his gate; but Kuan had such a screen. Only the ruler of a State, when meeting another such ruler, may use cup-mounds;[1] but Kuan used one. If even Kuan is to be cited as an expert in ritual, who is not an expert in ritual?

23 When talking to the Grand Master[2] of Lu about music, the Master said, Their music[3] in so far as one can find out about it began with a strict unison. Soon the musicians were given more liberty;[4] but the tone remained harmonious, brilliant, consistent, right on till the close.

24 The guardian of the frontier-mound at I[5] asked to be presented to the Master, saying, No gentleman arriving at this frontier has ever yet failed to accord me an interview. The Master's followers presented him. On going out the man said, Sirs, you must not be disheartened by his failure. It is now a very long while[6] since the Way prevailed in the world. I feel sure that Heaven intends to use your Master as a wooden bell.[7]

25 The Master spoke of the Succession Dance[8] as being[9] perfect beauty and at the same time perfect goodness;

1 A mound upon which to stand pledge-cups; see textual notes.
2 The *maestro*, music-master, who was always a blind man.
3 The music of the ancients.
4 To improvise.
5 On the borders of the State of Wei.
6 Sages appear at regular intervals. One is now due.
7 A rattle, used to arouse the populace in times of night-danger, and in general by heralds and town-criers; cf. *Li Chi*, Yüeh-ling. (Couvreur's translation, I, 343).
8 This dance (at any rate according to the later Confucian theory) mimed the peaceful accession of the legendary Emperor Shun; the War Dance mimed the accession by conquest of the Emperor Wu, who overthrew the Yin. See above, p. 85.
9 Or as we should say, 'as embodying'.

but of the War Dance as being perfect beauty, but not perfect goodness.

26 The Master said, High office filled by men of narrow views, ritual performed without reverence, the forms of mourning observed without grief – these are things I cannot bear to see!

BOOK IV

1 The Master said, It is Goodness that gives to a neighbourhood its beauty.[1] One who is free to choose, yet does not prefer to dwell among the Good – how can he be accorded the name of wise?[2]

2 The Master said, Without Goodness a man

> Cannot for long endure adversity,
> Cannot for long enjoy prosperity.

The Good Man rests content with Goodness; he that is merely wise pursues Goodness in the belief that it pays to do so.

3, 4 Of the adage[3] 'Only a Good Man knows how to like people, knows how to dislike them,' the Master said, He whose heart is in the smallest degree set upon Goodness will dislike no one.

5 Wealth and rank are what every man desires; but if they can only be retained to the detriment of the Way he professes, he must relinquish them. Poverty and

---

1 Cf. *Mencius*, II, 1, VII, 2.

2 A justification of the maxim, 'When right does not prevail in a kingdom, then leave it,' and of Confucius's own prolonged travels.

3 Cf. *Ta Hsüeh* ('The Great Learning'), commentary, X, 15. 'Only the Good man is considered capable of loving (*ai*) men, capable of hating them.' In the *Kuo Yü* (ch. 18), however, the saying is quite differently interpreted: 'Only a good man is safe to like and safe to dislike.... For if you like him, he will not take undue advantage of it; and if you dislike him, he will not resent it.' The words 'The Master said' at the beginning of paragraph 3 should be omitted, and paragraphs 3 and 4 taken together.

obscurity are what every man detests; but if they can only be avoided to the detriment of the Way he professes, he must accept them. The gentleman who ever parts company with Goodness does not fulfil that name. Never for a moment[1] does a gentleman quit the way of Goodness. He is never so harried but that he cleaves to this; never so tottering but that he cleaves to this.

6 The Master said, I for my part[2] have never yet seen one who really cared for Goodness, nor one who really abhorred wickedness. One who really cared for Goodness would never let any other consideration come first. One who abhorred wickedness would be so constantly doing Good that wickedness would never have a chance to get at him. Has anyone ever managed to do Good with his whole might even as long as the space of a single day? I think not. Yet I for my part have never seen anyone give up such an attempt because he had not the *strength* to go on. It may well have happened, but I for my part have never seen it.[3]

7 The Master said, Every man's faults belong to a set.[4] If one looks out for faults it is only as a means of recognizing Goodness.

8 The Master said, In the morning, hear the Way; in the evening, die content![5]

9 The Master said, A Knight whose heart is set upon the Way, but who is ashamed of wearing shabby clothes

1 Literally, 'for as long as it takes to eat' one bowl of rice. A common expression, simply meaning a very little while.
2 *Wo* as a nominative is more emphatic than *wu*.
3 It is the will not the way that is wanting.
4 i.e. a set of qualities which includes virtues.
5 The well-known saying *Vedi Napoili e poi mori* follows the same pattern. The meaning is, you will have missed nothing.

and eating coarse food, is not worth calling into counsel.

10 The Master said, A gentleman in his dealings with the world has neither enmities nor affections;[1] but wherever he sees Right he ranges himself beside it.

11 The Master said, Where gentlemen set their hearts upon moral force (*tê*),[2] the commoners set theirs upon the soil.[3] Where gentlemen think only of punishments, the commoners think only of exemptions.[4]

12 The Master said, Those[5] whose measures are dictated by mere expediency will arouse continual discontent.

13 The Master said, If it is really possible to govern countries by ritual and yielding, there is no more[6] to be said. But if it is not really possible, of what use is ritual?[7]

14 The Master said, He[8] does not mind not being in office; all he minds about is whether he has qualities that entitle him to office. He does not mind failing to get recognition; he is too busy doing the things that entitle him to recognition.

1 Reading uncertain, but general sense quite clear. See textual notes.
2 As opposed to physical compulsion. See additional notes.
3 They *an t'u*, 'are content with the soil', and prepared to defend it.
4 *Hui* means amnesties, immunities, exemptions, as opposed to what is 'lawful and proper'.
5 The rulers and upper classes in general.   6 See textual notes.
7 The saying can be paraphrased as follows: If I and my followers are right in saying that countries can be governed solely by correct carrying out of ritual and its basic principle of 'giving way to others', there is obviously no case to be made out for any other form of government. If on the other hand we are wrong, then ritual is useless. To say, as people often do, that ritual is all very well so long as it is not used as an instrument of government, is wholly to misunderstand the purpose of ritual.
8 The gentleman. But we might translate 'I do not mind', etc.

15 The Master said, Shên! My Way has one (thread) that runs right through it. Master Tsêng said, Yes. When the Master had gone out, the disciples asked, saying What did he mean? Master Tsêng said, Our Master's Way is simply this: Loyalty, consideration.[1]

16 The Master said, A gentleman takes as much trouble to discover what is right as lesser men take to discover what will pay.

17 The Master said, In the presence of a good man, think all the time how you may learn to equal him. In the presence of a bad man, turn your gaze within![2]

18 The Master said, In serving his father and mother a man may gently remonstrate with them. But if he sees that he has failed to change their opinion, he should resume an attitude of deference and not thwart them; may feel discouraged,[3] but not resentful.

19 The Master said, While father and mother are alive, a good son does not wander far afield; or if he does so, goes only where he has said he was going.[4]

20 The Master said, If for the whole three years of mourning a son manages to carry on the household exactly as in his father's day, then he is a good son indeed.[5]

1 Loyalty to superiors; consideration for the feelings of others, 'not doing to them anything one would not like to have done to oneself', as defined below, XV, 23. 'Loyalty and Consideration' is one of the Nine Virtues enumerated by the *I Chou Shu*, 29, I verso. Cf. also XV, 2 below.

2 'Within yourself scrutinize yourself'; *êrh* is the second person singular pronoun, not the conjunction?

3 See textual notes.

4 Particularly in order that if they die he may be able to come back and perform the rites of mourning.

5 Cf. I, 11.

21 The Master said, It is always better for a man to know the age of his parents. In the one case[1] such knowledge will be a comfort to him; in the other,[2] it will fill him with a salutary dread.

22 The Master said, In old days a man kept a hold on his words, fearing the disgrace that would ensue should he himself fail to keep pace with them.

23 The Master said, Those who err on the side of strictness are few indeed!

24 The Master said, A gentleman covets the reputation of being slow in word but prompt in deed.[3]

25 The Master said, Moral force (*tê*) never dwells in solitude; it will always bring neighbours.[4]

26 Tzu-yu said, In the service of one's prince repeated scolding[5] can only lead to loss of favour; in friendship, it can only lead to estrangement.

---

1 If he knows that they are not so old as one might think.
2 If he realizes that they are very old.
3 Cf. *The Way and Its Power*, p. 198.
4 Whenever one individual or one country substitutes *tê* for physical compulsion, other individuals or other countries inevitably follow suit.
5 Cf. XII, 23 and additional notes.

BOOK V

1 The Master said of Kung Yeh Ch'ang, Though he has suffered imprisonment, he is not an unfit person to choose as a husband; for it was not through any fault of his own. He married him to his daughter.

The Master said of Nan Jung,[1] In a country ruled according to the Way, he would not be overlooked; in a country not ruled according to the Way, he would manage to avoid capital punishment or mutilation. He married him to his elder brother's[2] daughter.

2 Of Tzu-chien[3] he said, A gentleman indeed is such a one as he! If the land of Lu were indeed without gentlemen, how could he have learnt this?

3 Tzu-kung asked saying, What do you think of me? The Master said, You are a vessel.[4] Tzu-kung said, What sort of vessel? The Master said, A sacrificial vase of jade![5]

4 Someone said, Jan Yung is Good, but he is a poor talker. The Master said, What need has he to be a good

1 The commentators identify Nan Jung with Nan-kung Kuo, son of Mêng I Tzu, head of the powerful Mêng Family. There is, however, no ground for this identification, nor any reason to suppose that Confucius ever formed so exalted a family connection.

2 According to later tradition Confucius's elder brother was a cripple and for this reason his duties devolved on Confucius.

3 The disciple Fu Tzu-chien, who figures in later legend as model governor of the town of Shan-fu. See additional notes.

4 A man of particular capacities, but lacking the general state of electness known as Jên (Goodness).

5 i.e. the highest sort of vessel.

talker? Those who down others with clap-trap are seldom popular. Whether he is Good, I do not know. But I see no need for him to be a good talker.

5 The Master gave Ch'i-tiao K'ai leave to take office, but he replied, 'I have not yet sufficiently perfected myself in the virtue of good faith.' The Master was delighted.

6 The Master said, The Way makes no progress. I shall get upon a raft and float out to sea.[1] I am sure Yu would come with me. Tzu-lu on hearing of this was in high spirits. The Master said, That is Yu indeed! He sets far too much store by feats of physical daring. It seems as though I should never get hold of the right sort of people.[2]

7 Mêng Wu Po[3] asked whether Tzu-lu was Good. The Master said, I do not know. On his repeating the question the Master said, In a country of a thousand war-chariots Yu could be trusted to carry out the recruiting. But whether he is Good I do not know. 'What about Ch'iu?'[4] The Master said, In a city of a thousand families or a baronial family with a hundred chariots he might do well as Warden. But whether he is Good, I do not know. 'What about Ch'ih?'[5] The Master said, Girt with

1 What Confucius proposes is, of course, to go and settle among the barbarians. Cf. III, 5 and IX, 13. A certain idealization of the 'noble savage' is to be found fairly often in early Chinese literature; cf. the eulogy of the barbarians put into the mouth of a Chinese whose ancestors had settled among them, *Shih Chi V*, and the maxim 'When the Emperor no longer functions, learning must be sought among the Four Barbarians,' north, west, east, and south *(Tso Chuan*, Chao kung seventeenth year).

2 Literally, 'get material'. Cf. *I Chou Shu* VIII, 1 verso. Yu (familiar name of Tzu-lu) figures in later legend as a converted swashbuckler, who constantly shocked Confucius by his pugnacity.

3 See above, II, 6.

4 The disciple Jan Ch'iu.

5 The disciple Kung-hsi Hua.

his sash, standing in his place at Court he might well be charged to converse with strangers and guests. But whether he is Good, I do not know.[1]

8 The Master in discussing Tzu-kung said to him, Which do you yourself think is the better, you or Hui?[2] He answered saying, I dare not so much as look at Hui. For Hui has but to hear one part in ten, in order to understand the whole ten. Whereas if I hear one part, I understand no more than two parts. The Master said, Not equal to him – you and I are not equal to him![3]

9 Tsai Yü[4] used to sleep during the day. The Master said, Rotten wood cannot be carved, nor a wall of dried dung be trowelled.[5] What use is there in my scolding him any more?

The Master said, There was a time when I merely listened attentively to what people said, and took for granted that they would carry out their words. Now I am obliged not only to give ear to what they say, but also to keep an eye on what they do. It was my dealings with Tsai Yü that brought about the change.

10 The Master said, I have never yet seen a man who was truly steadfast.[6] Someone answered saying, 'Shên Ch'êng.' The Master said, Ch'êng! He is at the mercy of his desires. How can *he* be called steadfast?

11 Tzu-kung said, What I do not want others to do to me, I have no desire to do to others. The Master said, Oh Ssu! You have not quite got to that point yet.

1 Jan Ch'iu is known to history as a faithful henchman of the Lu dictator. Kung-hsi Hua's ambition was to perfect himself in the etiquette of State ceremonies. See XI, 25.

2 See above, II, 9.   3 See p. 66.   4 See III, 21.

5 i.e. patterned with the trowel. To translate 'be plastered' destroys the parallelism.   6 Impervious to outside influences, intimidations, etc.

12 Tzu-kung said, Our Master's views concerning culture[1] and the outward insignia[2] of goodness, we are permitted to hear; but about Man's nature[3] and the ways of Heaven[4] he will not tell us anything at all.

13 When Tzu-lu heard any precept and was still trying unsuccessfully to put it into practice, his one fear was that he might hear some fresh precept.

14 Tzu-kung asked saying, Why was K'ung Wên Tzu called Wên ('The Cultured')?[5] The Master said, Because he was diligent[6] and so fond of learning that he was not ashamed to pick up knowledge even from his inferiors.

15 Of Tzu-ch'an[7] the Master said that in him were to be found four of the virtues that belong to the Way of the true gentleman. In his private conduct he was courteous, in serving his master he was punctilious, in providing for the needs of the people he gave them even more than their due; in exacting service from the people, he was just.

1 See Translator's Preface, p. 33.

2 *Chang* ('insignia') means literally 'emblems' (usually representations of birds, beasts or plants) figuring on banners or dresses to show the rank of the owner. Hence metaphorically, the outward manifestations of an inner virtue.

3 As it is before it has been embellished with 'culture'.

4 T'ien Tao. The Tao taught by Confucius only concerned human behaviour ('the ways of man'); he did not expound a corresponding Heavenly Tao, governing the conduct of unseen powers and divinities.

5 i.e. why was he accorded this posthumous title? See Introduction, p. 33. He was a statesman of the Wei State who died between 484 and 480 B.C. He figures in the chronicles as a disloyal and self-seeking minister.

6 There is perhaps a play on *wên* and *min* ('diligent'); the two words were pronounced very similarly in ancient Chinese.

7 Minister in the Cheng State; died 522 B.C.

16 The Master said, Yen P'ing Chung is[1] a good example of what one's intercourse with one's fellow-men should be. However long he has known anyone he always maintains the same scrupulous courtesy.

17 The Master said, Tsang Wên Chung[2] kept a Ts'ai tortoise[3] in a hall with the hill-pattern on its pillar tops and the duckweed pattern on its king-posts.[4] Of what sort, pray, was his knowledge?[5]

18 Tzu-chang asked saying, The Grand Minister Tzu-wên[6] was appointed to this office on three separate occasions, but did not on any of these three occasions display the least sign of elation. Three times he was deposed; but never showed the least sign of disappointment. Each time, he duly informed his successor concerning the administration of State affairs during his tenure of office. What should you say of him? The Master said, He was certainly faithful to his prince's interests. Tzu-chang said, Would you not call him Good? The Master said, I am not sure. I see nothing in that to merit the title Good.

(Tzu-chang said) When Ts'ui Tzu assassinated the

1 Or 'was'. The Ch'i minister Yen Tzu, famous for his wise counsels, died in 500 B.C.

2 Minister of Lu in the seventh century B.C.

3 The country of Ts'ai was famous for its tortoises.

4 Such decoration was proper only to the Emperor's ancestral temple and palace. Cf. *I Chou Shu* 48, end. Kuan Tzu (*Li Chi*, Tsa Ch'i, Couvreur's translation, II, 187) is accused of decorating his palace in the same way.

5 i.e. his knowledge of ritual. For a tortoise kept on a special terrace and smeared daily with the blood of four bulls, see *KuanTzu*, P'ien 75. Strictly speaking only rulers kept tortoises for use in divination (*Li Chi* X); ministers used the yarrow-stalks. But we find Tsang's grandson still in possession of a Ts'ai tortoise (*Tso Chuan*; Duke Hsiang twenty-third year); so perhaps the family claimed an hereditary privilege.

6 Middle of the seventh century B.C.

sovereign of Ch'i,[1] Ch'ên Wên Tzu[2] who held a fief of ten war chariots gave it up and went away. On arriving in another State, he said, 'I can see they are no better here than our minister Ts'ui Tzu'; and he went away. On arriving in the next country, he said, 'I can see they are no better here than our minister Ts'ui Tzu'; and went away. What should you say of him? The Master said, He was certainly scrupulous. Tzu-chang said, Would you not call him Good? The Master said, I am not sure. I see nothing in that to merit the title Good.

19 Chi Wên Tzu[3] used to think thrice before acting. The Master hearing of it said, Twice is quite enough.[4]

20 The Master said, Ning Wu Tzu[5] 'so long as the Way prevailed in his country showed wisdom; but when the Way no longer prevailed, he showed his folly'.[6] To such wisdom as his we may all attain; but not to such folly!

21 When the Master was in Ch'ên[7] he said, Let us go back, let us go back! The little ones[8] at home are headstrong and careless. They are perfecting themselves in all the showy insignia of culture without any idea how to use them.

1 In 548 B.C. The Duke of Ch'i had seduced his wife.
2 Another Ch'i minister.
3 Died 568 B.C.
4 Ch'êng Hao (A.D. 1032–1085) says that if one thinks more than twice, self-interest begins to come into play.
5 A minister of Wei (seventh century B.C.), famous for his blind devotion to his prince, whose enemies had incarcerated him in a deep dungeon. Here Ning managed to feed his prince through a tube.
6 Such was the judgment of the world.
7 About 492 B.C.?
8 Disciples.

22   The Master said, Po I and Shu Ch'i[1] never bore old ills in mind and had but the faintest feelings of rancour.

23 The Master said, How can we call even Wei-shêng Kao upright? When someone asked him for vinegar he went and begged it from the people next door, and then gave it as though it were his own gift.[2]

24 The Master said, Clever talk, a pretentious manner and a reverence that is only of the feet[3] – Tso Ch'iu Ming[4] was incapable of stooping to them, and I too could never stoop to them. Having to conceal one's indignation and keep on friendly terms with the people against whom one feels it – Tso Ch'iu Ming

---

1 Legendary brothers, almost always bracketed together in this way. The 'old ills' were the misdeeds of the last Yin ruler. When he was attacked by the Chou tribe, the brothers refused to take up arms against their sovereign, despite his great wickedness. Their lack of yüan ('rancour') was a classical theme; cf. VII, 14. This was shown by their attitude after each in turn had resigned his rights of accession to the rulership of the small State to which they belonged. Having proposed this act of 'cession' (jang), they carried it out loyally and uncomplainingly.

2 Wei-shêng Kao (see Chuang Tzu XXIX, 1, Chan Kuo Ts'ê, Yen stories, Pt. 1, Huai-nan Tzu XVII, end) is the legendary paragon of truthfulness. Confucius adopts the same formula as the rhyme:

> The Germans in Greek
> Are sadly to seek.
> All except Hermann;
> And Hermann is a German.

How rare, how almost non-existent a quality uprightness must be, Confucius bitterly says, if even into the legend of the most upright of all men there has crept an instance of falsity!

Translators have supposed Wei-shêng Kao to have been some actual contemporary of Confucius, whose conduct the Master was criticizing. This misses the whole point.

3 Cf. Ta Tai Li Chi, 49, where 'foot reverence' is coupled with 'mouth holiness'.

4 See additional notes.

was incapable of stooping to such conduct, and I too am incapable of stooping to such conduct.[1]

25 Once when Yen Hui and Tzu-lu were waiting upon him the Master said, Suppose each of you were to tell his wish. Tzu-lu said, I should like to have carriages and horses, clothes and fur rugs,[2] share them with my friends and feel no annoyance if they were returned to me the worse for wear. Yen Hui said, I should like never to boast of my good qualities nor make a fuss about the trouble I take on behalf of others. Tzu-lu said, A thing I should like is to hear the Master's wish. The Master said, In dealing with the aged, to be of comfort to them; in dealing with friends, to be of good faith with them; in dealing with the young, to cherish them.

26 The Master said, In vain have I looked for a single man capable of seeing his own faults and bringing the charge home against himself.

27 The Master said, In a hamlet of ten houses you may be sure of finding someone quite as loyal and true to his word as I. But I doubt if you would find anyone with such a love of learning.[3]

---

1 And am therefore unfitted for Court life, where such behaviour is the sole way to preferment.

2 See textual notes.

3 i.e. self-improvement in the most general sense. Not book-learning.

BOOK VI

1 The Master said, Now Yung,[1] for example. I should not mind setting him with his face to the south.[2] Jan Yung then asked about Tzu-sang Po-tzu.[3] The Master said, He too would do. He is lax.[4] Jan Yung said, I can understand that such a man might do as a ruler, provided he were scrupulous in his own conduct and lax only in his dealings[5] with the people. But you would admit that a man who was lax in his own conduct as well as in government would be too lax.[6] The Master said, What Yung says is quite true.

2 Duke Ai asked which of the disciples had a love of learning. Master K'ung answered him saying, There was Yen Hui. He had a great love of learning. He never vented his wrath upon the innocent nor let others suffer for his faults. Unfortunately the span of life allotted to him by Heaven was short, and he died. At present there are none or at any rate I have heard of none who are fond of learning.[7]

3 When Kung-hsi Hua was sent on a mission to Ch'i, Master Jan asked[8] that Hua's mother might be granted an allowance of grain. The Master said, Give her a

1 The disciple Jan Yung.   2 Trying him as a ruler.
3 Cf. the Tzu-sang of *Chuang Tzu* VI, 11.
4 This is a paradox, *chien* ('lax') being generally used in a bad sense.
5 i.e. in the exaction of taxes, corvées, and the like. I punctuate after *ching*, not after *chien*.
6 i.e. too lax to 'set with his face to the south'.   7 Cf. XI, 6.
8 i.e. asked the government (the Chi Family), in whose service he was.

cauldron[1] full. Jan said that was not enough. The Master said, Give her a measure.[2] Master Jan gave her five bundles.[3] The Master said, When Ch'ih[4] went to Ch'i he drove sleek horses and was wrapped in light furs. There is a saying, A gentleman helps out the necessitous; he does not make the rich richer still.

When Yüan Ssu was made a governor, he was given an allowance of nine hundred measures of grain, but declined it. The Master said, Surely you could find people who would be glad of it among your neighbours or in your village?

4 The Master said of Jan Yung, If the offspring of a brindled[5] ox is ruddy-coated[6] and has grown its horns, however much people might hesitate to use it,[7] would the hills and streams really reject it?

5 The Master said, Hui is[8] capable of occupying his whole mind for three months on end with no thought but that of Goodness. The others can do so, some for a day, some even for a month; but that is all.[9]

1 A merely nominal amount. Confucius disapproved of her being given any at all.

2 A good deal more; but still not a great deal.

3 Ten times (?) more than a measure. Jan entirely disregards Confucius's advice.

4 i.e. Kung-hsi Hua. He ought to have left behind sufficient provision for his mother.

5 i.e. one unsuitable for sacrifice.

6 All over. Only animals of one colour could be used for sacrifice.

7 In sacrificing to the hills and streams. The implication is that Jan Yung was of humble origin. This, says Confucius, ought not to prejudice us against him.

8 There is nothing to indicate whether this was said before or after Yen Hui's premature death.

9 On the strength of sayings such as this, Taoists claimed Yen Hui as an exponent of *tso-wang* ('sitting with blank mind'), the Chinese equivalent of *yoga*.

6 Chi K'ang-tzu[1] asked whether Tzu-lu was the right sort of person to put into office. The Master said, Yu is efficient. It goes without saying that he is capable of holding office. Chi K'ang-tzu said, How about Tzu-kung? Would he be the right sort of person to put into office? The Master said, He can turn his merits to account.[2] It goes without saying, that he is capable of holding office. Chi K'ang-tzu said, How about Jan Ch'iu? Would he be the right sort of person to put into office? The Master said, He is versatile. It goes without saying that he is capable of holding office.

7 The Chi Family[3] wanted to make Min Tzu-ch'ien governor of Pi.[4] Min Tzu-ch'ien said, Invent a polite excuse for me. If that is not accepted and they try to get at me again, I shall certainly install myself on the far side of the Wên.[5]

8 When Jan Kêng was ill, the Master went to enquire after him, and grasping his hand through the window said, It is all over with him! Heaven has so ordained it—[6] But that such a man should have such an illness! That such a man should have such an illness![7]

9 The Master said, Incomparable indeed was Hui! A handful[8] of rice to eat, a gourdful of water to drink, living

1 Became head of the actual administration of Lu in 492 B.C.
2 For *ta*, see additional notes.
3 i.e. the government. He would not serve a usurper.
4 The great stronghold of the Chi Family.
5 i.e. I shall take refuge in the neighbouring land of Ch'i, where I cannot be got at. He was faithful to the legitimate ruler, the Duke of Lu.
6 And we must not repine.
7 Later tradition very naturally explains the passage by saying that Jan Kêng's illness was leprosy. This fits in with the concluding words and also explains why Confucius did not enter the house.
8 Literally, a split bamboo-sectionful.

in a mean street – others would have found it unendurably depressing, but to Hui's cheerfulness it made no difference at all. Incomparable indeed was Hui![1]

10 Jan Ch'iu said, It is not that your Way does not commend itself to me, but that it demands powers I do not possess. The Master said, He whose strength gives out collapses during the course of the journey (the Way); but you deliberately draw the line.[2]

11 The Master said to Tzu-hsia, 'You must practise the ju^3 of gentlemen, not that of the common people.'

12 When Tzu-yu was Warden of the castle of Wu, the Master said, Have you managed to get hold of the right sort of people there? Tzu-yu said, There is someone called T'an-t'ai Mieh-ming who 'walks on no by-paths'.[4] He has not once come to my house except on public business.

13 The Master said, Mêng Chih-fan is no boaster. When his people were routed[5] he was the last to flee; but when they neared the city-gate, he whipped up his

1 Cf. *Mencius*, IV, 2, XXIX.

2 Metaphor of marking boundary-lines of estates or the like.

3 A word of very uncertain meaning. Perhaps 'unwarlikeness'. See additional notes. The meaning of the saying may be 'The unwarlikeness of gentlemen means a preference for *tê* (moral force), that of inferior people is mere cowardice.'

Hu came ultimately to be the general name for followers of the Confucian Way.

4 i.e. strictly follows our Way. There is probably some further point in this story, that is lost to us owing to our knowing so little about T'an-t'ai Mieh-ming.

5 At a battle with Ch'i outside the Lu capital in 484 B.C. To belittle his own achievements (the opposite of boasting) is the duty of a gallant gentleman. So a modern airman who had stayed behind to fight a rear action might say, 'I was in a funk all the time, but I couldn't get away; my engine was missing fire.'

horses, saying, It was not courage that kept me behind. My horses were slow.

14 The Master said, Without the eloquence of the priest[1] T'o and the beauty of Prince Ch'ao of Sung it is hard nowadays to get through.

15 The Master said, Who expects to be able to go out of a house except by the door? How is it then that no one follows this Way of ours?[2]

16 The Master said, When natural substance prevails over ornamentation,[3] you get the boorishness of the rustic. When ornamentation prevails over natural substance, you get the pedantry of the scribe. Only when ornament and substance are duly blended do you get the true gentleman.

17 The Master said, Man's very life is honesty, in that without it he will be lucky indeed if he escapes with his life.[4]

18 The Master said, To prefer it[5] is better than only to know it. To delight in it is better than merely to prefer it.

19 The Master said, To men who have risen at all above the middling sort, one may talk of things higher yet. But to men who are at all below the middling sort it is useless to talk of things that are above them.[6]

1 The *chu* ('priest') recited invocations addressed to the ancestors. Both T'o and Ch'ao flourished about 500 B.C.
2 Though it is the obvious and only legitimate way out of all our difficulties.
3 i.e. when nature prevails over culture.
4 I punctuate after *chih*, not after *yeh*.
5 The Way.
6 that belong to a higher stage of learning.

20 Fan Ch'ih asked about wisdom.[1] The Master said, He who devotes himself to securing for his subjects what it is right they should have, who by respect for the Spirits keeps them at a distance,[2] may be termed wise. He asked about Goodness. The Master said, Goodness cannot be obtained till what is difficult[3] has been duly done. He who has done this may be called Good.

21 The Master said, The wise man delights in water, the Good man delights in mountains. For the wise move; but the Good stay still. The wise are happy; but the Good, secure.[4]

22 A single change could bring Ch'i to the level of Lu; and a single change would bring Lu to the Way.

23 The Master said, A horn-gourd that is neither horn nor gourd! A pretty horn-gourd indeed, a pretty horn-gourd indeed.[5]

24 Tsai Yü asked saying, I take it a Good Man, even if he were told that another Good Man[6] were at the bottom of a well, would go to join him? The Master

1 i.e. to what rulers the title 'Wise' could be accorded.

2 When the Spirits of hills and streams do not receive their proper share of ritual and sacrifice they do not 'keep their distance', but 'possess' human beings, causing madness, sickness, pestilence, etc.

3 This only becomes intelligible when we refer to XIV, 2, where we see that the 'difficult thing' is to rid oneself of love of mastery, vanity, resentment, and covetousness.

4 For the origin of this saying, which has here taken on a form distorted by quietist influences, see additional note and Introduction, p. 23.

5 A particular sort of bronze goblet was called *ku*, which is written 'horn' beside 'gourd', though the object in question is not shaped like a gourd and is not a drinking-horn. The saying is, of course, a metaphorical way of lamenting over the political state of China, 'ruled over' by an Emperor who had no temporal power and local sovereigns whose rights had been usurped by their ministers.

6 See textual notes.

said, Why should you think so? 'A gentleman can be broken, but cannot be dented;[1] may be deceived, but cannot be led astray.'[2]

24 (Paraphrased). Tsai Yü, half playfully asked whether, since the Good always go to where other Good Men are, a Good Man would leap into a well on hearing that there was another Good Man at the bottom of it. Confucius, responding in the same playful spirit, quotes a maxim about the true gentleman, solely for the sake of the reference in it to *hsien*, which means 'throw down' into a pit or well, but also has the sense 'to pit', 'to dent'.

25 The Master said, A gentleman who is widely versed in letters and at the same time knows how to submit his learning to the restraints of ritual is not likely, I think, to go far wrong.

26 When the Master went to see Nan-tzu,[3] Tzu-lu was not pleased. Whereupon the Master made a solemn declaration[4] concerning his visit, saying, Whatsoever I have done amiss, may Heaven avert it,[5] may Heaven avert it!

27 The Master said, How transcendent is the moral power of the Middle Use![6] That it is but rarely found among the common people is a fact long admitted.[7]

1 Cf. *Shuo Yüan*, XVII: The gentleman (like jade) can be broken, but not bent.

2 i.e. deceived as to facts; but cannot be enticed into wrong conduct. Cf. *Mencius* V, 1, II, 4; Legge, p. 224.

3 The wicked concubine of Duke Ling of Wei.

4 See additional notes.

5 See textual notes.

6 Confucius's Way was essentially one of moderation: 'to exceed is as bad as to fall short'. See additional notes and Introduction, p. 30.

7 *Chiu i* constantly has an idiomatic sense of this sort, and does not mean simply 'a long while'. Cf. *Doctrine of the Mean*, III. Legge, p. 251.

28 Tzu-kung said, If a ruler not only conferred wide benefits upon the common people, but also compassed the salvation of the whole State, what would you say of him? Surely, you would call him Good? The Master said, It would no longer be a matter of 'Good'. He would without doubt be a Divine Sage.[1] Even Yao and Shun could hardly criticize him.[2] As for Goodness – you yourself desire rank and standing; then help others to get rank and standing. You want to turn your own merits to account; then help others to turn theirs to account – in fact, the ability to take one's own feelings as a guide – that is the sort of thing that lies in the direction of Goodness.[3]

1 See Translator's Preface, p. 11.
2 Cf. XIV, 45, and *Han Shih Wai Chuan*, VII, 9.
3 For *fang*, 'direction', cf. XI, 25.

BOOK VII

1, 2, 3 The Master said, I have 'transmitted what was taught to me without making up anything of my own'.[1] I have been faithful to and loved the Ancients. In these respects, I make bold to think, not even our old P'êng[2] can have excelled me. The Master said, I have listened in silence and noted what was said, I have never grown tired of learning nor wearied of teaching others what I have learnt. These at least are merits which I can confidently claim.[3] The Master said, The thought that 'I have left my moral power (*tê*) untended, my learning unperfected, that I have heard of righteous men, but been unable to go to them; have heard of evil men, but been unable to reform them'[4] – it is these thoughts that disquiet me.

4 In his leisure hours the Master's manner was very free-and-easy, and his expression alert and cheerful.

5 The Master said, How utterly have things gone to the bad with me! It is long now indeed since I dreamed that I saw the Duke of Chou.[5]

---

1 Cf. *Mo Tzu*, P'ien 46. 'A gentleman does not make anything up; he merely transmits.'

2 The Chinese Nestor. It is the special business of old men to transmit traditions.

3 For the idiom *ho yu*, 'there is no further trouble about', see above, IV, 13.

4 The passage in inverted commas consists of two rhymed couplets, and is probably traditional. For the rhymes, see Liu Pao-nan; and textual notes.

5 See Translator's Preface, p. 11.

6 The Master said, Set your heart upon the Way, support yourself by its power, lean upon Goodness, seek distraction in the arts.[1]

7 The Master said, From the very poorest upwards – beginning even with the man who could bring no better present than a bundle of dried flesh[2] – none has ever come to me without receiving instruction.

8 The Master said, Only one who bursts with eagerness do I instruct; only one who bubbles with excitement, do I enlighten. If I hold up one corner and a man cannot come back to me with the other three,[3] I do not continue the lesson.

9 If at a meal the Master found himself seated next to someone who was in mourning, he did not eat his fill. When he had wailed at a funeral, during the rest of the day he did not sing.[4]

10 The Master said to Yen Hui, The maxim

> *When wanted, then go;*
> *When set aside; then hide.*

is one that you and I could certainly fulfil. Tzu-lu said, Supposing you had command of the Three Hosts,[5] whom would you take to help you? The Master said, The man who was ready to 'beard a tiger or rush a river'[6] without caring whether he lived or died – that sort of man I should not take. I should certainly take

1 Music, archery and the like.   2 See additional notes.

3 Metaphor from laying out of field-plots?

4 Both of these are common ritual prescriptions. Cf. *Li Chi* III, fol. 6 and I, fol. 6.   5 i.e. the whole army.

6 Cf. *The Book of Songs*, No. 295, verse 6. The reply is clearly intended as a snub to the impulsive Tzu-lu. The song is one which I omit in my translation.

someone who approached difficulties with due caution and who preferred to succeed by strategy.

11 The Master said, If any means of escaping poverty presented itself that did not involve doing wrong, I would adopt it, even though my employment were only that of the gentleman who holds the whip.[1] But so long as it is a question of illegitimate means, I shall continue to pursue the quests that I love.[2]

12 The rites to which the Master gave the greatest attention were those connected with purification before sacrifice, with war and with sickness.[3]

13 When he was in Ch'i the Master heard the Succession,[4] and for three months did not know the taste of meat.[5] He said, 'I did not picture to myself that any music existed which could reach such perfection as this.'[6]

14 Jan Ch'iu said, Is our Master on the side of the Prince of Wei?[7] Tzu-kung said, Yes, I must ask him about that. He went in and said, What sort of people were Po I and

1 i.e. the most menial. 'Gentleman', *shih*, in such contexts is used with a slightly ironical intention, as one might say in French, 'le monsieur qui . . .' Cf. *Chuang Tzu* XV, 1.

2 The study of the Ancients.

3 A special sacrifice was held before the departure of military expeditions, and the sacrificial meat was distributed among the soldiers. The populace flocked to the Ancestral Shrines, wailing to the Ancestors for assistance. Sickness was exorcized by sacrifices to hills and streams.

4 See III, 25.

5 i.e. did not notice what he was eating.

6 The older commentators take 'this' to mean the land of Ch'i, i.e. 'I did not expect to find such music here in Ch'i.' This may be right.

7 When Duke Ling died in the summer of 493 B.C., the throne passed to his grandson, his son having previously abdicated his rights to the accession. Soon, however, the son went back on his word and attempted to oust the grandson from the throne.

Shu Ch'i?[1] The Master said, They were good men who lived in the days of old. Tzu-kung said, Did they repine? The Master said, They sought Goodness and got Goodness. Why should they repine? On coming out Tzu-kung said, Our Master is not on his side.

15 The Master said, He who seeks only coarse food to eat, water to drink and a bent arm for pillow, will without looking for it find happiness to boot.[2] Any thought of accepting wealth and rank by means that I know to be wrong is as remote from me as the clouds that float above.

16 The Master said, Give me a few more years, so that I may have spent a whole fifty in study,[3] and I believe that after all I should be fairly free from error.

17 The occasions upon which the Master used correct pronunciation[4] were when reciting the *Songs* or the *Books* and when practising ritual acts. At all such times he used the correct pronunciation.

1 See above, V, 22. The contrast is between Po I and Shu Ch'i on the one hand (they are always spoken of as though they were to all intents and purposes a single person) and Duke Ling's son on the other. The two 'good men of old' harboured no rancour after their act of cession; whereas Ling's son became discontented with his lot. Tzu-kung sounds Confucius indirectly upon his attitude, because the Master was at this time living in Wei and would have been loath to make an open pronouncement on the question.

2 For the idiom, see II, 18.

3 See textual notes. In common with most scholars, I follow the Lu version here. The Ku version introduces a reference to the *Book of Changes*. But there is no reason to suppose that the *Changes* had in Confucius's time been philosophized, or that he regarded it as anything but a book of divination.

4 Whereas in daily life he used the Lu dialect. See above, p. 66. Similarly the Swiss, for example, use their own dialect in daily life, but Hochdeutsch in church services or in reciting a poem by Schiller. Cf. *Hsün Tzu*, P'ien 4, A man of Yüeh is at ease in Yüeh speech, a man of Ch'u in Ch'u speech; gentlemen, in the 'correct pronunciation', *ya*, the same term as is used here. See further, additional notes.

18 The 'Duke of Shê'[1] asked Tzu-lu about Master K'ung (Confucius). Tzu-lu did not reply. The Master said, Why did you not say 'This is the character of the man: so intent upon enlightening the eager that he forgets his hunger, and so happy in doing so, that he forgets the bitterness of his lot and does not realize that old age is at hand.'[2] That is what he is.

19 The Master said, I for my part[3] am not one of those who have innate knowledge. I am simply one who loves the past and who is diligent in investigating it.

20 The Master never talked of prodigies, feats of strength, disorders[4] or spirits.

21 The Master said, Even when walking in a party of no more than three I can always be certain of learning from those I am with. There will be good qualities that I can select for imitation and bad ones that will teach me what requires correction in myself.

22 The Master said, Heaven begat the power (tê) that is in me. What have I to fear from such a one as Huan T'ui?[5]

23 The Master said, My friends, I know you think that there is something I am keeping from you. There is nothing at all that I keep from you. I take no steps

1 An adventurer, known originally as Shên Chu-liang; first mentioned in 523 and still alive in 475. The title 'Duke of Shê' was one which he had invented for himself.

2 According to the traditional chronology Confucius was sixty-two at the time when this was said.

3 *Wo*, emphatic as opposed to the simple nominative *wu*. Cf. *Hu Shih Wên Ts'un*, Vol. II, p. 13. Cf. p. 93 above.

4 Disorders of nature; such as snow in summer, owls hooting by day, or the like.

5 Minister of War in Sung. Cf. *Tso Chuan*, Duke Ai fourteenth year.

about which I do not consult you, my friends. Were it otherwise, I should not be Ch'iu.[1]

24 The Master took four subjects for his teaching: culture, conduct of affairs, loyalty to superiors and the keeping of promises.

25 The Master said, A Divine Sage[2] I cannot hope ever to meet; the most I can hope for is to meet a true gentleman. The Master said, A faultless man I cannot hope ever to meet; the most I can hope for is to meet a man of fixed principles. Yet where all around I see Nothing pretending to be Something,[3] Emptiness pretending to be Fulness, Penury pretending to be Affluence, even a man of fixed principles will be none too easy to find.

26 The Master fished with a line but not with a net; when fowling he did not aim at a roosting bird.[4]

27 The Master said, There may well be those who can do without knowledge; but I for my part am certainly not one of them. To hear much, pick out what is good and follow it, to see much and take due note of it,[5] is the lower[6] of the two kinds of knowledge.

1 Familiar name of Confucius. There is no evidence that Confucius is here disclaiming the possession of an esoteric doctrine. The wording (*hsing*, 'steps', '*démarches*') suggests that practical steps (with a view to office, patronage or the like) are all that is intended.

2 See Translator's Preface, p. 11.

3 An impotent cipher pretending to be a Duke, powerless tools of adventurers such as Yang Huo pretending to be Ministers.

4 See Translator's Preface, p. 29. For 'fowling', see *The Book of Songs,* p. 36.

5 As I do.

6 The higher being innate knowledge, which Confucius disclaims above, VII, 19. He thus (ironically) places himself at two removes from the hypothetical people who can dispense with knowledge, the three stages being, (1) those who do not need knowledge; (2) those who have innate knowledge; (3) those who accumulate it by hard work.

28 At Hu village[1] the people were difficult to talk to.[2] But an uncapped[3] boy presented himself for an interview. The disciples were in two minds about showing him in. But the Master said, In sanctioning his entry here I am sanctioning nothing he may do when he retires. We must not be too particular. If anyone purifies[4] himself in order to come to us, let us accept this purification. We are not responsible for what he does when he goes away.

29 The Master said, Is Goodness indeed so far away? If we really wanted Goodness, we should find that it was at our very side.

30 The Minister of Crime in Ch'ên asked whether Duke Chao of Lu knew the rites. Master K'ung said, He knew the rites. When Master K'ung had withdrawn, the Minister motioned Wu-ma Ch'i[5] to come forward and said, I have heard the saying 'A gentleman is never partial.' But it seems that some gentlemen are very partial indeed. His Highness[6] married into the royal family of Wu who belong to the same clan as himself, calling her Wu Mêng Tzu.[7] If his Highness knew the rites, who does not know the rites? Wu-ma Ch'i repeated this to the Master, who

1 Unknown. Probably one of the places Confucius passed through during his travels.

2 About the Way. Cf. XV, 7.

3 The 'capping' of boys marked their initiation into manhood.

4 A suppliant of any kind (whether asking a Master for teaching or Heaven for good crops) purifies himself by fasting and abstinence in order to enhance the power of his prayer. For abstinence before entertaining a teacher, cf. *Kuan Tzu*, P'ien 19, where the purification consists in washing in water from a new well, making a burnt offering, and ten days' abstinence and fasting.

5 Later regarded as a disciple of Confucius.

6 Duke Chao, reigned from 541 to 510 B.C.

7 He broke the rule of exogamy and hoped to pass this off by speaking of her in a way that might lead people to think she belonged to another clan, the Tzu.

said, I am a fortunate man. If by any chance I make a mistake, people are certain to hear of it![1]

31 When in the Master's presence anyone sang a song that he liked, he did not join in at once, but asked for it to be repeated and then joined in.

32 The Master said, As far as taking trouble goes,[2] I do not think I compare badly with other people. But as regards carrying out the duties of a gentleman in actual life, I have never yet had a chance to show what I could do.

33 The Master said, As to being a Divine Sage or even a Good Man, far be it from me to make any such claim. As for unwearying effort to learn and unflagging patience in teaching others,[3] those are merits that I do not hesitate to claim. Kung-hsi Hua said, The trouble is that we disciples cannot learn!

34 When the Master was very ill, Tzu-lu asked leave to perform the Rite of Expiation. The Master said, Is there such a thing?[4] Tzu-lu answered saying, There is. In one of the Dirges[5] it says, 'We performed rites of expiation for you, calling upon the sky-spirits above and the earth-spirits below.' The Master said, My expiation began long ago![6]

1 This is, of course, ironical. It would have been improper for Confucius to criticize his own late sovereign.

2 See textual notes.   3 Cf. *Mencius*, II, 1, II, 19.

4 i.e. is there any ancient authority for such a rite?

5 See Translator's Preface, p. 55.

6 What justifies me in the eyes of Heaven is the life I have led. There is no need for any rite now. In a fragment of one of the lost books of *Chuang Tzu* there is a parallel story in which Tzu-lu wants to take the omens about Confucius's chance of recovery, and Confucius says 'My omen-taking was done long ago!' See *T'ai P'ing Yü Lan* 849, fol. 1 verso. The reference was kindly sent to me by Dr. Gustav Haloun.

35 The Master said, Just as lavishness leads easily to presumption, so does frugality to meanness. But meanness is a far less serious fault than presumption.[1]

36 The Master said, A true gentleman is calm and at ease; the Small Man is fretful and ill at ease.

37 The Master's manner was affable yet firm, commanding but not harsh, polite but easy.

---

1 Cf. 111, 4. The lavishness of the Chi Family became presumption when it led them to have eight rows of dancers (III, 1) and thereby infringe upon a ducal prerogative

BOOK VIII

1 The Master said, Of T'ai Po[1] it may indeed be said that he attained to the very highest pitch of moral power. No less than three times he renounced the sovereignty of all things under Heaven, without the people getting a chance to praise him for it.

2 The Master said, Courtesy not bounded by the prescriptions of ritual becomes tiresome. Caution not bounded by the prescriptions of ritual becomes timidity, daring becomes turbulence, inflexibility becomes harshness.[2]

The Master said,[3] When gentlemen deal generously with their own kin, the common people are incited to Goodness. When old dependents are not discarded, the common people will not be fickle.

3 When Master Tsêng was ill he summoned his disciples

1 T'ai Po was the eldest son of King Tan, legendary ancestor of the Chou sovereigns. He renounced the Throne in favour of his youngest brother. *Jang* ('renunciation') is the virtue that engenders the greatest quantity of *tê* (moral power). No renunciation can be greater than to renounce 'the sovereignty of all things under Heaven'. Moreover, a *yin tê* (secret accretion of 'power') is always more redoubtable than an open one. The secrecy seems to have been achieved by giving it out that T'ai Po's flight to the lands of Wu and Yüeh was undertaken in order to collect medicines for Old King Tan, who was ill. (Chêng Hsüan makes a rather forced effort to enumerate three separate occasions upon which T'ai Po renounced his claims.)

2 See textual notes and compare XVII, 8.

3 The Pelliot MS. supplies these words, which have dropped out of the current version.

and said, Free my feet, free my hands. The *Song* says:

> In fear and trembling,
> With caution and care,
> As though on the brink of a chasm,
> As though treading thin ice.

But I feel now that whatever may betide I have got through safely, my little ones.[1]

4 When Master Tsêng was ill, Mêng Ching Tzu[2] came to see him. Master Tsêng spoke to him saying, When a bird is about to die its song touches the heart.[3] When a man is about to die, his words are of note.[4] There are three things that a gentleman, in following the Way, places above all the rest: from every attitude, every gesture that he employs he must remove all trace of violence or arrogance; every look that he composes in his face must betoken good faith; from every word that he utters, from every intonation, he must remove all trace of coarseness or impropriety. As to the ordering of ritual vessels and the like, there are those whose business it is to attend to such matters.

5 Master Tsêng said, Clever, yet not ashamed to consult those less clever than himself; widely gifted, yet not ashamed to consult those with few gifts; having, yet

---

1 While a man was dying four people held his hands and feet, 'one for each limb' (*Li Chi*, XXII). After death, the hands and feet were freed (*Li I Chih*, supplement to the *Hou Han Shu*, Part III, fol. 1). Tsêng says that he has got through safely, his moral course is run; there is no need to hold his hands and feet, which was done 'in case the dying man should in his death-struggle get into some "non-ritual" attitude'. He interprets the *Song* 295 as describing the heavy responsibilities of the man who has 'taken Goodness for his load'; see below, VIII, 7. For the anthropological connotations of 'freeing hands and feet', see additional notes.

2 Son of Mêng Wu Po (see II, 6). He appears to have been still alive in 430 B.C.   3 Cf. our belief concerning 'swan-songs'.

4 For 'la prescience reconnue aux mourants', cf. A. Lods, *Israel*, p. 260.

seeming not to have; full, yet seeming empty; offended against, yet never contesting – long ago I had a friend[1] whose ways were such as this.

6 Master Tsêng said, The man to whom one could with equal confidence entrust an orphan not yet fully grown[2] or the sovereignty of a whole State,[3] whom the advent of no emergency however great could upset – would such a one be a true gentleman? He I think would be a true gentleman indeed.

7 Master Tsêng said, The true Knight of the Way must perforce be both broad-shouldered and stout of heart; his burden is heavy and he has far to go. For Goodness is the burden he has taken upon himself; and must we not grant that it is a heavy one to bear? Only with death does his journey end; then must we not grant that he has far to go?

8 The Master said, Let a man be first incited by the *Songs*, then given a firm footing by the study of ritual, and finally perfected by music.

9 The Master said, The common people can be made to follow it;[4] they cannot be made to understand it.

10 The Master said, One who is by nature daring and is suffering from poverty will not long be law-abiding. Indeed, any men, save those that are truly Good, if their sufferings are very great, will be likely to rebel.[5]

---

1 It has been suggested that the friend in question was Yen Hui.
2 Literally, an orphan of six feet (i.e. four of our feet).
3 Literally, the command of a hundred leagues.
4 i.e. the Way.
5 Official interpretation, 'Men who are not truly Good, if you criticize them too severely, are likely to rebel.'

11 The Master said, If a man has gifts as wonderful as those of the Duke of Chou, yet is arrogant and mean, all the rest is of no account.

12 The Master said:

> One who will study for three years
> Without thought of reward[1]
> Would be hard indeed to find.

13 The Master said, Be of unwavering good faith, love learning, if attacked[2] be ready to die for the good Way. Do not enter a State that pursues dangerous courses, nor stay in one where the people have rebelled. When the Way prevails under Heaven, then show yourself; when it does not prevail, then hide. When the Way prevails in your own land, count it a disgrace to be needy and obscure; when the Way does not prevail in your land, then count it a disgrace to be rich and honoured.

14 The Master said, He who holds no rank in a State does not discuss its policies.

15 The Master said, When Chih the Chief Musician led the climax of the *Ospreys*,[3] what a grand flood of sound filled one's ears!

16 The Master said, Impetuous, but tricky! Ingenuous, but dishonest! Simple-minded, but capable of breaking promises![4] To such men I can give no recognition.

---

1 i.e. of obtaining a paid appointment. See textual notes.
2 Literally, 'on the defensive'.
3 See III, 20. For Chih, see XVIII, 9.
4 In old days (see XVII, 16) people at any rate had the merits of their faults.

17 The Master said, Learn as if you were following someone whom you could not catch up, as though it were someone you were frightened of losing.

18 The Master said, Sublime were Shun and Yü! All that is under Heaven was theirs, yet they remained aloof from it.

19 The Master said, Greatest, as lord and ruler, was Yao.[1] Sublime, indeed, was he. 'There is no greatness like the greatness of Heaven,' yet Yao could copy it. So boundless was it[2] that the people could find no name for it;[3] yet sublime were his achievements, dazzling the insignia of his culture!

20 Shun had five ministers and all that is under Heaven was well ruled. King Wu[4] said, I have ten[5] ministers. Master K'ung said, True indeed is the saying that 'the right material is hard to find'; for the turn of the T'ang and Yü dynasties[6] was the time most famous for this.[7] (As for King Wu),[8] there was a woman among his ten, so that in reality there were only nine men. Yet of all that is under Heaven he held two parts in three, using them in submissive service to the dynasty of Yin.[9] The moral power (*tê*) of Chou may, indeed, be called an absolutely perfect moral power!

1 For the legendary rulers Yao, Shun and Yü, see Introduction, p. 12. Cf. *Mencius*, III, 1, IV, 11.

2 i.e. Yao's *tê*.

3 So that it remained a *yin tê*, 'secret prestige'. Cf. above, VIII, 1.

4 The Warrior King, founder of the Chou dynasty.

5 His mother, and his nine brothers? See additional notes.

6 i.e. the accession of Shun.

7 i.e. for 'the right material', for an abundance of good ministers. Yet even then there were only five.

8 Some such words have dropped out of the text.

9 And by this act of cession (*jang*) building up the *tê* required for his subsequent campaign. For the whole paragraph, see additional notes.

21 The Master said, In Yü I can find no semblance of a flaw. Abstemious in his own food and drink, he displayed the utmost devotion in his offerings to spirits and divinities.[1] Content with the plainest clothes for common wear, he saw to it that his sacrificial apron and ceremonial head-dress were of the utmost magnificence. His place of habitation was of the humblest, and all his energy went into draining and ditching.[2] In him I can find no semblance of a flaw.

1 To ancestors, and spirits of hill, stream, etc.
2 For Yü, see Introduction, p. 12. For the question of rhyme in this paragraph, see textual notes.

BOOK IX

1 The Master seldom spoke of profit or fate or Goodness.[1]

2 A villager from Ta-hsiang said, Master K'ung is no doubt a very great man and vastly learned. But he does nothing to bear out this reputation. The Master, hearing of it, said to his disciples, What shall I take up? Shall I take up chariot-driving? Or shall it be archery? I think I will take up driving![2]

3 The Master said, The hemp-thread crown is prescribed by ritual.[3] Nowadays people wear black silk,[4] which is economical; and I follow the general practice. Obeisance below the daïs is prescribed by ritual. Nowadays people make obeisance after mounting the daïs. This is presumptuous, and though to do so is contrary to the general practice, I make a point of bowing while still down below.

4 There were four things that the Master wholly eschewed: he took nothing for granted,[5] he was never over-positive, never obstinate, never egotistic.

1 We may expand: Seldom spoke of matters from the point of view of what would pay best, but only from the point of view of what was right. He did not discuss whether Heaven determines all human actions (a question debated by the school of Mo Tzu in later days and evidently already raised in the time of Confucius). He refused to define Goodness or accord the title Good to any of his contemporaries.   2 See additional notes.

3 For wear at the ancestral sacrifice; made of threads twisted from a very thin yarn, very costly to manufacture.   4 See textual notes.

5 Chêng Hsüan (Pelliot MS.) reads the 'man' determinative at the side of i and interprets 'he never took anything for granted when he was not sure'. This is certainly right.

5 When the Master was trapped in K'uang,[1] he said, When King Wên perished, did that mean that culture (*wên*) ceased to exist?[2] If Heaven had really intended that such culture as his should disappear, a latter-day mortal would never have been able to link himself to it as I have done. And if Heaven does not intend to destroy such culture, what have I to fear from the people of K'uang?

6 The Grand Minister (of Wu?)[3] asked Tzu-kung saying, Is your Master a Divine Sage? If so, how comes it that he has many practical accomplishments?[4] Tzu-kung said, Heaven certainly intended[5] him to become a Sage; it is also true that he has many accomplishments. When the Master heard of it he said, The Grand Minister is quite right about me. When I was young I was in humble circumstances; that is why I have many practical accomplishments in regard to simple, everyday matters. Does it befit a gentleman to have many accomplishments? No, he is in no need of them at all.

Lao says that the Master said, It is because I have not been given a chance[6] that I have become so handy.

7 The Master said, Do I regard myself as a possessor of wisdom? Far from it. But if even a simple peasant comes

1 A border town held at various times by Chêng, Wei, Sung and Lu. For the legend as to why he was maltreated here, see additional notes. For 'trapped', see textual notes.

2 Literally, 'was not in this'. Cf. the common Chinese phrase 'Suppose there were a man in this,' i.e. 'suppose the case of a man who . . .' 'being in this' meaning 'existing'. Cf. *Mencius*, VI, 2, II, 3. 'Take the case of a man not strong enough to lift . . .'.

3 Probably P'i (adult name, Tzu-yü), who is mentioned in connection with Tzu-kung in 488 B.C.

4 Gentlemen do not stoop to practical accomplishments; much less the Sage.

5 But the wickedness of the world prevented it.

6 In public life. Lao is usually identified with the Ch'in Chang mentioned in *Tso Chuan*, Duke Chao, 20th year, and the Tzu-lao of *Chuang Tzu* XXV, 6.

in all sincerity and asks me a question, I am ready to thrash the matter out, with all its pros and cons, to the very end.

8 The Master said, The phoenix does not come; the river gives forth no chart.[1] It is all over with me![2]

9 Whenever he was visited by anyone dressed in the robes of mourning or wearing ceremonial head-dress, with gown and skirt, or a blind man, even if such a one were younger than himself, the Master on seeing him invariably rose to his feet, and if compelled to walk past him always quickened his step.[3]

10 Yen Hui said with a deep sigh, The more I strain my gaze up towards it,[4] the higher it soars. The deeper I bore down into it, the harder it becomes. I see it in front; but suddenly it is behind. Step by step the Master skilfully lures one on. He has broadened me with culture, restrained me with ritual. Even if I wanted to stop, I could not. Just when I feel that I have exhausted every resource, something seems to rise up, standing out sharp and clear.[5] Yet though I long to pursue it, I can find no way of getting to it at all.

11 When the Master was very ill, Tzu-lu caused some of the disciples to get themselves up as official retainers.[6] Coming to himself for a short while, the Master said,

1 The arrival of this magical bird and the sudden revelation of a magical chart were portents that heralded the rise of a Saviour Sage. See Introduction, p. 41.
2 Heaven does not intend to let me play a Sage's part.
3 A sign of respect.
4 Goodness.
5 Literally, 'overtoppingly', like a mountain-top or the top of a tree.
6 Such as he would have been entitled to, had he held office.

How like Yu, to go in for this sort of imposture! In pretending to have retainers when I have none, whom do I deceive? Do I deceive Heaven? Not only would I far rather die in the arms of you disciples than in the arms of retainers, but also as regards my funeral – even if I am not accorded a State Burial, it is not as though I were dying by the roadside.[1]

12 Tzu-kung said, Suppose one had a lovely jewel, should one wrap it up, put it in a box and keep it, or try to get the best price one can for it? The Master said, Sell it! Most certainly sell it! I myself am one who is waiting for an offer.[2]

13 The Master wanted to settle among the Nine Wild Tribes of the East.[3] Someone said, I am afraid you would find it hard to put up with their lack of refinement. The Master said, Were a true gentleman to settle among them there would soon be no trouble[4] about lack of refinement.

14 The Master said, It was only after my return from Wei to Lu that music was revised, Court pieces and Ancestral Recitations being at last properly discriminated.[5]

15 The Master said, I can claim that at Court I have

1 i.e. don't think I am worrying about whether I shall be buried with public honours. I know I can trust you to give me a decent burial; and that is all I ask for.

2 The question at issue is, of course, whether a man of talent should try to obtain office. Confucius declares that he himself is only too anxious to 'sell his jewel' (i.e. accept office), should any opportunity present itself.

3 For Confucius's ideas on the 'noble savage', see above, p. 100.

4 For ho yu, an idiom that cannot be translated literally, cf. VI, 6, VII, 2, IX, 15, and textual note on IV, 13.

5 The words of the Court pieces (ya) are contained in the second and third parts, the Recitations (sung) in the last of the four great divisions of the Book of Songs.

duly served the Duke and his officers; at home, my father and elder brother. As regards matters of mourning, I am conscious of no neglect, nor have I ever been overcome with wine. Concerning these things at any rate my mind is quite at rest.[1]

16 Once when the Master was standing by a stream, he said, Could one but go on and on[2] like this, never ceasing day or night!

17 The Master said, I have never yet seen anyone whose desire to build up his moral power was as strong as sexual desire.

18 The Master said, The case[3] is like that of someone raising a mound. If he stops working, the fact that it perhaps needed only one more basketful makes no difference; I stay where I am. Whereas even if he has not got beyond levelling the ground, but is still at work, the fact that he has only tilted one basketful of earth makes no difference. I go to help him.

19 The Master said, It was Hui whom I could count on always to listen attentively to anything I said.

20 The Master said of Yen Hui, Alas, I saw him go forward, but had no chance to see whither this progress would have led him in the end.[4]

---

1 Another instance of the idiomatic *ho yu*.

2 In one's moral striving, cf. *Mencius*, IV, 2, XVIII.

3 i.e. my attitude towards disciples in different stages of progress. A parallel passage in *Hsün Tzu* P'ien 28, makes the sense and construction of this passage quite clear.

4 This seems better than the traditional, 'I saw him make progress, and never saw him stand still.'

21 The Master said, There are shoots whose lot it is to spring up but never to flower; others whose lot it is to flower, but never bear fruit.[1]

22 The Master said, Respect the young. How do you know that they will not one day be all that you are now? But if a man has reached forty or fifty and nothing has been heard of him, then I grant there is no need to respect him.

23 The Master said, The words of the *Fa Yü*[2] (Model Sayings) cannot fail to stir us;[3] but what matters is that they should change our ways. The words of the *Hsüan Chü*[4] cannot fail to commend themselves to us; but what matters is that we should carry them out.[5] For those who approve but do not carry out, who are stirred, but do not change, I can do nothing at all.

24 The Master said, First and foremost, be faithful to your superiors, keep all promises, refuse the friendship of all who are not like you; and if you have made a mistake, do not be afraid of admitting the fact and amending your ways.[6]

25 The Master said, You may rob the Three Armies of their commander-in-chief, but you cannot deprive the humblest peasant of his opinion.

---

1 This surely refers to Yen Hui's early death.

2 Name of a collection of moral sayings? I suspect that it is the same as the *Fa Yen* twice quoted in *Chuang Tzu* (IV, 2, Wieger, 236, 237).

3 See textual notes.

4 Name of another collection of moral sayings, on the 'choice' and 'promotion' of the virtuous? See textual notes.

5 See p. 252.

6 Cf. I, 8.

26 The Master said, 'Wearing a shabby hemp-quilted gown, yet capable of standing unabashed with those who wore fox and badger.' That would apply quite well to Yu, would it not?

> Who harmed none, was foe to none,
> Did nothing that was not right.[1]

Afterwards Tzu-lu (Yu) kept on continually chanting those lines to himself. The Master said, Come now, the wisdom contained in them is not worth treasuring[2] to that extent!

27 The Master said,[3] Only when the year grows cold do we see that the pine and cypress are the last[4] to fade.

28 The Master said, he that is really Good can never be unhappy. He that is really wise can never be perplexed. He that is really brave is never afraid.[5]

29 The Master said, There are some whom one can join in study but whom one cannot join in progress along the Way; others whom one can join in progress along the Way, but beside whom one cannot take

---

1 Confucius quotes these two lines from *Songs*, No. 67.

2 Pun on two senses of *tsang* (1) excellent; (2) treasure, to treasure up, to store.

3 He is, however, only repeating a proverb.

4 *hou*, 'last', should probably be *pu* or *wu* ('not'). A similar saying in *Lü Shih Ch'un Ch'iu* (74, 2) refers to the Master's ordeals in Ch'ên and Ts'ai. Cf. *Chuang Tzu* XXVIII, 8.

5 Goodness, wisdom and courage are the Three Ways of the true gentleman. Cf. XIV, 30. Confucius always ranks courage below wisdom and wisdom below Goodness. In the original the first two clauses have become transposed. This is, however, a mere slip, as is shown by comparison with the parallel passage, XIV, 30. The *Chung Yung* ('Doctrine of the Mean'), XX, in reproducing the terms in the order wisdom, goodness, courage, merely betrays the influence of this corrupted passage.

one's stand;[1] and others again beside whom one can take one's stand, but whom one cannot join in counsel.

30   *The flowery branch of the wild cherry*
       How swiftly it flies back![2]
       It is not that I do not love you;
       But your house is far away.

The Master said, He did not really love her. Had he done so, he would not have worried about the distance.[3]

---

1 i.e. with whom one cannot collaborate in office. Cf. X, 3 and XVI, 13.

2 When one pulls it to pluck the blossom. Cf. *Songs*, 268, 1. Image of things that are torn apart after a momentary union. Evidently a verse from some song not included in our *Book of Songs*.

3 Men fail to attain to Goodness because they do not care for it sufficiently, not because Goodness 'is far away'. I think the old interpretation, which treats 29 and 30 as one paragraph, is definitely wrong.

BOOK X

1 At home in his[1] native village his manner is simple and unassuming, as though he did not trust himself to speak. But in the ancestral temple and at Court he speaks readily, though always choosing his words with care.

2 At Court when conversing with the Under Ministers his attitude is friendly and affable; when conversing with the Upper Ministers, it is restrained and formal. When the ruler is present it is wary, but not cramped.

3 When the ruler summons him to receive a guest, a look of confusion comes over his face and his legs seem to give beneath his weight. When saluting his colleagues he passes his right hand to the left, letting his robe hang down in front and behind; and as he advances with quickened step, his attitude is one of majestic dignity.

When the guest has gone, he reports the close of the visit, saying, 'The guest is no longer looking back.'

4 On entering the Palace Gate he seems to shrink[2] into himself, as though there were not room. If he halts, it must never be in the middle of the gate, nor in going through does he ever tread on the threshold.[3] As he

---

1 The gentleman's. See Translator's Preface, p. 48. In the text this has been altered to 'Master K'ung'. Throughout this Book the reader should refer constantly to the textual notes.

2 For shrinking, bowing, crawling, etc., see Translator's Preface, p. 50.

3 For the 'unluckiness' of thresholds, see Translator's Preface, p. 51.

passes the Stance[1] a look of confusion comes over his face, his legs seem to give way under him and words seem to fail him. While, holding up the hem of his skirt, he ascends the Audience Hall, he seems to double up and keeps in his breath, so that you would think he was not breathing at all. On coming out, after descending the first step his expression relaxes into one of satisfaction and relief. At the bottom of the steps he quickens his pace, advancing with an air of majestic dignity. On regaining his place he resumes his attitude of wariness and hesitation.

5 When carrying the tablet of jade,[2] he seems to double up, as though borne down by its weight. He holds it at the highest as though he were making a bow,[3] at the lowest, as though he were proffering a gift. His expression, too, changes to one of dread and his feet seem to recoil, as though he were avoiding something. When presenting ritual-presents, his expression is placid. At the private audience his attitude is gay and animated.

6 A gentleman[4] does not wear facings of purple or mauve, nor in undress does he use pink or roan.[5] In hot weather he wears an unlined gown of fine thread loosely woven, but puts on an outside garment before going out-of-doors.[6] With a black robe he wears black lamb-skin; with a robe of undyed silk, fawn. With a yellow

1 The place where the ruler takes up his stand when seeing off important guests?

2 Symbol of the ruler's feudal investiture; the *kuei*.

3 On a level with his forehead.

4 Here the compilers have forgotten to alter *chün-tzu* (gentleman) to K'ung Tzu (Confucius).

5 Usually translated 'purple'. But the term is applied to the coats of horses and cannot mean anything that we should call purple. These colours were reserved for times of fasting and mourning.

6 To do otherwise, would be like going out into the town in one's shirt-sleeves.

robe, fox fur.[1] On his undress robe the fur cuffs are long; but the right is shorter than the left.[2] His bed-clothes must be half as long again as a man's height.[3] The thicker kinds of fox and badger are for home wear. Except when in mourning, he wears all his girdle-ornaments.[4] Apart from his Court apron, all his skirts are wider at the bottom than at the waist. Lambskin dyed black and a hat of dark-dyed silk must not be worn when making visits of condolence.[5] At the Announcement[6] of the New Moon he must go to Court in full Court dress.

7, 8 When preparing himself for sacrifice he must wear the Bright Robe,[7] and it must be of linen. He must change his food and also the place where he commonly sits. But there is no objection to his rice being of the finest quality, nor to his meat being finely minced. Rice affected by the weather or turned he must not eat, nor fish that is not sound, nor meat that is high. He must not eat anything discoloured or that smells bad. He must not eat what is overcooked nor what is undercooked, nor anything that is out of season. He must not eat what has been crookedly cut, nor any dish that lacks its proper seasoning. The meat that he eats must at the very most not be enough to make his breath smell of meat rather than of rice. As regards wine, no limit is laid down; but

1 Cf. our black tie with black waistcoat.

2 To give him freedom of movement (pseudo K'ung An-kuo).

3 He does not, of course, undress, but simply draws the bed-clothes over him. According to Chu Hsi this refers only to one preparing for sacrifice.

4 Which are lucky talismans; or (in a more sophisticated vein of explanation) symbolic ornaments indicating his rank. Those of an ordinary gentleman were of jade.

5 i.e., 'plain' articles must be worn, approximating to those worn by the mourner. For these rules of dress, cf. *Li Chi*, XIII, fol. 3, and Introduction, p. 52.

6 See textual notes, and above, p. 90.

7 *Ming I*, the 'spirit robe' used during the period of purification. Cf. *Ming Ch'i*, 'spirit gear', the objects buried along with the dead in a tomb.

he must not be disorderly. He may not drink wine bought at a shop or eat dried meat from the market. He need not refrain from such articles of food as have ginger sprinkled over them; but he must not eat much of such dishes.[1]

After a sacrifice in the ducal palace, the flesh must not be kept overnight. No sacrificial flesh may be kept beyond the third day. If it is kept beyond the third day, it may no longer be eaten. While it is being eaten, there must be no conversation, nor any word spoken while lying down after the repast. Any article of food, whether coarse rice, vegetables, broth or melon, that has been used as an offering must be handled with due solemnity.

9 He must not sit on a mat that is not straight.[2]

10 When the men of his village are drinking wine he leaves the feast directly the village-elders have left. When the men of his village hold their Expulsion Rite,[3] he puts on his Court dress and stands on the eastern steps.[4]

11 When sending a messenger to enquire after someone in another country, he prostrates himself twice while speeding the messenger on his way. When K'ang-tzu[5] sent him some medicine he prostrated himself and accepted it; but said, As I am not acquainted with its properties, I cannot venture to taste it.[6]

1 All the above refers to periods of preparation for sacrifice. See Introduction, p. 56.   2 While eating sacrificial flesh?

3 The driving away of evil spirits at the close of the year; see additional and textual notes.

4 The place occupied by one who is presiding over a ceremony.

5 Head of the all-powerful Chi family. This sentence and the next paragraph obviously refer to Confucius himself.

6 A *chün-tzu* takes no medicine except that administered to him by a doctor whose father and grandfather have served the family. Compare the attachment of the English *chün-tzu* to the 'old family doctor'.

12 When the stables were burnt down, on returning from Court, he said, Was anyone hurt? He did not ask about the horses.

13 When his prince sends him a present of food, he[1] must straighten his mat and be the first to taste what has been sent. When what his prince sends is a present of uncooked meat, he must cook it and make a sacrificial offering. When his prince sends a live animal, he must rear it.[2] When he is waiting upon his prince at meal-times, while his prince is making the sacrificial offering, he (the gentleman) tastes the dishes. If he is ill and his prince comes to see him, he has himself laid with his head to the East with his Court robes thrown over him and his sash drawn across the bed. When the prince commands his presence he goes straight to the palace without waiting for his carriage to be yoked.[3]

14 On entering the Ancestral Temple, he asks about every detail.[4]

15 If a friend dies and there are no relatives to fall back on, he says, 'The funeral is my affair.' On receiving a present from a friend, even a carriage and horses, he does not prostrate himself. He does so only in the case of sacrificial meat being sent.

16 In bed he avoids lying in the posture of a corpse.[5] When at home he does not use ritual attitudes. When appearing before[6] anyone in mourning, however well he knows him, he must put on an altered expression,

1 The gentleman?　2 Not use it for food.
3 Cf. *Mencius*, V, 2, VII, 9.　4 Cf. III, 15.
5 i.e. with his face to the North, where lies the land of the Dead.
6 Or 'when he sees'. For different ways of writing the expression for 'mourning garb', see *Tz'u T'ung*, 434.

and when appearing before anyone in sacrificial garb, or a blind man, even informally, he must be sure to adopt the appropriate attitude. On meeting anyone in deep mourning he must bow across the bar of his chariot; he also bows to people carrying planks.[1] When confronted with a particularly choice dainty at a banquet, his countenance should change and he should rise to his feet. Upon hearing a sudden clap of thunder or a violent gust of wind, he must change countenance.

17 When mounting a carriage, he must stand facing it squarely and holding the mounting-cord. When riding he confines his gaze,[2] does not speak rapidly or point with his hands.[3]

18 (The gentleman) rises and goes at the first sign,[4] and does not 'settle till he has hovered'.[5] (A song) says:

> The hen-pheasant of the hill-bridge,
> Knows how to bide its time, to bide its time!
> When Tzu-lu made it an offering,
> It sniffed three times before it rose.[6]

1 Traditionally explained as meaning 'census tablets'.

2 Does not look about promiscuously. See textual notes.

3 Pointing is considered maleficent, unlucky, rude, as the case may be, in many parts of the world.

4 Of evil intentions on the part of the ruler; cf. *Lü Shih Ch'un Ch'iu*, P'ien 101, fol. 1. 'The *chün-tzu* is like a bird; if he is startled he rises.'

5 Is circumspect in choosing a new State in which to settle.

6 This quatrain (if such it is intended to be) resembles in content the songs by means of which the people commented on current political events. It is natural to interpret it as referring to the circumspect conduct of Confucius when the Chi Family (through the agency of Tzu-lu) invited him to return to Lu. One makes an offering to birds or animals whose behaviour suggests that they are sent by Heaven as omens or portents. For an anecdote of Tzu-lu and a pheasant, see *Lü Shih Ch'un Ch'iu*, 44, 1.

BOOK XI

1 The Master said, 'Only common people wait till they are advanced in ritual and music [before taking office]. A gentleman can afford to get up his ritual and music later on.' Even if I accepted this saying, I should still be on the side of those who get on with their studies first.[1]

2A The Master said, My adherents in Ch'ên and Ts'ai were none of them in public service.[2]

2B Those who worked by moral power were Yen Hui, Min Tzu-ch'ien, Jan Kêng and Jan Yung. Those who spoke well were Tsai Yü and Tzu-kung. Those who surpassed in handling public business were Jan Ch'iu and Tzu-lu; in culture and learning, Tzu-yu and Tzu-hsia.[3]

3 The Master said, Hui was not any help to me; he accepted everything I said.

---

1 This is the interpretation of Liu Pao-nan, founded on Chêng Hsüan. For the contrast between *chün-tzu* and *yeh-jên* cf. *Mencius*, III, 1, III, 14: 'If there were no *chün-tzu*, there would be no one to keep the common people (*yeh-jên*) in order; if there were no common people, there would be no one to produce food for the *chün-tzu*.'

2 Cf. *Mencius*, VII, 2, XVIII, where Confucius's difficulties in Ch'ên and Ts'ai are attributed to his being out of touch with the ruling classes in those States. The current interpretation 'Not one of them now comes near my door,' taken as a complaint of their infidelity, is comparatively recent.

3 This classification of the disciples is not put into the mouth of Confucius, as is clear from the form in which the names are given.

4 The Master said, Min Tzu-ch'ien is indeed a very good son. No one can take exception to what his parents or brothers have said of him.[1]

5 Nan Jung in reciting the *I* Song repeated the verse about the sceptre of white jade three times. (In consequence of which) Master K'ung gave him his elder brother's daughter to marry.[2]

6 K'ang-tzu of the Chi Family asked which of the disciples had a love of learning. Master K'ung replied, There was Yen Hui. He was fond of learning, but unfortunately his allotted span was a short one, and he died. Now there is none.

7 When Yen Hui died, his father Yen Lu begged for the Master's carriage, that he might use it to make the enclosure[3] for the coffin. The Master said, Gifted or not gifted,[4] you have spoken of your son and I will now speak of mine. When Li[5] died he had a coffin, but no enclosure. I did not go on foot in order that he might have an enclosure; for I rank next to the Great Officers[6] and am not permitted to go on foot.

8 When Yen Hui died, the Master said, Alas, Heaven has bereft me, Heaven has bereft me![7]

1 For the legend of his piety, see additional notes.

2 The Song in question is No. 271; see verse 5: A flaw in a white jade sceptre may be polished away; but a flaw in words cannot be repaired. 'Gave him his brother's daughter', cf. V. 1.

3 See additional notes.

4 Confucius thus apologizes for putting his son on a level with Yen Hui.

5 The name means 'carp-fish'. Later tradition makes him die later than Yen Hui.

6 It was the *shih* ('knights', 'gentlemen', those who fought in chariots and not afoot) who ranked after the Great Officers, and it is possible that Confucius ranked as 'leader of the *shih*'. See Translator's Preface, p. 27.

7 Recorded because Confucius rarely spoke of Heaven?

9 When Yen Hui died the Master wailed without restraint. His followers said, Master, you are wailing without restraint! He said, Am I doing so? Well, if any man's death could justify abandoned wailing, it would surely be this man's!

10 When Yen Hui died, the disciples wanted to give him a grand burial. The Master said it would be wrong to do so; nevertheless they gave him a grand burial. The Master said, Hui dealt with me as though I were his father. But I have failed to deal with him as though he were my son.[1] The fault however is not mine. It is yours, my friends!

11 Tzu-lu asked how one should serve ghosts and spirits. The Master said, Till you have learnt to serve men, how can you serve ghosts? Tzu-lu then ventured upon a question about the dead. The Master said, Till you know about the living, how are you to know about the dead?[2]

12A When Min Tzu-ch'ien stood by the Master's side in attendance upon him his attitude was one of polite restraint. That of Tzu-lu was one of impatient energy; that of Jan Ch'iu and of Tzu-kung was genial and affable.[3] The Master was pleased.

12B [The Master said],[4] A man like Yu[5] never dies in his bed.

---

1 Failed to assert my right to bury him in the way I thought suitable.

2 e.g. whether they are conscious, which was a much debated problem. See Translator's Preface, p. 26.

3 See textual note on X, 2.   4 There seems to be a hiatus in the text.

5 Tzu-lu. For his death in 480 B.C. during the accession struggles in Wei, see *Tso Chuan*, Ai kung, 15th year. Confucius may well have said this on hearing of Tzu-lu's death. The words are usually regarded as a prophecy.

13 When the men of Lu were dealing with the question of the Long Treasury, Min Tzu-ch'ien said, What about restoring it on the old lines? I see no necessity for rebuilding it on a new plan.[1] The Master said, That man is no talker; but when he does say anything, he invariably hits the mark.

14 The Master said, Yu's zithern has no right to be in my house at all.[2] Whereupon the disciples ceased to respect Tzu-lu. The Master said, The truth about Yu is that he has got as far as the guest-hall, but has not yet entered the inner rooms.[3]

15 Tzu-kung asked which was the better, Shih or Shang.[4] The Master said, Shih goes too far and Shang does not go far enough. Tzu-kung said, If that is so, then Shih excels. The Master said, To go too far is as bad as not to go far enough.

16 The head of the Chi Family was richer than the Duke of Chou;[5] but Ch'iu[6] when entrusted with the task of collecting his revenues for him, added to them and increased the yield. The Master said, He is no

1 The point of the remark is very uncertain. See additional and textual notes.

2 i.e. Tzu lu has no right to call himself a follower of my Way. The *sê* was a 25-stringed zithern.

3 Tzu-lu had an abundance of courage, which is the elementary virtue of the gentleman. But he lacked the two other virtues: wisdom and Goodness.

4 i.e. Tzu-chang or Tzu-hsia.

5 Huang K'an (sixth century) says that this does not refer to Tan, legendary founder of Lu, but to a subsequent Duke of Chou. Cf. however, *Hsün Tzu*, P'ien, 8, fol. 5, where the wealth of Tan is referred to.

6 i.e. Jan Ch'iu. The form in which the name is given suggests that these words were spoken by Confucius or a disciple and are not a statement of the compiler's.

follower of mine. My little ones, you may beat the drum and set upon him. I give you leave.[1]

17 [The Master said], Ch'ai[2] is stupid, Shen[3] is dull-witted, Shih[4] is too formal; Yu, too free and easy.[5]

18 The Master said, Hui comes very near to it.[6] He is often empty.[7] Ssu (Tzu-kung) was discontented with his lot and has taken steps to enrich himself.[8] In his calculations he often hits the mark.

19 Tzu-chang asked about the Way of the good people.[9] The Master said, He who does not tread in the tracks[10] cannot expect to find his way into the Inner Room.

20 The Master said (of someone), That his conversation is sound one may grant. But whether he is indeed a true gentleman or merely one who adopts outward airs of solemnity, it is not so easy to say.

21 Tzu-lu asked, When one hears a maxim, should one at once seek occasion to put it into practice? The Master said, Your father and elder brother are alive. How can

1 This is, of course, meant metaphorically. The same anecdote occurs in *Mencius*, IV, I, XIV.

2 Kao Ch'ai, associated with Tzu-lu in the Wei accession troubles.

3 Master Tsêng.

4 Tzu-chang. The meaning of the epithet *p'i* is very uncertain. See textual notes. Chu Hsi's 'it means that he was expert in ritual attitudes and deportment, but lacked sincerity' is not a philological gloss on *p'i*, but an application to this passage of what is said about Tzu-chang in XIX, 16.

5 Tradition represents Tzu-lu as a converted swashbuckler. See also textual notes.

6 To Goodness. The rest of the paragraph runs very awkwardly and is probably corrupt.   7 Hard up?

8 'Traded without official permission' is a possible interpretation.

9 Possibly a rival Way to that of Confucius, see Introduction, p. 24.

10 Of the Ancients.

you whenever you hear a maxim at once put it into practice? Jan Ch'iu asked, When one hears a maxim, should one at once seek occasion to put it into practice? The Master said, When one hears it, one should at once put it into practice.

Kung-hsi Hua said, When Yu asked, 'When one hears a maxim, should one at once put it into practice?' you said, You have a father and elder brother alive. But when Ch'iu asked, 'When one hears a maxim, should one at once put it into practice?' you said, 'When you hear it, put it into practice.' I am perplexed, and would venture to ask how this was. The Master said, Ch'iu is backward; so I urged him on. Yu is fanatical about Goodness;[1] so I held him back.

22 When the Master was trapped in K'uang,[2] Yen Hui fell behind. The Master said, I thought you were dead. Hui said, While you are alive how should I dare to die?

23 Chi Tzu-jan[3] asked whether Tzu-lu and Jan Ch'iu could be called great ministers. The Master said, I thought you were going to ask some really interesting question; and it is after all only a question about Yu and Ch'iu! What I call a great minister is one who will only serve his prince while he can do so without infringement of the Way, and as soon as this is impossible, resigns. But in the present case, so far as concerns Yu and Ch'iu, I should merely call them stop-gap ministers. Tzu-jan said, So you think they would merely do what they were told? The Master said, If called upon to slay their father or their prince, even *they* would refuse.

1 See textual notes.
2 See above, IX, 5. The story is also found in *Lü Shih Ch'un Ch'iu*, 17.
3 Brother of the head of the Chi Family.

24 Tzu-lu got Kao Ch'ai made Warden of Pi.[1] The Master said, You are doing an ill turn to another man's son. Tzu-lu said, What he will take charge of at Pi will be the peasants and the Holy Ground and Millet.[2] Surely 'learning consists in other things besides reading books'.[3] The Master said, It is remarks of that kind that make me hate glib people.[4]

25 Once when Tzu-lu, Tsêng Hsi, Jan Ch'iu and Kung-hsi Hua were seated in attendance upon the Master, he said, you consider me as a somewhat older man than yourselves. Forget for a moment that I am so.[5] At present you are out of office and feel that your merits are not recognized. Now supposing someone were to recognize your merits, what employment would you choose? Tzu-lu promptly and confidently replied, Give me a country of a thousand war-chariots, hemmed in by powerful enemies, or even invaded by hostile armies, with drought and famine to boot; in the space of three years I could endow the people with courage and teach them in what direction[6] right conduct lies.

Our Master smiled at him. What about you, Ch'iu? he said. Ch'iu replied saying, Give me a domain of sixty to seventy or say fifty to sixty (leagues), and in the space of three years I could bring it about that the common people should lack for nothing. But as to rites and music,[7] I should have to leave them to a real gentleman. What about you, Ch'ih?

1 See VI, 7.   2 See additional notes.

3 In which the 'stupid' (see XI, 17) Ch'ai was not proficient.

4 The pertness of Tzu-lu's remark consists of the fact that he throws in the Master's teeth a favourite Confucian maxim. Cf. I, 14 and Tzu-hsia's saying, I, 7.   5 See textual notes.

6 For *fang*, 'direction', cf. VI, 28. Courage, it will be remembered, is the lowest of the three virtues. Next comes wisdom; next Goodness.

7 Which are the perquisites of the upper classes as opposed to the common people.

(Kung-hsi Hua) answered saying, I do not say I could do this; but I should like at any rate to be trained for it. In ceremonies at the Ancestral Temple or at a conference or general gathering[1] of the feudal princes I should like, clad in the Straight Gown and Emblematic Cap, to play the part of junior assistant.

Tien,[2] what about you?

The notes of the zithern he was softly fingering died away; he put it down, rose and replied saying, I fear my words will not be so well chosen as those of the other three.[3] The Master said, What harm is there in that? All that matters is that each should name his desire.

Tsêng Hsi said, At the end of spring, when the making of the Spring Clothes[4] has been completed, to go with five times six newly-capped youths and six times seven uncapped boys, perform the lustration in the river I, take the air[5] at the Rain Dance altars, and then go home singing. The Master heaved a deep sigh and said, I am with Tien.

When the three others went away, Tsêng Hsi remained behind and said, What about the sayings of those three people? The Master said, After all, it was agreed that each should tell his wish; and that is just what they did.

Tsêng said, Why did you smile at Yu?

The Master said, 'Because it is upon observance of ritual that the governance of a State depends; and his words were lacking in the virtue of cession.[6] That is why I smiled at him.'

---

1 Scrupulously defined as 'Audiences' by the later ritualists, because in theory they were presided over by the Son of Heaven (the king of Chou).

2 i.e. Tsêng Hsi; he was the father of Master Tsêng.

3 Or 'I fear my choice will seem inferior to that of . . .'

4 A technical name for the clothes worn at the ceremony?

5 Cf. *Mencius*, II, 2, II, 1, where *fêng* means 'expose oneself to the wind'. Freak interpretations such as 'scatter', 'sing', 'sacrifice to the wind' are merely instances of wasted ingenuity.

6 *Jang*, 'giving up', 'ceding to others'.

'I suppose you were contrasting him with Ch'iu, who (by domain) certainly did not mean kingdom?'

'Where have you ever seen "a domain of sixty to seventy or fifty to sixty leagues" that was not a kingdom?'

'I suppose, then, you were contrasting him with Ch'ih, who was certainly not asking for a kingdom.'

'The business of the Ancestral Temple and such things as conferences and general gatherings can only be undertaken by feudal princes. But if Ch'ih were taking a minor part, what prince is there who is capable of playing a major one?'[1]

---

1 i.e. it is impossible to conceive of Kung-hsi Hua functioning on such an occasion except as the ruler of a Kingdom; so that, in effect, all three were asking for kingdoms.

BOOK XII

1 Yen Hui asked about Goodness. The Master said, 'He who can himself submit to ritual is Good.'[1] If (a ruler) could for one day 'himself submit to ritual', everyone under Heaven would respond to his Goodness. For Goodness is something that must have its source in the ruler himself; it cannot be got from others.

Yen Hui said, I beg to ask for the more detailed items of this (submission to ritual). The Master said, To look at nothing in defiance of ritual, to listen to nothing in defiance of ritual, to speak of nothing in defiance of ritual, never to stir hand or foot in defiance of ritual. Yen Hui said, I know that I am not clever; but this is a saying that, with your permission, I shall try to put into practice.[2]

2 Jan Jung asked about Goodness.[3] The Master said, Behave when away from home[4] as though you were in the presence of an important guest. Deal with the common people as though you were officiating at an important sacrifice. Do not do to others what you would not like yourself. Then there will be no feelings of opposition to you, whether it is the affairs of a State that you are handling or the affairs of a Family.[5]

1 In the *Tso Chuan* (Chao Kung, 12th year) Confucius is made to quote this as a saying from 'an old record'. The commentators, not understanding the archaic use of *k'o* ('able to') turned *k'o chi* into 'self-conquest', an error fruitful in edification; see above, p. 66.

2 A formula of thanks for instruction; cf. *Mencius*, I, 1, VII, 19.

3 i.e. ruling by Goodness, not by force.   4 i.e. in handling public affairs.

5 A ruling clan, such as that of the Chi in Lu.

Jan Yung said, I know that I am not clever; but this is a saying that, with your permission, I shall try to put into practice.

3 Ssu-ma Niu[1] asked about Goodness. The Master said, The Good (*jên*) man is chary (*jên*) of speech. Ssu-ma Niu said, So that is what is meant by Goodness – to be chary of speech? The Master said, Seeing that the doing of it is so difficult, how can one be otherwise than chary of talking about it?[2]

4 Ssu-ma Niu asked about the meaning of the term Gentleman. The Master said, The Gentleman neither grieves nor fears. Ssu-ma Niu said, So that is what is meant by being a gentleman – neither to grieve nor to fear? The Master said, On looking within himself he finds no taint; so why should he either grieve or fear?

5 Ssu-ma Niu grieved, saying, Everyone else has brothers; I alone have none.[3] Tzu-hsia said, I have heard this saying, 'Death and life are the decree of Heaven; wealth and rank depend upon the will of Heaven. If a gentleman attends to business and does not idle[4] away his time, if he behaves with courtesy to others and observes the rules of ritual, then all within the Four Seas[5] are his brothers.' How can any true gentleman grieve that he is without brothers?

1 A native of Sung; brother of Huan T'ui, VII, 22.

2 Here again Confucius is evasive about the meaning of Goodness. He first puns on *jên*, 'chary', and *jên*, 'goodness'; and then in his second reply answers as though his first reply had meant 'Goodness is a thing one ought to be chary of talking about.' The implication is that the questioner had not yet reached a stage at which the mysteries of *jên* could be revealed to him.

3 This may merely mean that his brother Huan T'ui, being an enemy of Confucius, could no longer be regarded by Niu as a brother. When Niu died in 481 B.C. he left behind him at least three brothers.

4 See textual notes.   5 That bound the universe.

6 Tzu-chang asked the meaning of the term 'illumined'. The Master said, He who is influenced neither by the soaking in of slander nor by the assault of denunciation may indeed be called illumined.[1] He who is influenced neither by the soaking in of slander nor by the assault of denunciation may indeed be called 'aloof'.

7 Tzu-kung asked about government. The Master said, Sufficient food, sufficient weapons, and the confidence of the common people. Tzu-kung said, Suppose you had no choice but to dispense with one of these three, which would you forgo? The Master said, Weapons. Tzu-kung said, Suppose you were forced to dispense with one of the two that were left, which would you forgo? The Master said, Food. For from of old death has been the lot of all men; but a people that no longer trusts its rulers is lost indeed.

8 Chi Tzu-ch'êng[2] said, A gentleman is a gentleman in virtue of the stuff he is made of. Culture cannot make gentlemen. Tzu-kung said, I am sorry, Sir, that you should have said that. For the saying goes that 'when a gentleman has spoken, a team of four horses cannot overtake his words'.[3]

Culture is just as important as inborn qualities; and inborn qualities, no less important than culture. Remove the hairs from the skin of a tiger or panther, and what is left looks just like the hairless hide of a dog or sheep.[4]

1 Cf. the section on posthumous titles in the *I Chou Shu*: 'He whom neither slander nor denunciation can influence is called clear-sighted', i.e. in his choice of subordinates.   2 A statesman of Wei.

3 Common people can say what they like, and no harm is done. But a person in your position will at once be quoted as an authority. I read a full stop after *shuo*.

4 The man of good birth is potentially capable of 'patterning his coat' with culture, and thus distinguishing himself from the common herd. But good birth alone, though essential as a basis for culture, is not enough to make a gentleman in the Confucian sense.

9 Duke Ai enquired of Master Yu, saying, It is a year of dearth, and the State has not enough for its needs. What am I to do? Master Yu replied, saying, Have you not got your tithes? The Duke said, Even with two-tenths instead of one, I still should not have enough. What is the use of talking to me about tithes? Master Yu said, When the Hundred Families[1] enjoy plenty, the prince necessarily shares in that plenty.[2] But when the Hundred Families have not enough for their needs, the prince cannot expect to have enough for his needs.

10 Tzu-chang asked what was meant by 'piling up moral force'[3] and 'deciding when in two minds'.[4] The Master said, 'by piling up moral force' is meant taking loyalty and good faith as one's guiding principles, and migrating to places where right prevails.[5] Again, to love a thing means wanting it to live, to hate a thing means wanting it to perish. But suppose I want something to live and at the same time want it to perish; that is 'being in two minds'.

> Not for her wealth, oh no!
> But merely for a change.[6]

1 All the people.   2 See textual notes.

3 No wonder Tzu-chang asked this question; for *ch'ung tê* (a very common expression in old texts) sometimes (e.g. *Hsi Tz'u* I, 7; *Tso Chuan*, Hsi Kung, 7th year) means 'to pile up *tê*, sometimes (e.g. *Tso Chuan*, Wên Kung, 2nd year), 'to do honour to, exalt possessors of *tê*'.

4 The two phrases in inverted commas rhyme, and no doubt Tzu-chang is asking for an explanation of a particular passage in an ancient rhymed text.

5 'If right prevails in a country, then serve it; if right does not prevail, then seek service elsewhere.'

6 Couplet from *Song* 105, 3, in which a lady says: I came all this long way to marry you, and you do not give me enough to eat. I shall go back to my country and home. Your thoughts are occupied with a new mate. If it is true that it is not because of her riches, then it is simply for the sake of a change. The last phrase ('only for a change') is susceptible of other interpretations. But it is clearly thus that Confucius understands it, and he uses this story of a man who got a wife from a far country, and then promptly neglected her in favour of someone taken up 'simply for a change', as an example of 'being in two minds', 'not knowing one's own mind'.

156

11 Duke Ching of Ch'i[1] asked Master K'ung about government. Master K'ung replied saying, Let the prince be a prince, the minister a minister, the father a father and the son a son. The Duke said, How true! For indeed when the prince is not a prince, the minister not a minister, the father not a father, the son not a son, one may have a dish of millet in front of one and yet not know if one will live to eat it.[2]

12 The Master said, Talk about 'deciding a lawsuit with half a word' — Yu is the man for that.

Tzu-lu never slept over a promise.[3]

13 The Master said, I could try a civil suit as well as anyone. But better still to bring it about that there were no civil suits![4]

14 Tzu-chang asked about public business. The Master said, Ponder over it untiringly at home; carry it out loyally when the time comes. (Literally, 'Home it untiringly, carry it out loyally.')

1 Died 490 B.C. The last of a long line of powerful and successful dukes. The closing years of his reign were clouded by the intrigues of the Ch'ên Family, which menaced the security of the dynasty (the prince was no longer a prince; ministers, i.e. the leaders of the Ch'ên faction, were no longer content to be ministers); and by succession-squabbles among his sons (the father no longer had the authority of a father; the sons were not content to be sons).

2 Figure of speech denoting utter insecurity. Legend makes Duke Ching haunted by the fear of death. Cf. *Lieh Tzu* VI, end. Advice very like that which Confucius gives here was given to Duke Ching's ancestor Duke Huan by Kuan Chung. See *Kuo Yü*, ch. VI, last fol., and *Han Shih Wai Chuan*, X, 9.

3 'He never agreed to do anything that could not be done till next day; for during the night circumstances might alter and prevent him from carrying out his word.' Such is the interpretation of the early commentators. Chu Hsi takes it in the sense of 'never putting off till the morrow'. Cf. *Shang Tzu's Su Chih*, 'dilatory government'.

4 Cf. *Ta Hsüeh* ('Great Learning'), Commentary, Para. 4.

15 Repetition of VI, 25.

16 The Master said, The gentleman calls attention to the good points in others; he does not call attention to their defects. The small man does just the reverse of this.

17 Chi K'ang-tzu asked Master K'ung about the art of ruling. Master K'ung said, Ruling (*chêng*) is straightening (*chêng*). If you lead along a straight way, who will dare go by a crooked one?

18 Chi K'ang-tzu was troubled by burglars. He asked Master K'ung what he should do. Master K'ung replied saying, If only you were free from desire, they would not steal even if you paid them to.[1]

19 Chi K'ang-tzu asked Master K'ung about government, saying, Suppose I were to slay those who have not the Way in order to help on those who have the Way, what would you think of it? Master K'ung replied saying, You are there to rule, not to slay. If you desire what is good, the people will at once be good. The essence of the gentleman is that of wind; the essence of small people is that of grass. And when a wind passes over the grass, it cannot choose but bend.[2]

20 Tzu-chang asked what a knight must be like if he is to be called 'influential'.[3] The Master said, That depends on what you mean by 'influential'. Tzu-chang replied saying, If employed by the State, certain to win fame, if

1 This is a rhetorical way of saying that if K'ang-tzu did not accumulate valuables, he would not be robbed. But coupled with this meaning is the suggestion that the ruler's moral force operates directly on the people, as a magic, not merely as an example.

2 Cf. *Mencius*, III, 1, II, 4.

3 *Ta*, able to turn his *tê* to account. See VI, 6.

employed by a Ruling Family, certain to win fame. The Master said, That describes being famous; it does not describe being influential. In order to be influential a man must be by nature straightforward and a lover of right. He must examine men's words and observe their expressions, and bear in mind the necessity of deferring to others.[1] Such a one, whether employed by the State or by a Ruling Family, will certainly be 'influential'; whereas the man who wins fame may merely have obtained, by his outward airs, a reputation for Goodness which his conduct quite belies. Anyone who makes his claims with sufficient self-assurance is certain to win fame in a State, certain to win fame in a Family.

21 Once when Fan Ch'ih was taking a walk with the Master under the trees at the Rain Dance altars, he said, May I venture to ask about 'piling up moral force', 'repairing shortcomings' and 'deciding when in two minds'?[2] The Master said, An excellent question. 'The work first; the reward afterwards'; is not that piling up moral force? 'Attack the evil that is within yourself;[3] do not attack the evil that is in others.' Is not this 'repairing shortcomings'?

> 'Because of a morning's blind rage
> To forget one's own safety
> And even endanger one's kith and kin'[4]

is that not a case of 'divided mind'?

---

1 See additional notes.

2 See above, para. 10. Here all three phrases rhyme; the phrases supplied by Confucius also rhyme, and are presumably quotations from a didactic poem.

3 See textual notes.

4 A rhyming triplet. Not knowing the full context either of the poem which the disciple quotes or of the one which Confucius utilizes in his reply, we cannot hope to understand the exact force of this passage.

22 Fan Ch'ih asked about the Good (ruler). The Master said, He loves men. He asked about the wise (ruler). The Master said, He knows men. Fan Ch'ih did not quite understand.[1] The Master said, By raising the straight and putting them on top of the crooked, he can make the crooked straight.[2] Fan Ch'ih withdrew, and meeting Tzu-hsia said to him, Just now I was with the Master and asked him about the wise (ruler). He said, By raising the straight and putting them on top of the crooked he can make the crooked straight. What did he mean?

Tzu-hsia said, Oh, what a wealth of instruction is in those words! When Shun had all that is under Heaven, choosing from among the multitude he raised up Kao Yao,[3] and straightway Wickedness disappeared. When T'ang had all that is under Heaven, choosing from among the multitude he raised up I Yin;[4] and straightway Wickedness disappeared.

23 Tzu-kung asked about friends. The Master said, inform them loyally and guide them discreetly. If that fails, then desist. Do not court humiliation.

24 Master Tsêng said, The gentleman by his culture collects friends about him, and through these friends promotes Goodness.

1 This applies only to the second answer.
2 See above, II, 19.
3 See *The Book of Songs*, p. 268.
4 See *The Book of Songs*, p. 278.

BOOK XIII

1 Tzu-lu asked about government. The Master said, Lead them; encourage them! Tzu-lu asked for a further maxim. The Master said, Untiringly.

2 Jan Yung, having become steward of the Chi Family, asked about government. The Master said, Get as much as possible done first by your subordinates.[1] Pardon small offences. Promote men of superior capacity. Jan Yung said, How does one know a man of superior capacity, in order to promote him? The Master said, Promote those you know, and those whom you do not know other people will certainly not neglect.[2]

3 Tzu-lu said, If the prince of Wei were waiting for you to come and administer his country for him, what would be your first measure? The Master said, It would certainly be to correct language. Tzu-lu said, Can I have heard you aright? Surely what you say has nothing to do with the matter. Why should language be corrected? The Master said, Yu! How boorish you are! A gentleman, when things he does not understand are mentioned, should[3] maintain an attitude of reserve. If language is incorrect, then what is said does not concord with what was meant; and if what is said does not concord with what was meant, what is to be done cannot be effected. If what is to be done cannot be

1 So that your time may not be taken up with petty preliminaries.
2 i.e. will certainly bring to your notice.
3 See textual notes.

effected,[1] then rites and music will not flourish. If rites and music do not flourish, then mutilations and lesser punishments will go astray. And if mutilations and lesser punishments go astray, then the people have nowhere to put hand or foot.

Therefore the gentleman uses only such language as is proper for speech, and only speaks of what it would be proper to carry into effect. The gentleman, in what he says, leaves nothing to mere chance.[2]

4 Fan Ch'ih asked the Master to teach him about farming. The Master said, You had much better consult some old farmer. He asked to be taught about gardening. The Master said, You had much better go to some old vegetable-gardener. When Fan Ch'ih had gone out, the Master said, Fan is no gentleman! If those above them love ritual, then among the common people none will dare to be disrespectful. If those above them love right, then among the common people none will dare to be disobedient. If those above them love good faith, then among the common people none will dare depart from the facts.[3] If a gentleman is like that, the common people will flock to him from all sides with their babies strapped to their backs. What need has he to practise farming?[4]

5 The Master said, A man may be able to recite the three hundred *Songs*; but, if when given a post in the

1 The 'chain-argument' clanks rather heavily in English; but it is essential to preserve the form of the original.

2 The whole of this highly elaborate, literary paragraph bears the stamp of comparatively late date. See Introduction, p. 16. The links in chain-arguments of this kind are always rhetorical rather than logical; and it would be a waste of time to seek for a causal sequence. Later Confucian literature supplies many examples of such rhetorical 'chains'. For *kou*, 'chance', see additional notes.

3 Bear false witness in lawsuits.   4 See additional notes.

government, he cannot turn his merits to account, or when sent on a mission to far parts he cannot answer particular questions,[1] however extensive his knowledge may be, of what use is it to him?

6 The Master said, If the ruler himself is upright, all will go well even though he does not give orders. But if he himself is not upright, even though he gives orders, they will not be obeyed.

7 The Master said, In their politics Lu and Wei are still brothers.[2]

8 The Master said of the Wei grandee Ching,[3] He dwelt as a man should dwell in his house. When things began to prosper with him, he said, 'Now they[4] will begin to be a little more suitable.' When he was better off still, he said, 'Now they will be fairly complete.' When he was really rich, he said, 'Now I shall be able to make them quite beautiful.'

9 When the Master was going to Wei, Jan Ch'iu drove him. The Master said, What a dense population! Jan Ch'iu said, When the people have multiplied, what next should be done for them? The Master said, Enrich them. Jan Ch'iu said, When one has enriched them, what next should be done for them? The Master said, Instruct them.

---

1 Besides delivering his message, he must be able to give an answer of his own to particular enquiries relative to this message.

2 On the rise of the Chou dynasty to power, Lu was given to the fourth and Wei to the seventh son of King Wên. The saying expresses, one may suppose, the disillusionment of Confucius on finding that things in Wei were no better than in Lu. In early times, however, it was understood as a commendation of Wei.

3 Flourished about 558 B.C.

4 My household rites. For *kou*, see textual notes.

10 The Master said, If only someone were to make use of me, even for a single year, I could do a great deal; and in three years I could finish off the whole work.

11 The Master said, 'Only if the right sort of people had charge of a country for a hundred years would it become really possible to stop cruelty and do away with slaughter.' How true the saying is!

12 The Master said, If a Kingly Man[1] were to arise, within a single generation Goodness would prevail.

13 The Master said, Once a man has contrived to put himself aright, he will find no difficulty at all in filling any government post. But if he cannot put himself aright, how can he hope to succeed in putting others right?[2]

14 Once when Master Jan came back from Court,[3] the Master said, Why are you so late? He replied, saying, There were affairs of State. The Master said, You must mean private business. If there had been affairs of State, although I am not used,[4] I too should have been bound to hear of them.

15 Duke Ting[5] asked if there were any one phrase that sufficed to save a country. Master K'ung replied saying, No phrase could ever be like that.[6] But here is one that comes near to it. There is a saying among men: 'It is

1 See Translator's Preface, p. 42.

2 The play on *chêng* 'to straighten, put right' and *chêng* 'to govern' makes this passage impossible to translate satisfactorily.

3 From the Court of the Chi Family, who had usurped the Duke's powers.

4 i.e. have no official post.

5 See above, III, 19.

6 The stop should come after *jo shih*.

hard to be a prince and not easy to be a minister.' A ruler who really understood that it was 'hard to be a prince' would have come fairly near to saving his country by a single phrase.

Duke Ting said, Is there any one phrase that could ruin a country? Master K'ung said, No phrase could ever be like that. But here is one that comes near to it. There is a saying among men: 'What pleasure is there in being a prince, unless one can say whatever one chooses, and no one dares to disagree?'[1] So long as what he says is good, it is of course good also that he should not be opposed. But if what he says is bad, will it not come very near to his ruining his country by a single phrase?

16 The 'Duke' of Shê[2] asked about government.[3] The Master said, When the near approve and the distant approach.

17 When Tzu-hsia was Warden of Chü-fu,[4] he asked for advice about government. The Master said, Do not try to hurry things. Ignore minor considerations. If you hurry things, your personality will not come into play.[5] If you let yourself be distracted by minor considerations, nothing important will ever get finished.

18 The 'Duke' of Shê addressed Master K'ung saying, In my country there was a man called Upright Kung.[6]

---

1 This saying also occurs in *Han Fei Tzu*, P'ien, 36.

2 See above VII, 18. Cf. *Han Fei Tzu*, P'ien, 38 and *Mo Tzu*, P'ien, 46 (*Kêng Chu*).

3 i.e. about the tokens of good government.

4 A town in Lu.

5 For *ta*, see VI, 6.

6 A legendary paragon of honesty; see *Huai-nan Tzu*, ch. XIII, fol. 6, where he is coupled with Wei-sheng Kao, *Han Fei Tzu*, P'ien, 49, and *Lü Shih Ch'un Ch'iu*, P'ien, 54. See also textual notes.

His father appropriated a sheep, and Kung bore witness against him. Master K'ung said, In my country the upright men are of quite another sort. A father will screen his son, and a son his father – which incidentally[1] does involve a sort of uprightness.

19 Fan Ch'ih asked about Goodness. The Master said, In private life, courteous, in public life, diligent, in relationships, loyal. This is a maxim that no matter where you may be, even amid the barbarians of the east or north, may never be set aside.

20 Tzu-kung asked, What must a man be like in order that he may be called a true knight (of the Way)? The Master said, he who

> In the furtherance of his own interests
> Is held back by scruples,
> Who as an envoy to far lands
> Does not disgrace his prince's commission

may be called a true knight.

Tzu-kung said, May I venture to ask who would rank next? The Master said, He whom his relatives commend for filial piety, his fellow-villagers, for deference to his elders. Tzu-kung said, May I venture to ask who would rank next? The Master said, He who always stands by his word, who undertakes nothing that he does not bring to achievement. Such a one may be in the humblest[2] possible circumstances, but all the same we must give him the next place.

Tzu-kung said, What would you say of those who are now conducting the government? The Master said, Ugh! A set of peck-measures,[3] not worth taking into account.

1 For the idiom see II, 18 and VII, 15.
2 For *k'êng k'êng*, see textual notes and XIV, 42.
3 'Mere thimblefuls', as we should say.

21 The Master said, If I cannot get men who steer a middle course to associate with, I would far rather have the impetuous and hasty.[1] For the impetuous at any rate assert themselves; and the hasty have this at least to be said for them, that there are things they leave undone.[2]

22 The Master said, The men of the south have a saying, 'Without stability[3] a man will not even make a good *shaman* or witch-doctor.'[4] Well said! Of the maxim: if you do not stabilize an act of *tê*, you will get evil by it (instead of good), the Master said, They (i.e. soothsayers) do not simply read the omens.[5]

23 The Master said, The true gentleman is conciliatory but not accommodating. Common people are accommodating but not conciliatory.[6]

24 Tzu-kung asked, saying, What would you feel about a man who was loved by all his fellow-villagers? The Master said, That is not enough.

What would you feel about a man who was hated by all his fellow-villagers? The Master said, That is not enough. Best of all would be that the good people in his village loved him and the bad hated him.

1 than the timid and conscientious. See textual notes.

2 Cf. *Mencius*, VII, 2, XXXVII.

3 Play on *hêng* (1) a rite for stabilizing, perpetuating the power of good omens and auspicious actions (see additional notes); (2) steadfast, in the moral sense.

4 For '*shaman* or witch-doctor' the *Li Chi* (33, fol. 3) has 'diviner by the yarrow stalks'.

5 To 'read the omens' is the first step in any undertaking. Cf. our own word 'inaugurate'. In its moral application Confucius's remark means that it is not enough to embark on the Way; the real test is whether one can continue in it. For 'evil' see textual notes.

6 'Accommodating' (*t'ung*) means ready to sacrifice principles to agreement. Cf. the common phrase *kou t'ung*, 'to agree somehow or other', i.e. at all costs.

25 The Master said, The true gentleman is easy to serve, yet difficult to please.[1] For if you try to please him in any manner inconsistent with the Way, he refuses to be pleased; but in using the services of others he only expects of them what they are capable of performing. Common people are difficult to serve, but easy to please. Even though you try to please them in a manner inconsistent with the Way, they will still be pleased; but in using the services of others they expect them (irrespective of their capacities) to do any work that comes along.

26 The Master said, The gentleman is dignified, but never haughty; common people are haughty, but never dignified.

27 The Master said, Imperturbable, resolute, tree-like,[2] slow to speak – such a one is near to Goodness.

28 Tzu-lu asked, What must a man be like, that he may be called a true knight of the Way? The Master said, he must be critical and exacting,[3] but at the same time indulgent. Then he may be called a true knight. Critical and exacting with regard to the conduct of his friends; indulgent towards his brothers.

29, 30 The Master said, Only when men of the right sort[4] have instructed a people for seven years ought there to be any talk of engaging them in warfare. The Master said, To lead into battle a people that has not first been instructed is to betray them.[5]

1 Cf. *Hsün Tzu*, P'ien, 27, end.
2 Or 'wooden', i.e. simple. But see textual notes.
3 See textual notes.
4 i.e. followers of the Way. The 'instruction' is, of course, in virtue, not in the use of arms.
5 Cf. *Mencius*, VI, 2, VIII, 2, and *Ku-liang Chuan*, Duke Hsi, 23rd year.

BOOK XIV

1 Yüan Ssu asked about compunction.[1] The Master said, When a country is ruled according to the Way, (the gentleman) accepts rewards. But when a country is not ruled according to the Way, he shows compunction in regard to rewards.

2 Of the saying 'He upon whom neither love of mastery, vanity, resentment nor covetousness have any hold may be called Good,' the Master said, Such a one has done what is difficult;[2] but whether he should be called Good I do not know.

3 The Master said, The knight of the Way who thinks only of sitting quietly at home is not worthy to be called a knight.[3]

4 The Master said, When the Way prevails in the land, be bold in speech and bold in action. When the Way does not prevail, be bold in action but conciliatory in speech.

5 The Master said, One who has accumulated moral power (*tê*) will certainly also possess eloquence; but he who has eloquence does not necessarily possess moral

1 With regard to accepting rewards. It will be remembered that it was Yüan Ssu (see above, VI, 3) who was rebuked for refusing a salary. The omission of his surname has led to the supposition that he was the compiler of this chapter.

2 Cf. VI, 20.

3 See Translator's Preface, p. 27.

power. A Good Man will certainly also possess courage; but a brave man is not necessarily Good.

6 Nan-kung Kuo[1] asked Master K'ung, saying, Yi[2] was a mighty archer and Ao shook the boat;[3] yet both of them came to a bad end.[4] Whereas Yü and Chi, who devoted themselves to agriculture, came into possession of all that is under Heaven.[5]

At the time our Master made no reply, but when Nan-kung had withdrawn he said, He is a true gentleman indeed, is that man! He has a right appraisal of 'virtue's power' (tê),[6] has that man!

7 The Master said, It is possible to be a true gentleman and yet lack Goodness. But there has never yet existed a Good man who was not a gentleman.

8 The Master said, How can he be said truly to love,[7] who exacts no effort from the objects of his love? How can he be said to be truly loyal, who refrains from admonishing the object of his loyalty?

9 The Master said, When a ducal mandate was being prepared[8] P'i Ch'ên[9] first made a rough draft, Shih Shu[10]

1 Son of Mêng I Tzu; see II, 5.

2 A legendary hero. His name is cognate to the word for rainbow.

3 Shook his enemies out of it, at the great battle in which he destroyed the Shên-hsün clan. See also textual notes.

4 Yi was slain by his minister Shu (or Cho) of Han. Shu's son Ao was in turn slain by Shao K'ang. For the legend, see *Tso Chuan*, Hsiang Kung, 4th year, and the *T'ien Wên*, verse 90 (Conrady-Erkes edition, p. 246).

5 For Great Yü drained the land and so made it suitable for agriculture. Hou Chi, from whom the Chou people were descended, was (as his name implies; *chi* = millet) the patron deity of agriculture.

6 As opposed to physical strength such as that displayed by Yi and Ao.

7 As a father loves a son or a prince his people.

8 In the State of Chêng.

9 Flourished in the middle of the sixth century B.C.

10 Grandson of Duke Mou of Chêng; died in 506 B.C.

checked and revised it, Tzu-yü[1] the Receiver of Envoys amended and embellished it; Tzu-ch'an[2] of Tung-li gave it amplitude and colour.

10, 11 Someone asked about Tzu-ch'an. The Master said, A kindly[3] man! Asked about Tzu-hsi[4] he said, That man! That man! Asked about Kuan Chung[5] he said, This is the sort of man he was: he could seize the fief of Pien with its three hundred villages[6] from its owner, the head of the Po Family; yet Po, though he 'lived on coarse food'[7] to the end of his days, never uttered a single word of resentment.[8] The Master said, To be poor and not resent it[9] is far harder than to be rich, yet not presumptuous.[10]

12 The Master said, Mêng Kung Ch'o would have done well enough as Comptroller of the Chao or Wei

1 Perhaps Yü Chieh, great-grandson of Duke Mou. He is the 'Receiver of Envoys Tzu-yü of Chêng' mentioned in *Tso Chuan*, Hsiang kung, 29th year.　2 See p. 102.

3 The word (see above, p. 96) is often used in a bad sense. Kindliness is often a feeble amends for neglect of duty. Thus Tzu-ch'an took people across the rivers in his own carriage; but he ought to have mended the bridges. *Mencius*, IV, 2, I, 2.

4 A famous minister of the Ch'u State; assassinated in 479 B.C. According to the accounts of him in the *Tso Chuan* he did and said much of which Confucius would certainly have approved. The exclamation with which his name is here received is, however, certainly one of disapprobation. The story that he prejudiced his prince against Confucius was probably merely invented to explain this passage.

5 See III, 22.

6 Cf. *Hsün Tzu*, P'ien, 7, fol. 1.

7 A stock expression, merely meaning 'in humble circumstances'.

8 So great was Kuan Chung's prestige. This is the tenor of many stories about Kuan Chung. He struck with an arrow the man who was afterwards to become Duke Huan of Ch'i; yet the Duke forgave him and made him Prime Minister. He broke all the sumptuary laws; yet it never occurred to the people of Ch'i to regard him as 'presumptuous'.

9 As the head of the Po Family managed to do.

10 In which respect, according to Confucius's view (see III, 22), Kuan Chung signally failed.

families; but he was not fit to be a State minister even in T'êng or Hsüeh.[1]

13 Tzu-lu asked what was meant by 'the perfect man'. The Master said, If anyone had the wisdom of Tsang Wu Chung,[2] the uncovetousness of Mêng Kung Ch'o, the valour of Chuang Tzu of P'ien[3] and the dexterity of Jan Ch'iu,[4] and had graced these virtues by the cultivation of ritual and music, then indeed I think we might call him 'a perfect man'.

He said, But perhaps to-day we need not ask all this of the perfect man. One who, when he sees a chance of gain, stops to think whether to pursue it would be right; when he sees that (his prince) is in danger, is ready to lay down his life; when the fulfilment of an old promise is exacted, stands by what he said long ago – him indeed I think we might call 'a perfect man'.

14 The Master asked Kung-ming Chia[5] about Kung-shu Wên-tzu,[6] saying, Is it a fact that your master neither 'spoke nor laughed nor took'? Kung-ming Chia replied saying, The people who told you this were exaggerating. My master never spoke till the time came to do so;

1 Let alone in a great State like Lu. Mêng Kung Ch'o was a Lu politician who flourished about 548 B.C. The Chao and Wei were noble families in Chin.

2 Middle of the sixth century; grandson of Tsang Wên Chung, V, 17.

3 The paragon of legendary prowess. See *Hsin Hsü*, VIII.

4 It is very odd to find the disciple Jan Ch'iu ranged alongside of worthies who belonged to a past generation and contrasted with the men of 'to-day'. I suspect that some earlier member of the Jan family is intended, perhaps Jan Shu, whose marksmanship at a battle between Ch'i and Lu (516 B.C.) is mentioned in the *Tso Chuan*. The familiar name of Jan Ch'iu might then easily have been substituted by a scribe.

5 Presumably a retainer of Kung-shu Wên-tzu.

6 Spoken of as 'very aged' in 504 B.C., and apparently dead in 497 B.C., the year (according to the traditional chronology) of Confucius's first visit to Wei, Wen-tzu's native place. See *Tso Chuan*, Ting Kung, 6th year and 13th year.

with the result that people never felt that they had had too much of his talk. He never laughed unless he was delighted; so people never felt they had had too much of his laughter. He never took[1] unless it was right to do so, so that people never felt he had done too much taking. The Master said, Was that so? Can that really have been so?

15 The Master said, Tsang Wu Chung occupied the fief of Fang and then demanded from (the Duke of) Lu that (his brother) Wei should be allowed to take the fief over from him. It is said that he applied no pressure upon his prince; but I do not believe it.[2]

16 The Master said, Duke Wên of Chin could rise to an emergency, but failed to carry out the plain dictates of ritual. Duke Huan of Ch'i carried out the dictates of ritual, but failed when it came to an emergency.[3]

17 Tzu-lu said, When Duke Huan put to death (his brother) Prince Chiu, Shao Hu gave his life in an attempt to save the prince; but Kuan Chung did not.[4] Must one not say that he fell short of Goodness? The Master said, That Duke Huan was able to convene the

1 Took rewards.

2 In 550 Tsang Wu Chung, accused of plotting a revolt, was obliged to go into exile. On his way he seized the fief of Fang, and then sent word to the Duke offering to proceed into exile and relinquish Fang, on condition that he should be allowed to hand the fief over to his brother Tsang Wei. The request was granted. (*Tso Chuan*, Duke Hsiang, 23rd year.) The later commentators fail to realize that 'Wei' is a proper name and unsuccessfully attempt to turn it into *wei*, 'to do'. Translators have followed suit.

3 See additional and textual notes.

4 Both Kuan Chung and Shao Hu were supporting Prince Chiu's claim to the dukedom. Prince Hsiao Po (afterwards to become Duke Huan) murdered his brother Prince Chiu and seized the ducal throne; whereupon Kuan Chung, the great opportunist, transferred his allegiance to the murderer.

rulers of all the States without resorting to the use of his war-chariots was due to Kuan Chung. But as to his[1] Goodness, as to his Goodness!

18 Tzu-kung said, I fear Kuan Chung was not Good. When Duke Huan put to death his brother Prince Chiu, Kuan Chung so far from dying on Chiu's behalf became Duke Huan's Prime Minister. The Master said, Through having Kuan Chung as his Minister Duke Huan became leader of the feudal princes, uniting and reducing to good order all that is under Heaven; so that even to-day the people are benefiting by what he then did for them. Were it not for Kuan Chung we might now be wearing our hair loose and folding our clothes to the left![2] We must not expect from him what ordinary men and women regard as 'true constancy' — to go off and strangle oneself in some ditch or drain, and no one the wiser.

19 Kung-shu Wên-tzu, when summoned to office by the Duke (of Wei), brought with him and presented to the Duke his retainer Chuan,[3] the same Chuan who became a State officer. The Master hearing of it[4] said, With good reason was he accorded the title Wên.[5]

20 The Master referred to Duke Ling of Wei as being no follower of the true Way. K'ang-tzu[6] said, How is it

1 i.e. Kuan Chung's.

2 As the barbarians do. Duke Huan stemmed the great invasion of the Ti tribes.

3 Or Hsien. It is necessary slightly to paraphrase this sentence in order to bring out the meaning with clarity.

4 As a historical event; not at the time when it happened.

5 Cf. *I Chou Shu*, 54, fol. 1, 'He who helps commoners to rank and position is called Wên.' So various were Kung-shu Wên-tzu's merits that the business of choosing his posthumous title was unusually difficult. See *Li Chi*, IV, fol. 5.

6 The head of the Chi Family.

then that he does not come to grief? Master K'ung said, He has Chung-shu Yü[1] to deal with foreign envoys and guests, the priest T'o[2] to regulate the ceremonies in his ancestral temple and Wang-sun Chia[3] to command his armies. Why then should he come to grief?

21 The Master said, Do not be too ready to speak of it,[4] lest the doing of it should prove to be beyond your powers.

22 When Ch'ên Hêng assassinated Duke Chien of Ch'i, Master K'ung washed his head and limbs,[5] went to Court and informed Duke Ai of Lu, saying, Ch'ên Hêng has slain his prince. I petition that steps should be taken to punish him. The Duke said, You had better inform the Three.[6] Master K'ung said, As I rank next to the Great Officers,[7] I could not do otherwise than lay this information before you. And now your Highness says 'Inform the Three?' He then went to the Three and informed them. They refused his petition. Master K'ung said, As I rank next to the Great Officers, I could not do otherwise than lay this petition before you.

23 Tzu-lu asked him how to serve a prince. The Master said, Never oppose him by subterfuges.[8]

24 The Master said, The gentleman can influence those who are above him; the small man can only influence those who are below him.

---

1 Known posthumously as K'ung Wên Tzu. See V, 14.
2 See VI, 14.   3 See III, 13.
4 Goodness. Cf. XII, 3.
5 As became a suppliant. The assassination took place in 481 B.C.
6 The heads of the three great families Chi, Shu and Mêng.
7 Cf. XI, 7. This anecdote, in a very similar form, occurs in the *Tso Chuan*, Ai, 14th year.
8 But if you have to oppose him, do so openly.

25 The Master said, In old days men studied for the sake of self-improvement; nowadays men study in order to impress other people.[1]

26 Ch'ü Po Yū[2] sent a messenger to Master K'ung. Master K'ung bade the man be seated and asked of him saying, What is your master doing? He replied, saying, My master is trying to diminish the number of his failings;[3] but he has not hitherto been successful. When the messenger had gone away, the Master said, What a messenger, what a messenger![4]

27, 28 When the Master said, He who holds no rank in a State does not discuss its policies,[5] Master Tsêng said, 'A true gentleman, even in his thoughts, never departs from what is suitable to his rank.'[6]

29 The Master said, A gentleman is ashamed to let his words outrun his deeds.[7]

30 The Master said, The Ways of the true gentleman are three. I myself have met with success in none of them. For he that is really Good is never unhappy, he that is really wise is never perplexed, he that is really

1 Cf. *Hsün Tzu*, P'ien, 1.

2 A famous Wei minister. See below, XV, 6.

3 Or 'is trying to lessen his offence'. Ch'ü Po Yü may have promised to get Confucius a post in Wei and failed to do so. The message may mean that he is still trying, but has not yet succeeded arranging anything.

4 This is usually taken as an exclamation of approval. I very much doubt if that is so.

5 See above, VIII, 14.

6 Tsêng illustrates Confucius's saying by quoting an old maxim, which also figures, in practically identical form, in the first appendix (*Hsiang*) of the *Book of Changes*, section 52. In my paper on the *Book of Changes* (*Bulletin of the Museum of Far Eastern Antiquities*, No. 5), I quote this saying as though it occurred in the text of the *Book* itself, an error which I take this opportunity of correcting.

7 See textual notes.

brave is never afraid. Tzu-kung said, That, Master, is your own Way![1]

31 Tzu-kung was always criticizing other people. The Master said, It is fortunate for Ssu that he is so perfect himself as to have time to spare for this. I myself have none.

32 The Master said, (A gentleman) does not grieve that people do not recognize his merits; he grieves at his own incapacities.

33 The Master said, Is it the man who 'does not count beforehand upon the falsity of others nor reckon upon promises not being kept', or he who is conscious beforehand of deceit, that is the true sage?[2]

34 Wei-shêng Mou said to Master K'ung, 'Ch'iu,[3] what is your object in going round perching now here, now there? Is it not simply to show off the fact that you are a clever talker?' Master K'ung said, I have no desire to be thought a clever talker; but I do not approve of obstinacy.[4]

35 The Master said, The horse Chi[5] was not famed for its strength but for its inner qualities (*tê*).

36 Someone said, What about the saying 'Meet resentment with inner power (*tê*)'?[1] The Master said, In that

1 Is precisely how you yourself behave. Usually taken as referring to Confucius's disclaimer ('I myself have met with success in none', etc.) and meaning, 'So you yourself say; (but we know that is only due to your modesty, and do not take your words literally).'

2 See additional and textual notes.

3 Familiar name of Confucius, the form of address is discourteous. It is surmised that Wei-shêng Mou was a recluse.

4 It is no use going on and on trying to convert a prince. After a time one must give it up, and try elsewhere.

5 A famous horse of ancient times. A rhymed couplet.

case, how is one to meet inner power? Rather, meet resentment with upright dealing and meet inner power with inner power.

37 The Master said, The truth is, no one knows me![2] Tzu-kung said, What is the reason that you are not known? The Master said, I do not 'accuse Heaven, nor do I lay the blame on men'.[3]

But the studies[4] of men here below are felt on high, and perhaps after all I am known; not here, but in Heaven!

38 Kung-po Liao spoke against Tzu-lu to the Chi Family. Tzu-fu Ching-po[5] informed the Master saying, I fear my master's[6] mind has been greatly unsettled by this. But in the case of Kung-po Liao, I believe my influence is still great enough to have his carcase exposed in the market-place. The Master said, If it is the will of Heaven that the Way shall prevail, then the Way will prevail. But if it is the will of Heaven that the Way should perish, then it must needs perish. What can Kung-po Liao do against Heaven's will?

39 The Master said, Best of all, to withdraw from one's generation; next to withdraw to another land; next to leave because of a look; next best to leave because of a word.[7]

1 The same saying is utilized in the *Tao Tê Ching*, ch. 63. It originally meant 'Let the ruler meet discontent among his subjects with *tê* and not with violence.' Confucius here uses it in a much more general sense.

2 No ruler recognizes my merits and employs me.

3 'A gentleman neither accuses Heaven nor blames men.' *Mencius*, II, 2, XIII, 1.   4 The self-training consisting in the study of antiquity.

5 A retainer of the Chi Family, friendly with Tzu-kung.

6 Chi K'ang-tzu's.

7 This continues the theme of the last paragraph. If *Tao* (the Way) does not prevail, it is better to flee altogether from the men of one's generation, rather than to go round 'perching first here, then there' as Confucius himself had unsuccessfully done, or to wait till the expression of the ruler's face betrays that he is meditating some enormity; or worst of all, to wait till his words actually reveal his intention.

40 The Master said, The makers[1] were seven. . . .

41 Tzu-lu was spending the night at the Stone Gates.[2] The gate-keeper said, Where are you from? Tzu-lu said, From Master K'ung's. The man said, He's the one who 'knows it's no use, but keeps on doing it', is that not so?

42 The Master was playing the stone-chimes, during the time when he was in Wei. A man carrying a basket passed the house where he and his disciples had established themselves. He said, How passionately he beats his chimes! When the tune was over, he said, How petty and small-minded![3] A man whose talents no one recognizes has but one course open to him – to mind his own[4] business! 'If the water is deep, use the stepping-stones; if it is shallow, then hold up your skirts.'[5] The Master said, That is indeed[6] an easy way out!

43 Tzu-chang said, The Books[7] say, 'When Kao Tsung was in the Shed of Constancy,[8] he did not speak for

1 i.e. inventors, 'culture-heroes', originators of fire, agriculture, metallurgy, boats, carriages, the potter's wheel, the loom. Their names are variously given. It is natural to suppose that the compilers could not agree as to which names Confucius had enumerated, and therefore left the paragraph unfinished.

2 On the frontiers of Lu and Ch'i? Both this and the next paragraph belong to popular legend rather than to the traditions of the school. Cf. Book XVIII.

3 Cf. XIII, 20. He sees in Confucius's passionate playing an expression of discontent at his failure to get office.

4 See textual notes.

5 In *Song* 54. The meaning here is, 'Take the world as you find it.'

6 *Kuo* here means '*en effet*', not 'effective', 'resolute'. Cf. *Mencius*, IV, 2, XXXII.

7 See *Shu Ching*, Wu Yi. Cf. *Kuo Yü*, 20, fol. 2

8 i.e. in mourning for his father. The *liang-an* was a penthouse set up for the habitation of a mourner against the wall of a tomb. Kao Tsung's traditional date is 1324–1266 B.C.

three years.' What does this mean? The Master said, Not Kao Tsung in particular. All the men of old did this. Whenever a prince died, the ministers (of the last prince) all continued in their offices, taking their orders from the Prime Minister;[1] and this lasted for three years.

44 The Master said, So long as the ruler loves ritual,[2] the people will be easy to handle.

45 Tzu-lu asked about the qualities of a true gentleman. The Master said, He cultivates in himself the capacity to be diligent in his tasks. Tzu-lu said, Can he not go further than that? The Master said, He cultivates in himself the capacity to ease the lot of other people.[3] Tzu-lu said, Can he not go further than that? The Master said, He cultivates in himself the capacity to ease the lot of the whole populace. If he can do that, could even Yao or Shun find cause to criticize him?[4]

46 Yüan Jang sat waiting for the Master in a sprawling position.[5] The Master said, Those who when young show no respect to their elders achieve nothing worth mentioning when they grow up. And merely to live on, getting older and older, is to be a useless pest.[6]

And he struck him across the shins with his stick.

47 A boy from the village of Ch'uëh used to come

1 Cf. *Mencius*, III, 1, II, 4.
2 i.e. carries on immemorial usages and customs.
3 Other gentlemen.   4 Cf. VI, 28.
5 Whereas he ought to have been standing when his teacher arrived and only to have sat down when told to do so.
6 This paragraph is usually translated in a way which makes it appear that Yüan Jang was an old man, whom Confucius brutally reproaches with 'being old and not dying'. It is, on the contrary, clear that he was a young man, like the boy of the next paragraph.

with messages. Someone asked about him, saying, Is he improving himself?[1] The Master said, Judging by the way he sits in grown-up people's places and walks alongside of people older than himself, I should say he was bent upon getting on quickly rather than upon improving himself.

1 i.e. taking advantage of his visits to the house of Confucius.

BOOK XV

1 Duke Ling of Wei asked Master K'ung about the marshalling of troops. Master K'ung replied saying, About the ordering of ritual vessels I have some knowledge; but warfare is a thing I have never studied. Next day he resumed his travels.[1] In Ch'ên supplies fell short and his followers became so weak that they could not drag themselves on to their feet. Tzu-lu came to the Master and said indignantly, Is it right that even gentlemen should be reduced to such straits? The Master said, A gentleman can withstand hardships; it is only the small man who, when submitted to them, is swept off his feet.[2]

2 The Master said, Ssu,[3] I believe you look upon me as one whose aim is simply to learn and retain in mind as many things as possible. He replied, That is what I thought. Is it not so? The Master said, No; I have one (thread) upon which I string them all.[4]

3 The Master said, Yu,[5] Those who understand moral force (*tê*) are few.

4 The Master said, Among those that 'ruled by inactivity'[6] surely Shun may be counted. For what action

---

1 There is a similar story in the *Tso Chuan*, Ai Kung, 11th year.
2 As though by a flood.   3 Familiar name of Tzu-kung.
4 Cf. IV, 15.   5 Familiar name of Tzu-lu.
6 *Wu-wei*, the phrase applied by the Taoists to the immobility of self-hypnosis.

did he take? He merely placed himself gravely and reverently with his face due south;[1] that was all.

5 Tzu-chang asked about getting on with people. The Master said, Be loyal and true to your every word, serious and careful in all you do; and you will get on well enough, even though you find yourself among barbarians. But if you are disloyal and untrustworthy in your speech, frivolous and careless in your acts, even though you are among your own neighbours, how can you hope to get on well? When standing,[2] see these principles ranged before you; in your carriage, see them resting on the yoke. Then you may be sure that you will get on. Tzu-chang accordingly inscribed the maxim upon his sash.

6 The Master said, Straight and upright indeed was the recorder Yü![3] When the Way prevailed in the land he was (straight) as an arrow; when the Way ceased to prevail, he was (straight) as an arrow. A gentleman indeed is Ch'ü Po Yü.[4] When the Way prevailed in his land, he served the State; but when the Way ceased to prevail, he knew how to 'wrap it[5] up and hide it in the folds of his dress'.

1 The position of the ruler. Shun was a Divine Sage (*shêng*) whose *tê* was so great that it sufficed to guide and transform the people.

2 In your place at Court. For 'ranged', see textual notes.

3 Having failed to persuade Duke Ling of Wei to use the services of Ch'ü Po Yü, the recorder Yü gave directions that when he (the recorder) died his body should not receive the honours due to a minister, as a posthumous protest against the Duke Ling's offences. The story is told in *Han Shih Wai Chuan*, 7, and many other places.

4 Ch'ü Po Yü left Wei owing to the tyrannical conduct of Duke Hsien in 559 B.C. No tense is expressed in the first clause. I say 'is' because in XIV, 26, Ch'ü Po Yü appears to be still alive. It is, however, not very probable that he was, as legend asserts, still alive when Confucius visited Wei in 495 B.C.

5 His jewel; i.e. his talents.

7 The Master said, Not to talk to[1] one who could be talked to, is to waste a man. To talk to those who cannot be talked to, is to waste one's words. 'He who is truly wise never wastes a man';[2] but on the other hand, he never wastes his words.

8 The Master said, Neither the knight who has truly the heart of a knight nor the man of good stock who has the qualities that belong to good stock[3] will ever seek life at the expense of Goodness; and it may be that he has to give his life in order to achieve Goodness.

9 Tzu-kung asked how to become Good. The Master said, A craftsman, if he means to do good work, must first sharpen his tools. In whatever State you dwell

Take service with such of its officers as are worthy,
Make friends with such of its knights as are Good.

10 Yen Hui asked about the making of a State. The Master said, One would go by the seasons of Hsia;[4] as State-coach for the ruler one would use that of Yin,[5] and as head-gear of ceremony wear the Chou hat.[6] For music one would take as model the Succession Dance,[7] and would do away altogether with the tunes of Chêng;[8] one

---

1 About the Way. Cf. VII, 28.
2 I suspect that this is a proverbial saying.
3 The written forms of *chih* and *jên* are here half-punningly insisted upon.
4 It was believed that in the Hsia dynasty the year began in the spring.
5 Which were less ornate than those of Chou, say the commentators. But this is a mere guess. *Han Fei Tzu*, P'ien, 10, says that the Yin invented state coaches.
6 Which had some resemblance to our scholastic mortar-board.
7 See above, III, 25 and VII, 13.
8 The words to these tunes are in the seventh book of the *Songs*. But it was probably to the character of the music not to that of the words that Confucius objected. See additional notes.

would also keep clever talkers at a distance. For the tunes of Chêng are licentious and clever talkers are dangerous.

11 The Master said, He who will not worry about what is far off will soon find something worse[1] than worry close at hand.

12 The Master said, In vain have I looked for one whose desire to build up his moral power was as strong as sexual desire.[2]

13 The Master said, Surely one would not be wrong in calling Tsang Wên Chung[3] a stealer of other men's ranks? He knew that Liu-hsia Hui was the best man for the post, yet would not have him as his colleague.[4]

14 The Master said, To demand much from oneself and little from others is the way (for a ruler) to banish discontent.

15 The Master said, If a man does not continually ask himself 'What am I to do about this, what am I to do about this?' there is no possibility of my doing anything about him.

16 The master said, Those who are capable of spending a whole day together without ever once discussing questions of right or wrong, but who content themselves[5] with performing petty acts of clemency,[6] are indeed difficult.[7]

1 Yu is a much stronger word than lü.
2 Cf. IX, 17.   3 See V, 17.
4 'Degraded him', says the Tso Chuan, Wên Kung, 2nd year. For Liu-hsia Hui, see below, XVIII, 2.
5 'Satisfy their consciences', as we should say.
6 See textual notes.
7 To lead into the Way.

17 The Master said, The gentleman who takes the right as his material to work upon and ritual as the guide in putting what is right into practice, who is modest in setting out his projects and faithful in carrying them to their conclusion, he indeed is a true gentleman.

18 The Master said, A gentleman is distressed by his own lack of capacity; he is never distressed at the failure of others to recognize his merits.

19 The Master said, A gentleman has reason to be distressed if he ends his days without making a reputation for himself.[1]

20 The Master said, 'The demands that a gentleman makes are upon himself; those that a small man makes are upon others.'[2]

21 The Master said, A gentleman is proud, but not quarrelsome, allies himself with individuals, but not with parties.

22 The Master said, A gentleman does not

> Accept men because of what they say,
> Nor reject sayings, because the speaker is
> what he is.

23 Tzu-kung asked saying, Is there any single saying that one can act upon all day and every day?[3] The Master said,

---

1 Which contradicts the saying before. As both sayings completely lack context, it would be a waste of time to try to reconcile the contradiction.
2 This is a proverbial saying, capable of many interpretations. To the Taoists it meant 'Seek Tao in yourself (through the practice of quietism) and not in the outside world.'
3 For *chung shên*. Cf. IX, 26.

Perhaps the saying about consideration:[1] 'Never do to others what you would not like them to do to you.'[2]

24 The Master said, In speaking of the men of the day I have always refrained from praise and blame alike. But if there is indeed anyone whom I have praised, there is a means by which he may be tested. For the common people here round us are just such stuff as the three dynasties[3] worked upon in the days when they followed the Straight Way.

25 The Master said, I can still remember the days when a scribe left blank spaces,[4] and when someone using a horse (for the first time)[5] hired a man to drive it.[6] But that is all over now!

26 The Master said, Clever talk can confound the workings of moral force, just as small impatiences can confound great projects.

27 The Master said, When everyone dislikes a man, enquiry is necessary; when everyone likes a man, enquiry is necessary.

28 The Master said, A man can enlarge his Way; but there is no Way that can enlarge a man.[7]

---

1 Ch. IV, 15.

2 Cf. V, 11.

3 Hsia, Yin and Chou.

4 When in doubt; instead of trusting to his imagination.

5 Some such words must have slipped out. Pao Hsien's (first century A.D.) commentary suggests that they were still there in his text.

6 Another instance of diffidence, parallel to 'leaving blanks'. See additional notes.

7 Without effort on his part. Play on 'Way' and 'road'. 'A man can widen a road . . . ', etc.

29 The Master said, To have faults and to be making no effort to amend them is to have faults indeed![1]

30 The Master said, I once spent a whole day without food and a whole night without sleep, in order to meditate.[2] It was no use. It is better to learn.[3]

31 The Master said, A gentleman, in his plans, thinks of the Way; he does not think how he is going to make a living. Even farming sometimes entails[4] times of shortage; and even learning may incidentally lead to high pay. But a gentleman's anxieties concern the progress of the Way; he has no anxiety concerning poverty.

32 The Master said, He whose wisdom brings him into power, needs Goodness to secure that power. Else, though he get it, he will certainly lose it. He whose wisdom brings him into power and who has Goodness whereby to secure that power, if he has not dignity wherewith to approach the common people, they will not respect him. He whose wisdom has brought him into power, who has Goodness whereby to secure that power and dignity wherewith to approach the common people, if he handle them contrary to the prescriptions of ritual, is still a bad ruler.[5]

1 Whereas one should never condemn one who is amending his faults. The *Ku-liang Chuan* (Hsi, 22) adds two words, which give a very different turn to the saying. See textual notes.

2 See II, 15.

3 This paragraph reads at first sight as though it were the record of a personal experience. In reality it is meant in a much more general way. *Hsün Tzu* (P'ien, I, fol. 2) quotes the proverb 'I spent a whole day meditating; I should have done better to learn. I stood on tip-toe in order to get a good view; I should have done better to climb a hill.'

4 For the idiom, see II, 18; VII, 15; XIII, 18 and XIX, 6.

5 This paragraph with its highly literary, somewhat empty elaboration, and its placing of ritual on a pinnacle far above Goodness, is certainly one of the later additions to the book. For the chain-like rhetorical development, cf. XIII, 3.

33 The Master said, It is wrong for a gentleman to have knowledge of menial matters[1] and proper that he should be entrusted with great responsibilities. It is wrong for a small man to be entrusted with great responsibilities, but proper that he should have a knowledge of menial matters.

34 The Master said, Goodness is more to the people than water and fire. I have seen men lose their lives when 'treading upon' water and fire; but I have never seen anyone lose his life through 'treading upon' Goodness.[2]

35 The Master said, When it comes to Goodness one need not avoid competing with one's teacher.

36 The Master said, From a gentleman consistency is expected, but not blind fidelity.

37 The Master said, In serving one's prince one should be

> Intent upon the task,
> Not bent upon the pay.

38 The Master said, There is a difference[3] in instruction but none in kind.

1 The usual interpretation is 'It is impossible for us to recognize a gentleman when he is merely employed in small matters.' But I do not see how such a sense can be forced out of the text as it stands. For the undesirability of a gentleman's having miscellaneous accomplishments, cf. IX, 6.

2 A symbolic 'treading upon fire' is still used in China as a rite of purification. According to the *Lun-hêng* (P'ien, 45) a processional wading along the river was part of the rain-making ceremony. Confucius says that Goodness (on the part of the ruler) is a greater and safer purifier than even water or fire.

3 Between us and the Sages. Any of us could turn into a Yao or Shun, if we trained ourselves as they did. Cf. XVII, 2, and *Mencius*, II, 1, II, 28.

39 The Master said, With those who follow a different Way it is useless to take counsel.

40 The Master said, In official speeches[1] all that matters is to get one's meaning through.

41 The Music-master Mien came to see him. When he reached the steps, the Master said, Here are the steps.[2] When he reached the mat, the Master said, Here is the mat. When everyone was seated the Master informed him saying, So-and-so is here, So-and-so is there. When the Music-master Mien had gone, Tzu-chang asked saying, 'Is that the recognized way to talk to a Music-master?' The Master said, Yes, certainly it is the recognized way to help a Music-master.

1 *Tz'u* means pleas, messages, excuses for being unable to attend to one's duties, etc.
2 Music-masters were blind.

BOOK XVI

1 (1) The Head of the Chi Family decided to attack Chuan-yü.[1] (2) Jan Ch'iu and Tzu-lu[2] came to see Master K'ung and said to him, The Head of the Chi Family has decided to take steps with regard to Chuan-yü. (3) Master K'ung said, Ch'iu, I fear you must be held responsible for this crime. (4) Chuan-yü was long ago appointed by the Former Kings[3] to preside over the sacrifices to Mount Tung-mêng. Moreover, it lies within the boundaries of our State, and its ruler is a servant of our own Holy Ground and Millet. How can such an attack be justified?

(5) Jan Ch'iu said, It is our employer who desires it. Neither of us two ministers desires it. (6) Master K'ung said, Ch'iu, among the sayings of Chou Jên[4] there is one which runs: 'He who can bring his powers into play steps into the ranks;[5] he who cannot, stays behind.' Of what use to anyone are such counsellors as you, who see your master tottering, but do not give him a hand, see him falling, but do not prop him up? (7) Moreover, your plea is a false one. For if a tiger or wild buffalo escapes from its cage or a precious ornament of tortoise-shell or jade gets broken in its box, whose fault is it?[6]

1 A small independent State within the borders of Lu.
2 Who were in the service of the Chi Family.
3 The Chou Emperors.
4 An ancient sage. Further sayings by him are quoted in *Tso Chuan*, Yin Kung, 6th year, and Chao Kung, 5th year. I fancy he is the same person as the Ch'ih Jên of the *Shu Ching* (P'an Kêng, Part I).
5 Military metaphor, here applied to politics.
6 i.e. it is the fault of the person in charge of these things.

(8) Jan Ch'iu said, The present situation is this: Chuan-yü is strongly fortified and is close to Pi.[1] If he does not take it now, in days to come it will certainly give trouble to his sons or grandsons. (9) Master K'ung said, Ch'iu, a true gentleman, having once denied that he is in favour of a course, thinks it wrong to make any attempt to condone that course. (10) Concerning the head of a State or Family I have heard the saying:

> He is not concerned lest his people should
>   be poor,
> But only lest what they have should be
>   ill-apportioned.
> He is not concerned lest they should be few,
> But only lest they should be divided against
>   one another.[2]

And indeed, if all is well-apportioned, there will be no poverty; if they are not divided against one another, there will be no lack of men.[3] (11) If such a state of affairs exists, yet the people of far-off lands still do not submit, then the ruler must attract them by enhancing the prestige (*tê*) of his culture; and when they have been duly attracted,[4] he contents them. And where there is contentment there will be no upheavals.

(12) To-day with you two, Yu and Ch'iu, acting as counsellors to your master, the people of far lands do not submit to him, and he is not able to attract them. The State itself is divided and tottering, disrupted and cleft, but he can do nothing to save it and is now planning to wield buckler and axe within the borders of his own land. I am afraid that the troubles of the Chi Family

1 The chief castle of the Chi Family.

2 The text of this little poem is slightly corrupt. See textual notes.

3 The words *an wu ch'ing* have become displaced. They belong after *an chih*, 21 characters further on; see textual notes.

4 For the ideas underlying this passage, see Introduction, p. 33.

are due not to what is happening in Chuan-yü, but to what is going on behind the screen-wall of his own gate.[1]

2 Master K'ung said, When the Way prevails under Heaven all orders concerning ritual, music and punitive expeditions are issued by the Son of Heaven himself. When the Way does not prevail, such orders are issued by the feudal princes; and when this happens, it is to be observed that ten generations rarely pass before the dynasty falls. If such orders are issued by State Ministers, five generations rarely pass before they lose their power. When the retainers[2] of great Houses seize a country's commission,[3] three generations rarely pass before they lose their power. When the Way prevails under Heaven, policy is not decided by Ministers; when the Way prevails under Heaven, commoners[4] do not discuss public affairs.

3 Master K'ung said, Power over the exchequer was lost by the Ducal House[5] five generations ago, and government has been in the hands of Ministers[6] for four generations. Small wonder that the descendants of the Three Huan[7] are fast losing their power!

1 His own lack of *tê* and the fact that he has had advisers.

2 Such as Yang Huo, who seized power in Lu in 505 B.C.

3 The *ming* of a State is the charge whereby the Emperor appoints its feudal lord.

4 People not belonging to the Imperial family.

5 Surrendered by the Duke to the Three Families.

6 The heads of the Chi Family. The first three paragraphs of this book seem to form a connected unity. It was under Chi K'ang-tzu (succeeded in 492 B.C.) that Tzu-lu and Jan Ch'iu were colleagues. If we take paragraph 3 as having been spoken subsequent to 492 B.C., the five powerless Dukes must be Ch'êng, Hsiang, Chao, Ting and Ai; and the four Ministers, Chi Wu-tzu, Chi P'ing-tzu, Chi Huan-tzu and Chi K'ang-tzu. But it would be a mistake to try to fit into too strict a chronology sayings that may be purely legendary. For the late date of Book XVI, see Introduction, p. 18.

7 The Three Families, Chi, Mêng and Shu.

4 Master K'ung said, There are three sorts of friend that are profitable, and three sorts that are harmful. Friendship with the upright, with the true-to-death and with those who have heard much is profitable. Friendship with the obsequious,[1] friendship with those who are good at accommodating their principles, friendship with those who are clever at talk[2] is harmful.

5 Master K'ung said, There are three sorts of pleasure that are profitable, and three sorts of pleasure that are harmful. The pleasure got from the due ordering of ritual and music, the pleasure got from discussing the good points in the conduct of others, the pleasure of having many wise friends is profitable. But pleasure got from profligate enjoyments, pleasure got from idle gadding about, pleasure got from comfort and ease is harmful.

6 Master K'ung said, There are three mistakes that are liable to be made when waiting upon a gentleman. To speak before being called upon to do so; this is called forwardness.[3] Not to speak when called upon to do so; this is called secretiveness. To speak without first noting the expression of his face; this is called 'blindness'.[4]

7 Master K'ung said, There are three things against which a gentleman is on his guard. In his youth, before his blood and vital humours[5] have settled down, he is on his guard against lust. Having reached his prime, when the blood and vital humours have finally hardened, he is on his guard against strife. Having reached old age, when the blood and vital humours are already decaying, he is on his guard against avarice.

1,2,3 See textual notes.   4 Cf. *Hsün Tzu*, P'ien, 1, end.
5 The physiological theories which underlie this paragraph are, I suspect, considerably posterior to Confucius.

8 Master K'ung said, There are three things that a gentleman fears: he fears the will of Heaven, he fears great men,[1] he fears the words of the Divine Sages. The small man does not know the will of Heaven and so does not fear it. He treats great men with contempt, and scoffs at the words of the Divine Sages.

9 Master K'ung said, Highest are those who are born wise. Next are those who become wise by learning. After them come those who have to toil painfully in order to acquire learning. Finally, to the lowest class of the common people belong those who toil painfully without ever managing to learn.

10 Master K'ung said, The gentleman has nine cares. In seeing he is careful to see clearly, in hearing he is careful to hear distinctly, in his looks he is careful to be kindly; in his manner to be respectful, in his words to be loyal, in his work to be diligent. When in doubt he is careful to ask for information; when angry he has a care for the consequences, and when he sees a chance of gain, he thinks carefully whether the pursuit of it would be consonant with the Right.

11, 12 Master K'ung said, 'When they see what is good, they grasp at it as though they feared it would elude them. When they see what is not good, they test it cautiously, as though putting a finger into hot water.' I have heard this saying; I have even seen such men.[2] 'It is by dwelling in seclusion that they seek the fulfilment of their aims; it is by deeds of righteousness that they extend the influence of their Way.' I have heard this

1 *Ta-jen* means (1) giants; (2) ministers, persons in authority; (3) morally great, as in *Mencius*, IV, 2, VI: IV, 2, XI and XII, etc. Probably the meaning here is 'morally great'; that is to say, people like Confucius himself.

2 These two clauses are accidentally inverted in the original.

saying; but I have never seen such men. 'Duke Ching of Ch'i had a thousand teams of horses; but on the day of his death the people could think of no good deed for which to praise him.[1] Po I and Shu Ch'i[2] starved at[3] the foot of Mount Shou-yang; yet the people sing their praises down to this very day.' Does not this saying illustrate the other?[4]

13 Tzu-ch'in[5] questioned Po Yü[6] saying, As his son[7] you must after all surely have heard something different from what the rest of us hear. Po Yü replied saying, No. Once when he was standing alone and I was hurrying[8] past him across the courtyard, he said, Have you studied the *Songs*? I replied saying, No. (He said) If you do not study the *Songs*, you will find yourself at a loss in conversation. So I retired and studied the *Songs*. Another day he was again standing alone, and as I hurried across the courtyard, he said, Have you studied the rituals? I replied saying, No. (He said) If you do not study the rituals, you will find yourself at a loss how to take your stand.[9] So I retired and studied the rituals. These two things I heard from him.

Tzu-ch'in came away delighted, saying, I asked about one point, but got information about three. I learnt

1 This is clearly the same formula as VIII, 1 (end), where, however, it is used in praise and not, as here, in condemnation.

2 See V, 22.

3 This form of the preposition, which occurs twice here but nowhere else in the *Analects*, marks the passage as a quotation from some other text. Moreover, the passage is closed by a formula (*ch'i ssu chih wei*) which regularly follows quotations.

4 i.e. are not Po I and Shu Ch'i examples of people who dwelt in seclusion to fulfil their aims, by deeds of righteousness extended the influence of the Way?

5 See I, 10.

6 Confucius's son; see XI, 7.

7 *Tzu* here means 'son' and not 'you, my master'.

8 As a sign of respect.

9 On public occasions.

about the *Songs*, about the rituals, and also learnt that a gentleman keeps his son at a distance.[1]

14 The wife of the ruler of a State is referred to by the ruler as 'That person'. She refers to herself as Little Boy. The people of the country call her 'That person of the Prince's'. When speaking of her to people of another State the ruler calls her 'This lonely one's little prince'. But people of another State likewise call her 'That person of the Prince's'.[2]

1 The reasons why a gentleman must not teach his own son are discussed in *Mencius*, IV, I, XVIII. There is a definite ritual severance between father and son. A father may not carry his son in his arms. A son may not, when sacrifice is being made to his deceased father, act as the 'medium' into whom the spirit of the deceased passes. See *Li Chi*, I, fol. 5.

2 This paragraph is a passage on etiquette from some old handbook of ritual, and was probably inserted here merely because it was found along with the manuscript of this *p'ien* ('chapter'). See additional notes, and cf. *Li Chi*, II, fol. 3.

BOOK XVII

1 Yang Huo[1] wanted to see Master K'ung; but Master K'ung would not see him. He sent Master K'ung a sucking pig. Master K'ung, choosing a time when he knew Yang Huo would not be at home, went to tender acknowledgment; but met him in the road. He spoke to Master K'ung, saying, 'Come here, I have something to say to you.' What he said was, 'Can one who hides his jewel[2] in his bosom and lets his country continue to go astray be called Good? Certainly not. Can one who longs to take part in affairs, yet time after time misses the opportunity to do so − can such a one be called wise? Certainly not.[3] The days and months go by, the years do not wait upon our bidding.' Master K'ung said, All right;[4] I am going to serve.

2 The Master said, By nature, near together; by practice far apart.[5]

3 The Master said, It is only the very wisest and the very stupidest who cannot change.

1 See XVI, 2, note. For the anecdote, cf. *Mencius*, III, 2, VII, 3. For 'sent' see textual notes.   2 i.e. his talents. Cf. XV, 6.

3 Yang Huo answers his own rhetorical questions, a common formula in Chinese.

4 The form of assent Confucius uses implies reluctance. This story, like those in Books XVIII and XIII, certainly originated in non-Confucian circles and comes from the same sort of source as the Confucius Anecdotes in the Taoist works *Chuang Tzu* and *Lieh Tzu*.

5 This proverbial saying has wide possibilities of application. It here presumably means that goodness is a matter of training and application and not an inborn quality.

4 When the Master went to the walled town of Wu,[1] he heard the sound of stringed instruments and singing. Our Master said with a gentle[2] smile, 'To kill a chicken one does not use an ox-cleaver.'[3] Tzu-yu replied saying, I remember once hearing you say, 'A gentleman who has studied the Way will be all the tenderer towards his fellow-men; a commoner who has studied the Way will be all the easier to employ.' The Master said, My disciples, what he says is quite true. What I said just now was only meant as a joke.

5 Kung-shan Fuiao,[4] when he was holding the castle of Pi in revolt (against the Chi Family), sent for the Master, who would have liked to go; but Tzu-lu did not approve of this and said to the Master, After having refused in so many cases, why go to Kung-shan of all people? The Master said, It cannot be for nothing[5] that he has sent for me. If anyone were to use me, I believe I could make a 'Chou in the east'.[6]

6 Tzu-chang asked Master K'ung about Goodness. Master K'ung said, He who could put the Five into practice everywhere under Heaven would be Good. Tzu-chang begged to hear what these were. The Master said, Courtesy, breadth, good faith, diligence and clem-

1 Where Tzu-yu was in command. See VI, 12.   2 See textual notes.

3 A saying of proverbial type meaning, in effect, that in teaching music to the inhabitants of this small town Tzu-yu is 'casting pearls before swine'. The proverb may well have had a second, balancing clause, here alluded to, but not expressed; such as, 'To teach commoners one does not use a zithern.'

4 Warden of Pi, the chief stronghold of the Chi Family. He revolted in 502, but in 498 he fled to Ch'i and later to Wu where he is said to have plotted, in a spirit of petty revenge, against his native State of Lu.

5 Confucius believes that Kung-shan intends to restore the Duke to his rightful powers.

6 Create a second Golden Age, comparable to the early days of the Chou dynasty.

ency. 'He who is courteous is not scorned, he who is broad wins the multitude, he who is of good faith is trusted by the people, he who is diligent succeeds in all he undertakes, he who is clement can get service from the people.'[1]

7 Pi Hsi[2] summoned the Master, and he would have liked to go. But Tzu-lu said, I remember your once saying, 'Into the house of one who is in his own person doing what is evil, the gentleman will not enter.' Pi Hsi is holding Chung-mou[3] in revolt. How can you think of going to him? The Master said, It is true that there is such a saying. But is it not also said that there are things 'so hard that no grinding will ever wear them down', that there are things 'so white that no steeping will ever make them black'? Am I indeed to be forever like the bitter gourd that is only fit to hang up,[4] but not to eat?[5]

8 The Master said, Yu, have you ever been told of the Six Sayings about the Six Degenerations?[6] Tzu-lu replied, No, never. (The Master said) Come, then; I will tell you. Love of Goodness without love of learning[7] degenerates into silliness. Love of wisdom without love of learning degenerates into utter lack of principle. Love of keeping promises without love of learning degenerates into villainy.[8] Love of uprightness without love of learning[9] degenerates into harshness. Love of courage

1 This is almost certainly a quotation from some text of the *Shu Ching*. Cf. XX, 1, where most of it reappears.
2 A Chin officer.
3 A town in Wei, captured by the Chin (in 490?).
4 Till it is dry and can be used as a vessel.
5 Play on two senses of *shih* (1) to eat; (2) to get a salary, an official post.
6 See textual notes.
7 i.e. learning the Way of the ancients.
8 i.e. keeping regrettable pacts and promises to the detriment of *i* ('what is right under the circumstances').
9 Like that of Upright Kung, XIII, 18.

200

without love of learning degenerates into turbulence.[1] Love of courage without love of learning degenerates into mere recklessness.

9 The Master said, Little ones, Why is it that none of you study the *Songs*? For the *Songs* will help you to incite people's emotions, to observe their feelings, to keep company, to express your grievances. They may be used at home in the service of one's father; abroad, in the service of one's prince.[2] Moreover, they will widen your acquaintance with the names[3] of birds, beasts, plants and trees.

10 The Master addressed Po Yü[4] saying, Have you done the *Chou Nan* and the *Shao Nan*[5] yet? He who has not even done the *Chou Nan* and the *Shao Nan* is as though he stood with his face pressed against a wall!

11 The Master said, Ritual, ritual! Does it mean no more than presents of jade and silk?[6] Music, music! Does it mean no more than bells and drums?[7]

12 The Master said, To assume an outward air of fierceness when inwardly trembling is (to take a comparison from low walks of life) as dishonest as to sneak into places where one has no right to be, by boring a hole or climbing[8] through a gap.

1 The tendency to fling oneself into any revolutions or upheavals that are going on in the world around one.

2 For the uses of the *Songs* here inculcated, see *The Book of Songs*, p. 335.

3 i.e. the 'correct names', the names in the ancient Court dialect used in ritual, as opposed to the local names.

4 Son of Confucius. See XVI, 13.

5 The first two books of the *Songs*.

6 Cf. *Hsün Tzu*, P'ien, 27, fol. 1.

7 For the particle *yün*, see my paper in *Bulletin of the School of Oriental Studies*, Vol. VII, Pt. III, 1934.

8 See textual notes.

13 The Master said, The 'honest villager' spoils[1] true virtue (*tê*).

14 The Master said, To tell in the lane what you have heard on the highroad is to throw merit (*tê*) away.

15 The Master said, How could one ever possibly serve one's prince alongside of such low-down creatures? Before they have got office, they think about nothing but how to get it; and when they have got it, all they care about is to avoid losing it. And so soon as they see themselves in the slightest danger of losing it, there is no length to which they will not go.

16 In old days the common people had three faults, part[2] of which they have now lost. In old days the impetuous were merely impatient of small restraints; now they are utterly insubordinate. In old days the proud were stiff and formal; now they are touchy and quarrelsome. In old days simpletons were at any rate straightforward; but now 'simple-mindedness' exists only as a device of the impostor.

17 The Master said, Clever talk and a pretentious manner are seldom found in the Good.[3]

18 The Master said, I hate to see roan killing red, I hate to see the tunes of Chêng[4] corrupting Court music, I hate to see sharp mouths overturning kingdoms and clans.

---

1 As we should say 'Spoils the market for . . .'. For a long discussion of this saying, see *Mencius*, VII, 2, XXXVII.

2 What follows is a paradox, for we expect to hear that the people have improved; whereas it turns out that the 'lost parts' were redeeming features.

3 Identical with I, 3.

4 See XV, 10. Cf. also *Mencius*, VII, 2, XXXVII.

19 The Master said, I would much rather not have to talk. Tzu-kung said, If our Master did not talk, what should we little ones have to hand down about him? The Master said, Heaven does not speak; yet the four seasons run their course thereby,[1] the hundred creatures, each after its kind, are born thereby. Heaven does no speaking!

20 Ju Pei[2] wanted to see Master K'ung. Master K'ung excused himself on the ground of ill-health. But when the man who had brought the message was going out through the door he took up his zithern and sang, taking good care that the messenger should hear.

21 Tsai Yü[3] asked about the three years' mourning,[4] and said he thought a year would be quite long enough: 'If gentlemen suspend their practice of the rites[5] for three years, the rites will certainly decay; if for three years they make no music, music will certainly be destroyed.'[6] (In a year) the old crops have already vanished, the new crops have come up, the whirling drills have made new fire.[7] Surely a year would be enough?

The Master said, Would you then (after a year) feel at ease in eating good rice and wearing silk brocades? Tsai

1 By command of Heaven.

2 Of whom practically nothing is known. He had evidently disgraced himself.

3 See V, 9.

4 For parents. Three years is often interpreted as meaning 'into the third year', i.e. 25 months.

5 The mourning for parents entailed complete suspension of all ordinary activities.

6 A traditional saying. Cf. *Shih Chi*, ch. 28, beginning.

7 The ritualists describe four 'fire-changing' rites, one for each season, the new fire being in each case kindled on the wood of a tree appropriate to the season. But perhaps the only actual 'fire-changing', when all fires were put out and after three days rekindled from a new ritually-obtained flame, was in the spring. See *Hou Han Shu*, LXI, fol. 6, recto and *Chou Li*, ch. 57 (commentary).

Yü said, Quite at ease. (The Master said) If you would really feel at ease, then do so. But when a true gentleman is in mourning, if he eats dainties, he does not relish them, if he hears music, it does not please him, if he sits in his ordinary seat, he is not comfortable. That is why he abstains from these things. But if you would really feel at ease, there is no need for you to abstain.

When Tsai Yü had gone out, the Master said, How inhuman[1] Yü is! Only when a child is three years old does it leave its parents' arms. The three years' mourning is the universal mourning everywhere under Heaven.[2] And Yü – was he not the darling of his father and mother for three years?

22 The Master said, Those who do nothing all day but cram themselves with food and never use their minds are difficult.[3] Are there not games such as draughts?[4] To play them would surely be better than doing nothing at all.

23 Tzu-lu said, Is courage to be prized by a gentleman? The Master said, A gentleman gives the first place to Right. If a gentleman has courage but neglects Right, he becomes turbulent. If a small man has courage but neglects Right, he becomes a thief.

1 *Jên* is here used in its later sense, 'possessing human feelings', 'kind'. This chapter, it will be remembered (see Introduction, p. 15), shows many signs of late date.

2 The whole object of this paragraph is to claim Confucius as a supporter of the three years' mourning. This custom was certainly far from being 'universal', and was probably not ancient. Cf. *Mencius*, III, 1, III, where the people of Têng protest that even in Lu 'the former princes none of them practised it'.

3 Cf. XV, 16.

4 For draughts, see *Tso Chaun*, Duke Hsiang, 25th year, end. It no doubt resembled the current game of *wei-ch'i*. I think *po* (cognate with *po* 'to strike', cf. Japanese *utsu*, 'to strike', i.e. make a move in board-games) is to be taken with *i* and is not the name of a separate game.

24 Tzu-kung said, Surely even the gentleman must have his hatreds? The Master said, He has his hatreds. He hates those who point out what is hateful in others.[1] He hates those who dwelling in low estate[2] revile all who are above them. He hates those who love deeds of daring but neglect ritual. He hates those who are active and venturesome, but are violent in temper.[3] I suppose you also have your hatreds? Tzu-kung said,[4] I hate those who mistake cunning[5] for wisdom. I hate those who mistake insubordination for courage. I hate those who mistake tale-bearing for honesty.

25 The Master said, Women and people of low birth are very hard to deal with. If you are friendly with them, they get out of hand, and if you keep your distance, they resent it.[6]

26 The Master said, One who has reached the age of forty and is still disliked will be so till the end.

1 Cf. *Kuan Tzu*, P'ien, 66, end.
2 *liu* has been wrongly inserted here on the analogy of XIX, 20.
3 See textual notes.
4 This 'said' has accidentally been transferred to the clause above.
5 See textual notes.
6 Like Liu Pao-nan, I take *nü-tzu* in its ordinary sense of 'women' as opposed to 'men', and *hsiao jên* in its ordinary sense of 'cads' as opposed to gentlemen. The standard interpreters soften the saying by making it apply to 'maids and valets'.

BOOK XVIII

1 'The lord of Wei fled from him,[1] the lord of Chi suffered slavery at his hands, Pi Kan rebuked him and was slain.' Master K'ung said, In them the Yin had three Good men.

2 When Liu-hsia Hui[2] was Leader of the Knights,[3] he was three times dismissed. People said to him, Surely you would do well to seek service elsewhere? He said, If I continue to serve men in honest ways, where can I go and not be three times dismissed? If, on the other hand, I am willing to serve men by crooked ways, what need is there for me to leave the land of my father and mother?

3 Duke Ching of Ch'i received Master K'ung; he said, To treat him on an equality with the head of the Chi Family is impossible. I will receive him as though he ranked between the head of the Chi and the head of the Mêng. (At the interview) he said, I am old and have no use for you. Whereupon Master K'ung left (the land of Ch'i).[4]

---

1 i.e. from the tyrant Chou, last sovereign of the Yin dynasty. The lord of Wei was his step-brother. The lords of Chi and Pi Kan were his uncles. For his enormities, see *The Way and Its Power*, p. 126.

2 See XV, 13.

3 A comparatively humble post. Its occupant was chiefly concerned with criminal cases.

4 As pointed out in the Introduction, Book XVIII is wholly legendary in content. The Confucius who ranked above the head of the Mêng family is already well on the way towards apotheosis.

4 The people of Ch'i sent[1] to Lu a present of female musicians,[2] and Chi Huan-tzu[3] accepted them. For three days no Court was held, whereupon Master K'ung left Lu.

5 Chieh Yü,[4] the madman of Ch'u, came past Master K'ung, singing as he went:

> Oh phoenix, phoenix
> How dwindled is your power!
> As to the past, reproof is idle,
> But the future may yet be remedied.
> Desist, desist![5]
> Great in these days is the peril of those who
>   fill office.

Master K'ung got down,[6] desiring to speak with him; but the madman hastened his step and got away, so that Master K'ung did not succeed in speaking to him.

6 Ch'ang-chü and Chieh-ni[7] were working as plough-mates together. Master K'ung, happening to pass that way, told Tzu-lu to go and ask them where the river could be forded. Ch'ang-chü said, Who is it for whom you are driving? Tzu-lu said, For K'ung Ch'iu. He said, What, K'ung Ch'iu of Lu? Tzu-lu said, Yes, he. Ch'ang-chü said, In that case he already knows where the ford

---

1 See textual notes.

2 In order to weaken the power of the government. A common folk-lore theme.

3 The father of Chi K'ang-tzu; died 492. This is the only passage in the *Analects* where he is directly mentioned.

4 See *Chuang Tzu*, IV, 8, where this typically Taoist, anti-Confucian story is told in a slightly longer form. For the 'madman', see also *Chuang Tza*, I, 4 and VII, 2, *Hsin Hsü*, III. *Han Fei Tzu*, P'ien, 20. *Chan Kuo T'sê*, Ch'in stories, Pt. II.

5 See textual notes.   6 From his carriage.

7 The names recall in their formation those of the fictitious personages in *Chuang Tzu* and *Lieh Tzu*.

is.[1] Tzu-lu then asked Chieh-ni. Chieh-ni said, Who
are you? He said, I am Tzu-lu. Chieh-ni said, You are a
follower of K'ung Ch'iu of Lu, are you not? He said,
That is so. Chieh-ni said, Under Heaven there is none
that is not swept along by the same flood.[2] Such is the
world and who can change it? As for you, instead of
following one who flees from this man and that, you
would do better to follow one who shuns this whole
generation of men. And with that he went on covering
the seed.

Tzu-lu went and told his master, who said ruefully,
One cannot herd with birds and beasts. If I am not to
be a man among other men, then what am I to be?[3] If
the Way prevailed under Heaven, I should not be trying
to alter things.

7 Once when Tzu-lu was following (the Master) he fell
behind and met an old man carrying a basket[4] slung
over his staff. Tzu-lu asked him, saying, Sir, have you
seen my master? The old man said, You who

> With your four limbs do not toil,
> Who do not sift the five grains,[5]

who is your master? And with that he planted his staff
in the ground and began weeding, while Tzu-lu stood
by with his hands pressed together.[6]

He kept Tzu-lu for the night, killed a fowl, prepared
a dish of millet for his supper and introduced him to his
two sons. Tzu-lu said, It is not right to refuse to serve
one's country. The laws of age and youth may not be

1 Or should do; for he claims to be a Sage.
2 See textual notes.
3 I think the second yü, like the first, is interrogative.
4 Cf. XIV, 20.
5 Who would not know how to choose the right seed for sowing. The
five kinds of grain are rice, two kinds of millet, wheat and pulse.
6 The palms pressed together in an attitude of respect.

set aside. And how can it be right for a man to set aside the duty that binds minister to prince, or in his desire to maintain his own integrity, to subvert the Great Relationship?[1] A gentleman's service to his country consists in doing such right as he can. That the Way does not prevail, he knows well enough beforehand.

Next day[2] Tzu-lu went on his way and reported what had happened. The Master said, He is a recluse, and told Tzu-lu to go back and visit him again. But on arriving at the place he found that the old man had gone away.[3]

8 Subjects whose services were lost to the State: Po I, Shu Ch'i,[4] Yü Chung,[5] I I, Chu Chang,[6] Liu-hsia Hui, Shao-lien.[7] The Master said, Those of them who 'would neither abate their high resolve nor bring humiliation upon themselves' were, I suppose, Po I and Shu Ch'i. It means that[8] Liu-hsia Hui and Shao-lien did abate their high resolve and bring humiliation upon themselves. 'Their words were consonant with the Relationships, their deeds were consonant with prudence; this and no more,' means that Yü Chung and I I, on the

1 This is the only book in the *Analects* in which the term *lun*, 'relationship', which figures so prominently in later Confucianism, makes its appearance.

2 In the original this clause down to 'gone away' follows the words 'his two sons'. This makes the whole story run very awkwardly; see T.T. 2036. The clauses have certainly become accidentally inverted.

3 Fearing that Confucius might recommend him for public service? Compare the very similar story, *Chuang Tzu*, XXV, 5.

4 For Po I and Shu Ch'i, see V, 22.

5 Brother of T'ai Po, VIII, 1.

6 I I and Chu Chang are unknown. I suspect that Chu Chang at any rate is not a proper name at all, but a corruption of part of the sentence. This was clearly suspected by Lu Tê-ming (*c.* 600 A.D.).

7 For Liu-hsia Hui, see XV, 13. Shao-lien is said to have been an 'eastern barbarian'.

8 Confucius seems here to be commenting on some text which is unknown to us.

contrary, lived in seclusion and refrained from comment. They secured personal integrity; and when set aside maintained due balance.[1] As for me, I am different from any of these. I have no 'thou shalt' or 'thou shalt not'.

9 The Chief Musician Chih[2] betook himself to Ch'i; Kan, the leader of the band at the second meal,[3] betook himself to Ch'u, Liao (leader of the band at the third meal) went to Ts'ai, and Ch'üeh (leader of the band at the fourth meal) went to Ch'in. The big drummer Fang Shu went within[4] the River, the kettle-drummer Wu went within the River Han, the Minor Musician Yang and Hsiang, the player of the stone-chimes, went within the sea.[5]

10 The Duke of Chou addressed the Duke of Lu,[6] saying: A gentleman never discards[7] his kinsmen; nor does he ever give occasion to his chief retainers to chafe at not being used. None who have been long in his service does he ever dismiss without grave cause. He does not expect one man to be capable of everything.[8]

1 See above, note 1. For variants, see textual notes. This whole paragraph is certainly corrupt. Liu-hsia Hui hung on to office despite every rebuff, and cannot be counted as a 'lost subject'. After the name of I I some phrase must have followed meaning 'Those who concealed their discontent', or the like. See textual notes.

2 Cf. VIII, 15. It is natural to suppose that this migration took place when Duke Chao of Lu fled to Ch'i in 517 B.C.

3 Or 'at the second course'.

4 i.e. to the north of.

5 to an island. This paragraph and the two which follow it are stray fragments arbitrarily inserted at the end of the Book. Cf. the terminations of Books X and XVI.

6 His son.

7 The original sense of the maxim may have been 'never reserves all his largesses for his own kinsmen'.

8 Cf. XIII, 25.

11 Chou had its Eight Knights:

Elder-brother Ta	(d'ât)
Elder-brother Kua	(g'uât)
Middle-brother T'u	(t'ut)
Middle-brother Hu	(hut)
Younger-brother Yeh	(zia)
Younger-brother Hsia	(g'a)
Youngest-brother Sui	(d'uâ)
Youngest-brother Kua	(Kuâ)[1]

1 A sign that a country had reached the maximum of plenty and fertility was that one woman should bear four pairs of twins. Cf. the similar set of twins mentioned in Tsang Wên Chung's great discourse, *Tso Chuan*, Duke Wên, 18th year. The present set is unknown elsewhere, and commentators cannot decide in what reign the happy phenomenon took place. I give the names in their approximate ancient pronunciation, to show that they form a sort of jingle. 'The names go in pairs, as becomes those of twins,' says Huang K'an. For the pronunciation of the last name I follow Lu Tê-ming.

BOOK XIX

1 Tzu-chang said, A knight who confronted with danger is ready to lay down his life, who confronted with the chance of gain thinks first of right, who judges sacrifice by the degree of reverence shown and mourning by the degree of grief[1] – such a one is all that can be desired.

2 Tzu-chang said, He who sides with moral force (*tê*) but only to a limited extent,[2] who believes in the Way, but without conviction – how can one count him as with us, how can one count him as not with us?

3 The disciples of Tzu-hsia asked Tzu-chang about intercourse with others. Tzu-chang said, What does Tzu-hsia tell you? He replied saying, Tzu-hsia says:

> Go with those with whom it is proper to go;
> Keep at a distance those whom it is proper to
>   keep at a distance.

Tzu-chang said, That is different from what I have been told:

> A gentleman reverences those that excel, but
>   'finds room'[3] for all;
> He commends the good and pities the incapable.

Do I myself greatly excel others? In that case I shall certainly find room for everyone. Am I myself inferior

---

1 And not by the elaborateness of the ceremonies. For the first part of the saying, Cf. XIV, 13.

2 Saying for example that *tê* has its uses, but that the ultimate appeal must always be to physical compulsion.   3 i.e. tolerates.

to others? In that case, it would be others who would keep me at a distance. So that the question of keeping others at a distance does not arise.[1]

4 Tzu-hsia said, Even the minor walks[2] (of knowledge) have an importance of their own. But if pursued too far they tend to prove a hindrance; for which reason a gentleman does not cultivate them.

5 Tzu-hsia said, He who from day to day is conscious of what he still lacks, and from month to month never forgets what he has already learnt, may indeed be called a true lover of learning.

6 Tzu-hsia said,

One who studies widely and with set purpose,
Who questions earnestly, then thinks for
    himself about what he has heard

— such a one will incidentally[3] achieve Goodness.

7 Tzu-hsia said, Just as the hundred[4] apprentices must live in workshops to perfect themselves in their craft, so the gentleman studies, that he may improve himself in the Way.

8 Tzu-hsia said, When the small man goes wrong, it is always on the side of over-elaboration.[5]

1 Literally, what becomes of that (ch'i in such usages corresponds to the Latin iste) 'keeping others at a distance' of yours?

2 Such as agriculture, medicine, etc. The idea that specialized knowledge is incompatible with true gentility prevailed in England till well towards the close of the nineteenth century.

3 Cf. II, 18, VII, 15, XIII, 18 and XV, 21.

4 i.e. all the different sorts of . . .

5 Lu Tê-ming does not gloss this character, and therefore presumably read wên in its ordinary pronunciation. I see no reason to read it in the 'departing tone', with the meaning 'gloss over', 'make excuses'. The sole authority for the usual interpretation is the pseudo K'ung An-kuo.

9 Tzu-hsia said, A gentleman has three varying aspects: seen from afar, he looks severe, when approached he is found to be mild, when heard speaking he turns out to be incisive.

10 Tzu-hsia said, A gentleman obtains the confidence of those under him, before putting burdens upon them. If he does so before he has obtained their confidence, they feel that they are being exploited.[1] It is also true that he obtains the confidence (of those above him) before criticizing them. If he does so before he has obtained their confidence, they feel that they are being slandered.

11 Tzu-hsia said, So long as in undertakings of great moral import a man does not 'cross the barrier', in undertakings of little moral import he may 'come out and go in'.[2]

12 Tzu-yu said, Tzu-hsia's disciples and scholars, so long as it is only a matter of sprinkling and sweeping floors, answering summonses and replying to questions, coming forward and retiring, are all right. But these are minor matters. Set them to anything important, and they would be quite at a loss.

Tzu-hsia, hearing of this, said, Alas, Yen Yu is wholly mistaken. Of the Way of the True Gentleman it is said:

If it be transmitted to him before he is ripe[3]
By the time he is ripe, he will weary of it.

1 See textual notes.
2 In matters such as loyalty, keeping promises, obedience to parents, the laws which govern his conduct are absolute. In lesser matters he is allowed a certain latitude. Several early writers attribute the saying to Confucius himself.
3 See textual notes.

Disciples may indeed be compared to plants and trees. They have to be separately treated according to their kinds.

In the Way of the Gentleman there can be no bluff. It is only the Divine Sage who embraces in himself both the first step and the last.

13 Tzu-hsia said, The energy that a man has left[1] over after doing his duty to the State, he should devote to study; the energy that he has left after studying, he should devote to service of the State.

14 Tzu-yu said, The ceremonies of mourning should be carried to the extreme that grief dictates, and no further.

15 Tzu-yu said, My friend Chang does 'the things that it is hard to be able to do';[2] but he is not yet Good.

16 Master Tsêng said, Chang is so self-important. It is hard to become Good when working side by side with such a man.

17 Master Tsêng said, I once heard the Master say, Though a man may never before have shown all that is in him, he is certain to do so when mourning for a father or mother.

18 Master Tsêng said, I once heard the Master say, Filial piety such as that of Mêng Chuang Tzu[3] might in other respects be possible to imitate; but the way in which he changed neither his father's[4] servants nor his father's domestic policy, that would indeed be hard to emulate.

1 Cf. I, 6.   2 Cf. XIV, 2.
3 Died in 550 B.C.
4 Mêng Hsien Tzu, died in 554 B.C.

215

19 When the Chief of the Mêng Family[1] appointed Yang Fu as Leader of the Knights,[2] Yang Fu[3] came for advice to Master Tsêng. Master Tsêng said, It is long since those above lost the Way of the Ruler and the common people lost their cohesion. If you find evidence of this, then be sad and show pity rather than be pleased at discovering such evidence.

20 Tzu-kung said, The tyrant Chou[4] cannot really have been as wicked as all this! That is why a gentleman hates to 'dwell on low ground'. He knows that all filth under Heaven tends to accumulate there.

21 Tzu-kung said, The faults of a gentleman are like eclipses of the sun or moon. If he does wrong, everyone sees it. When he corrects his fault, every gaze is turned up towards him.

22 Kung-sun Ch'ao of Wei[5] asked Tzu-kung, From whom did Chung-ni[6] derive his learning? Tzu-kung said, The Way of the kings Wên and Wu has never yet utterly fallen to the ground. Among men,[7] those of great understanding have recorded the major principles of this Way and those of less understanding have recorded the minor principles. So that there is no one who has not access to the Way of Wên and Wu. From

1 Mêng Wu Po, who succeeded to the headship of the clan in 481 B.C. Usually explained as meaning Mêng I Tzu, predecessor of Mêng Wu Po. But in his time (if we are to follow the traditional chronology) Master Tsêng would have been too young to be consulted. It must be remembered, however, that the Confucian legend was not built up by people who had chronological tables open in front of them.

2 A post involving the judging of criminal cases. See above, p. 9.

3 Unknown.   4 See above, p. 206.

5 So called to distinguish him from a number of Kung-sun Chaos in other countries.   6 i.e. Confucius.

7 The usual interpretation: 'It is still here among men', implies a very abrupt construction.

whom indeed did our Master *not* learn? But at the same time, what need had he of any fixed and regular teacher?

23 Shu-sun Wu-shu[1] talking to some high officers at Court said, Tzu-kung is a better man than Chung-ni. Tzu-fu Ching-po[2] repeated this to Tzu-kung. Tzu-kung said, Let us take as our comparison the wall round a building. My wall only reaches to the level of a man's shoulder, and it is easy enough to peep over it and see the good points of the house on the other side. But our Master's wall rises many times a man's height, and no one who is not let in by the gate can know the beauty and wealth of the palace that, with its ancestral temple, its hundred ministrants, lies hidden within. But it must be admitted that those who are let in by the gate are few; so that it is small wonder His Excellency should have spoken as he did.

24 Shu-sun Wu-shu having spoken disparagingly of Chung-ni, Tzu-kung said, It is no use; Chung-ni cannot be disparaged. There may be other good men; but they are merely like hillocks or mounds that can easily be climbed. Chung-ni is the sun and moon that cannot be climbed over. If a man should try to cut himself off from them, what harm would it do to the sun and moon? It would only show that he did not know his own measure.

25 Tzu-ch'in[3] said to Tzu-kung, This is an affectation of modesty. Chung-ni is in no way your superior. Tzu-kung said, You should be more careful about what you say. A gentleman, though for a single word he may be set down as wise, for a single word is set down as a fool. It would be as hard to equal our Master as to climb up

1 Flourished *c.* 500 B.C.   2 Cf. XIV, 38.
3 See I, 10, and XVI, 13.

on a ladder to the sky. Had our Master ever been put in control of a State or of a great Family, it would have been as is described in the words: 'He raised them, and they stood, he led them and they went. He steadied them as with a rope, and they came. He stirred them, and they moved harmoniously. His life was glorious, his death bewailed.'[1] How can such a one ever be equalled?

1 Probably a quotation from a *lei* (funeral eulogy).

BOOK XX

1 Yao said, Oh you, Shun!

> Upon you in your own person now rests the
>   heavenly succession;[1]
> Faithfully grasp it by the centre.
> The Four Seas may run dry;[2]
> But this heavenly gift lasts forever.

Shun too, when giving his charge to Yü ... (hiatus).

(T'ang)[3] said, I, your little son Li, venture to sacrifice
a black ox and tell you, oh most august sovereign God,
that those who are guilty[4] I dare not spare; but God's
servants I will not slay. The decision is in your heart, O
God.

If I in my own person do any wrong, let it never be
visited upon the many lands. But if anywhere in the
many lands wrong be done, let it be visited upon my
person.[5]

> When Chou gave its great largesses,
> It was the good who were enriched:
> 'Although I have my Chou kinsmen,

---

1 See additional notes.

2 i.e. 'sooner shall the sea run dry, than this gift ...'. For *yung-chung*, cf.
Shu Ching, Metal Casket, 10.

3 Founder of the Yin dynasty, when informing the Supreme Ancestor
of his (T'ang's) accession. Li was his personal name.

4 The Hsia, whom T'ang had defeated.

5 This 'scape-goat' formula is constantly referred to in early Chinese
literature. Mo Tzu (Universal Love, Pt. III), after quoting this same passage,
says that T'ang 'did not scruple to make of himself a sacrificial victim'.
The passage has been reinterpreted in a very drastic fashion.

They are less to me than the Good Men.[1]
If among the many families
There be one that does wrong,
Let the wrong be visited on me alone.'

(King Wu)[2] paid strict attention to weights and measures, reviewed the statutes and laws, restored disused offices, and gave a polity to all the four quarters of the world. He raised up States that had been destroyed, reestablished lines of succession that had been broken, summoned lost subjects back to prominence, and all the common people under Heaven gave their hearts to him. What he cared for most was that the people should have food, and that the rites of mourning and sacrifice should be fulfilled.

He who is broad[3] wins the multitude, he who keeps his word is trusted by the people, he who is diligent succeeds in all he undertakes, he who is just is the joy (of the people).

2 Tzu-chang asked Master K'ung, saying, What must a man do, that he may thereby be fitted to govern the land? The Master said, He must pay attention to the Five Lovely Things[4] and put away from him the Four Ugly Things. Tzu-chang said, What are they, that you call the Five Lovely Things? The Master said, A gentleman 'can be bounteous without extravagance, can get work out of people without arousing resentment, has longings but is never covetous, is proud but never insolent, inspires awe but is never ferocious'.

Tzu-chang said, What is meant by being bounteous without extravagance? The Master said, If he gives to

1 i.e. those who distinguished themselves in the campaign against Yin. The speaker is presumably King Wu.
2 Or the Duke of Chou?
3 'He who is broad' down to 'undertakes' occurs also in XVII, 6.
4 For these enumerations, cf. XVI, 4–8.

the people only such advantages as are really advantageous[1] to them, is he not being bounteous without extravagance? If he imposes upon them only such tasks as they are capable of performing, is he not getting work out of them without arousing resentment? If what he longs for and what he gets is Goodness, who can say that he is covetous? A gentleman, irrespective of whether he is dealing with many persons or with few, with the small or with the great, never presumes to slight them. Is not this indeed being 'proud without insolence'? A gentleman sees to it that his clothes and hat are put on straight, and imparts such dignity to his gaze that he imposes on others. No sooner do they see him from afar than they are in awe. Is not this indeed inspiring awe without ferocity?

Tzu-chang said, What are they, that you call the Four Ugly Things? The Master said, Putting men to death, without having taught them (the Right); that is called savagery. Expecting the completion of tasks, without giving due warning; that is called oppression. To be dilatory about giving orders, but to expect absolute punctuality, that is called being a tormentor. And similarly, though meaning to let a man have something, to be grudging about bringing it out from within, that is called behaving like a petty functionary.

3 The Master said, He who does not understand the will of Heaven cannot be regarded as a gentleman. He who does not know the rites cannot take his stand.[2] He who does not understand words,[3] cannot understand people.

1 For example, if he promotes agriculture instead of distributing doles and largesses.

2 Cf. XVI, 13.

3 i.e. cannot get beneath the surface-meaning and understand the state of mind that the words really imply. Cf. *Mencius*, II, 1, II, 17. Para. 3 was lacking in the Lu version.

ADDITIONAL NOTES

II, 18 *tsai ch'i chung* is an idiom (cf. VII, 15, XIII, 18, XV, 31, XIX, 6) which can never be translated literally. It is used of results that occur incidentally without being the main object of a certain course of action.

III, 1 Eight teams of dancers.

The exact number of performers is in every ritual a matter of extreme importance. The Chi Family's crime consisted in usurping rites which were proper only to the Ducal House; or, possibly, proper only to the Emperor. They were 'making the twigs heavy and the trunk light' the surest way to ruin.

III, 8 An alternative interpretation of Confucius's reply is 'In painting, the plain colour (i.e. the white) is put on last', because otherwise it would get soiled. This explanation lands us in all kinds of difficulties, and is based, I think, on a misunderstanding of a passage in the *Chou Li*, LXXIX (p. 17; Biot's translation, II, 516), which in reality means: 'When birds, beasts and snakes are combined with the symbols of the four seasons and with the five colours in their proper arrangements, and are thus duly displayed, this is called "skilled work". In the business of painting (i.e. of decorating the personal possessions of officials with designs appropriate to their rank) plain work comes after (i.e. is not considered so highly).'

'Plain work' is painted in the appropriate colours, but lacks the birds, beasts and snakes that decorate the appurtenances of the mighty. Confucius uses the same maxim as the *Chou Li*, but reinterprets it as meaning not 'In painting plain work is not so highly esteemed,' but 'The painting comes after the plain groundwork.'

The *Chou Li* commentary tries to force upon 'plain work' the impossible sense of 'application of white pigment', thus making the last sentence totally disconnected from the context.

III, 15 The poem *T'ien Wên* is supposed to embody the questions asked by the poet Ch'ü Yüan when he visited the shrines of former kings and ministers, and to concern legends depicted on the walls of these shrines.

III, 16 According to the *Chou Li* (XXI, 52) the local archery meeting was made the occasion for a general review of conduct, 'points' in the competition being given for (1) not quarrelling; (2) correct deportment; (3) *chu-p'i*, explained as meaning 'skill in archery'; (4) singing; (5) dancing.

It is clear, then, that the *Chou Li* does not give to *chu* the meaning 'give chief place to'; it is, however, equally clear that in the *Lun Yü* passage *chu* can only bear this meaning. Moreover, the mention in *Lun Yü* of 'strength' suggests that 'piercing the hide' and not merely hitting the mark is what is meant.

III, 21 *Shê* ('holy ground') was an earth-mound at the borders of a town or village, interpreted as symbolizing the whole soil of the territory in which it stood. It was often associated with a sacred tree or grove, and with a block or pillar of wood[1] which served as a 'stance'

1 In other parts of the world objects analogous to the *chu* vary within comparatively small areas between being made of stone and being made of wood. The typical Chinese *chu* has always been a wooden object; but *chu* of other materials including stone probably also existed.

(resting-place) for spirits. This wooden object was called *chu*; see textual notes. In parallel passages the question at issue is what sort of wood was used in making the *chu*. This passage is generally taken as referring to the trees of the Holy Ground and not to the material of the *chu*.

The *fêng*, a terminal earth-mound where a road reached the borders of a State, is analogous to the *shê*, and the same official was responsible for the maintenance of both.

IV, 11 The Chu Hsi interpretation is 'The gentleman thinks of *tê*, the small man of material comfort; the gentleman, of punishments (i.e. justice); the small man of favours.' In his conversations (section on *Lun Yü* in *Chu Tzu Ch'üan Shu*) he records that Yin Shun (1071–1142) construed the sentence as I have done; and Huang K'an (sixth century) notes this rendering as an alternative one. The absence of any 'then', 'in that case' in the second and fourth clauses makes the sentence obscure, and I fancy that *tsê* ('then') has been suppressed in order to admit of an interpretation such as Chu Hsi's, by people who unlike Confucius, believed in government by penalties. Chu Hsi's interpretation of *huai-t'u* is hopelessly forced.

IV, 26 The character that I have translated 'repeated scolding' means literally 'to enumerate'. Hence to 'enumerate people's faults', to 'tick off'. Cf. *Shih Chi*, ch. 86, fol. 4.

It is taken in this sense here by Yü Yüeh[1] (died 1906). The *Chi Chieh* gives it the meaning 'quick', 'hasty'. Cf. *Lieh Tzu*, II, 8: 'Anyone who is good at swimming can quickly learn . . .', and *Chuang Tzu*, XIX, 4. But Chêng Hsüan, the great Han dynasty commentator, explains it

1 H.P. 1391,10.

as meaning 'enumerating one's own services'. Finally, the current explanation gives it the meaning 'numerously', 'repeatedly'. Comparison with XII, 23 seems to show that this last explanation is right.

V, 2 For this saying, set in the context of a longer anecdote, see *K'ung Tzu Chia Yü*, XIX (Tzu-lu Ch'u Chien) and *Shuo Yüan*, VII. A work called *Fu Tzu* (i.e. sayings of Master Fu) was current until the first century A.D., and the stories about Fu's ideal governorship which are found in works of the third century B.C. and onwards may be extracts from *Fu Tzu*. See G. Haloun, *Asia Major*, VIII, fasc. 3, pp. 437 *seq*. But there is no reason to suppose that any of these stories supplies us with the original context of this saying in the *Analects*.

V, 21 This saying exists in two forms. The version of the *Analects* reoccurs *verbatim* in the *Ju-lin Chuan* (ch. 121 of the *Shih Chi*) and, apart from the insertion of one superfluous character,[1] also in the Life of Confucius[2] (ch. 47 of the *Shih Chi*). But in another passage[3] of the Life and in *Mencius*[4] Confucius is made to say 'Let us return ... the little ones ... push themselves forward and grab' (the opposite of the essential principle *jang*, 'yield', 'give place to others'). 'They cannot forget their beginnings' (i.e. they are always lapsing back into the old ways of greed and push that are inconsistent with my Way of Goodness).

V, 24 When later Confucians were attempting to make Confucius in some way responsible (either as author or editor) for the whole of early Chinese literature, they turned Tso Ch'iu Ming into a disciple of Confucius and

---

1 *Wu* ('I') is inserted before 'do not know how to'; which does not make sense.   2 Chavannes' translation, V, p. 359.
3 Chavannes, V, 343.   4 VII, 2, XXXVII.

credited him with the authorship (under the Master's direction) of the *Tso Chuan* chronicle. Nothing further is known about him.

VI, 6 *Ta* means 'to put through', 'penetrate'. So (1) To 'put oneself through', to turn one's *tê* to account, to get on in the world, to progress; to get one's meaning or one's doctrines through, i.e. to 'put them across'. (2) To get through, penetrate, i.e. understand.

VI, 11 From the Han dynasty onwards the word *ju*, which is of very uncertain origin, was applied to those who devoted themselves to the study of the *Songs*, the *Books*, the ritual treatises, etc., and hence to followers of Confucius in general. It seems, however, to have originally been a contemptuous nickname given by the warlike people of Ch'i to their more pacific neighbours in Lu. Cf. *Tso Chuan*, Ai kung, 21st year. But since the word occurs only this once in the *Analects*, without adequate context, it is impossible to know for certain what meaning the compilers attached to it.

VI, 21 This saying, in the form in which it now occurs, is completely Taoistic, save that the word Good (Goodness) has been substituted for 'Tao'. Taoism, it is true, drew its vocabulary and ideas partly from a stock common to all early Chinese thought. But nowhere else in the *Analects* is it suggested that anyone save the *Shêng* (Divine Sage) can achieve his ends by inactivity, and as this passage stands it is impossible not to give it a more general application. But comparison with other sayings in the *Analects* and elsewhere suggests that this saying originally had a very different form. In XV, 32, it is *shou* 'keeping what one has gained'[1] (and not *shou*

1 See textual notes.

'longevity') which is the consequence of Goodness, but cannot result from wisdom alone. Moreover, in the *Kuliang Chuan*[1] we twice get the saying 'The wise man schemes (*lü*) ... the Good man keeps' ('secures', *shou*) what the scheming has achieved. Both passages are concerned with politics, not with the moral life of the individual, and mean that State successes gained by cleverness will not be permanent; only the State that is based on Goodness can have any permanence.

As it stands, the saying runs very awkwardly. It is first said that the Good man delights (*lo*) in mountains and then that it is the wise man who 'delights'; whereas the Good man is long-lived (*shou*) as opposed to 'delighting' (*lo*). I cannot help believing that the original sense of the last two phrases was: 'The wise ruler schemes; but the Good ruler alone can give permanent effect to schemes,' as in the *Ku-liang Chuan*.

The Good 'stay still', because their effects are achieved by *tê* ('moral force') not by *li* ('physical force'). The dictum easily passes into the vocabulary of full-blown, systematic quietism.

Pao Hsien, in the first century, takes the whole saying as referring to the ruler. But it is usually taken to refer to the individual in general, and is interpreted in a completely Taoist sense: all exercise of the emotions destroys the soul and leads to early death.

VI, 26 'Made a solemn declaration', literally 'arrowed it'. Here metaphorical; but probably the character 'arrow' has its ideogrammatic sense and is not a phonetic substitute. For the use of a bundle of arrows in oath-taking, see H. Maspero (Mélanges chinois et bouddhiques, III, p. 270). *Le Serment dans la procédure judiciaire....* The bundle of arrows is a symbol of the

1 Yin 2 and Huan 18.

unbreakable, in contrast with a single arrow, that can easily be snapped. Cf. the memorial inscription of the Mongol leader Mêng-ku (13th century) by Yao Sui[1] (A.D. 1238–1314): He broke an arrow and swore saying: 'May every act in which I am not utterly faithful to the Khan be snapped like this!' We see here that it is against his acts and not against himself that the speaker invokes destruction. Confucius's *yeh chih* is generally translated 'crush (reject, forsake) me'. But the text says 'it' not 'me', following a formula similar to that of the Mongol oath. There is no evidence that *yeh* can mean 'reject'. Nor is there any suggestion in the text that improper conduct had taken place between Nan-tzu and Confucius, but only that his seeing her at all, as a means of obtaining influence at the Wei Court, was improper.

VI, 27 It is upon this passage that the whole Confucian philosophy of compromise, of 'too much is as bad as too little', is built. What *chung-yung* meant to start with is very doubtful. To the compilers of the *Analects*, I do not think it meant anything different from *chung tao*, the Middle Way. But the interpretation 'middle and usual', i.e. 'traditional', is a quite possible one.

A Confucian treatise of very mixed content, strongly tinged with Taoism, deals in several passages with the power of *chung-yung*, and bears these two words as its title. (It is known in Europe as the *Doctrine of the Mean*.) The material that this treatise contains is partly, at any rate, as old as the first half of the third century; but the unification of China is referred to, and the actual compilation of the work must be as late as the end of the third century B.C.

Is there not, however, some connection between this passage and *Song* 142, which recounts the virtues of

1 Collected Works, XIV, 1 verso.

Chung Shan Fu? The 6th verse says: 'Moral force (*tê*) is light as a hair; but among the people there are few that can lift it' (i.e. that can use it).

I suspect that in its original form the saying was parallel to that about T'ai Po in VIII, 1, and ran: 'How transcendent was the *tê* of Chung Shan Fu (Minister of King Hsüan of Chou). That among the people there are few (who know how to use *tê*) is an old story!' in allusion to *Song* 142, verse 6. The two characters *shan* and *fu*, written too close one above the other, were later misread as a single character *yung*. This however is merely a tentative suggestion.

VII, 7 As in modern Chinese school-fees are called 'the bundle of dried flesh', it would not occur to the average reader that *shu-hsiu* in this passage could possibly mean anything but 'a bundle of dried flesh', brought as a humble present to the teacher. This, however, was not the view of many outstanding commentators. Chêng Hsüan (died A.D. 200) says it means 'fourteen years old': the Master accepted any pupil who had attained to years of discretion. The alternatives arise in this way: *Shu* = to tie, tie one's belt. *Hsiu* = 'to put right', 'to cure'; hence to 'cure' meat, so that 'tied cured' means 'a bundle of dried flesh' or one who has 'tied his belt and put himself to rights', i.e. has donned the garb of manhood. There is, however, no trace of this idiom till Han times; whereas 'dried flesh', as a humble form of offering, occurs in texts which have every chance of being pre-Han. I therefore think that Huang K'an (sixth century) was right in championing the 'dried flesh' theory against the view of Chêng Hsüan.

VII, 17 There is not much doubt that *ya* ('refined', 'standard', 'correct' as applied to speech) is etymologically the same word as the ethnic term Hsia, the common name of the Chinese, as opposed to the barbarians. Mo Tzu calls the third part of the *Book of Songs* 'Ta Hsia' instead of the usual *Ta Ya*.[1]

To avoid the implication that Confucius sometimes spoke in his native dialect, Ch'êng Hao in the eleventh century interpreted *ya* as meaning not 'standard', but 'standardly', i.e. frequently. Hence Legge's 'His frequent themes were...'. But Chêng Hsüan interprets the passage exactly as I have done.

VII, 18 It is the 'Duke' of Shê who is the subject of the following anecdote. There was once a man who said he had a passion for dragons. He was always talking about them, and had them painted all over the walls of his house. After all, he said, there is nothing pleasanter to look at than a dragon. One day a huge, shiny, slimy paw flopped on to his window-sill; soon a green and golden scaly face reared itself up at the window and grinned a dank greeting. The lover of dragons was beside himself with terror. He fled shrieking to the hall, where he tripped over the oozing, slithery tail which the monster had thrust in friendly salutation through the doorway of the house.

The story is told as a warning against insincere enthusiasms. (See Waley, *Introduction to the Study of Chinese Painting*, p. 37.)

VIII, 3 The passage quoted from the *Li Chih I* refers, it must be admitted, to the death of an emperor, not a private person.

Trussing up of various kinds and the placing of heavy weights on the body occur in many parts of the world, in some cases before death, in some cases after it. Where such practices take place after death, they are explained

1 The variant has been smoothed away from Mo Tzu's text by modern editors.

by anthropologists as being due to fear of the dead returning to life.[1] Where they occur before death this explanation obviously does not hold good. The question is complicated by the fact that in China (and probably elsewhere?) many practices originally belonging to the period preceding death were in less primitive days delayed until death had actually taken place; see De Groot, *The Religious Systems of China*, I, p. 9.

VIII, 15 The interpretation of *shih* ('began') as 'when he first entered on his duties' seems to date from Sung times.

VIII, 20 King Wu's statement that he had 'ten ministers' is found in several passages of old literature; e.g. *Tso Chuan*, Duke Hsiang, 28th year.[2]

IX, 2 The commentators take the villager's 'vastly learned', etc. not as irony but as praise; for to achieve a reputation in any one line is unworthy of a *chün-tzu*. This seems to make Confucius's comment unintelligible. I take the villager to be a boorish, ignorant man who does not know that a true gentleman ought not to be known as a specialist in any one line.

IX, 5 The people of K'uang are supposed to have mistaken Confucius for the adventurer Yang Huo (see XVII, 1) who had formerly created a disturbance in K'uang. The mistake was made more natural by the fact that Confucius's carriage was being driven by a man who had previously been associated with Yang Huo.

1 Cf. Frazer, *The Fear of the Dead in Primitive Religion*, 2 vols., 1933 and 1934.

2 The omission of the word 'ministers' in some early versions (e.g. the T'ang Scriptures on Stone) was a doctrinal not a philological emendation. It is unfilial to speak of a mother as being 'minister' (literally 'servant') to her son.

X, 10 For the No (expulsion rite) see *Chou Li*, ch. 48 and 54. The exorcist accompanied by four 'Madmen' (see *The Book of Songs*, p. 222) 'wearing over their heads a bear's skin with four eyes of yellow metal (copper or gold?), clad in a black coat and red skirt, grasping halberd and raising shield, leads all the house-servants and performs the No of the season, searching the house and driving out noxious influences'.

In many parts of Europe the whole household still visits every corner of the house and outbuildings on New Year's Eve, banging forks on dish-covers and so on, in order to drive out the Old Year.

The *Chi Chieh* says that Confucius stood on the eastern steps of the ancestral shrine during this ceremony 'in order to reassure the ancestral spirits' of the house, who might otherwise have taken flight along with the 'noxious influences'. In T'ang times the No was stylized as a Court dance.

XI, 4 Min Tzu-ch'ien's mother died when he was a child and his father married again. One day when he was driving his father's carriage he let the reins slip. His father found that he was wearing such thin gloves that his hands were numbed with cold. On going home he looked at the gloves worn by the two children born to him by his second wife and found that they were thick and warm. He said to his wife, 'I married you solely in order to have someone to look after my motherless children. Now I can see that you have been imposing upon me. Leave my home at once!' Tzu-ch'ien said, 'If my step-mother remains, one child will be imperfectly clad; but if she goes, several children will be cold.' His father said no more about it. (Fragment of lost portions of *Shuo Yüan*, quoted under heading 'filial piety' in *I Wên Lei Chü*.)

XI, 7 *Kuo* (the word translated 'enclosure') meant, as may be seen most clearly from the paragraph on 'Inspecting the *kuo* and grave-figures' in *I Li*, XII, a protection for the coffin made by laying beams longways and crossways, like the framework at the top of a well. Excavation has confirmed this; Cf. S. Umehara, *Selected Relics from the Chin-ts'un Tombs, Lo-yang*. Kyōto, 1937, Figure 3.

In later times *kuo* meant an 'outer coffin', a 'shell'. In Japan the term 'stone *kuo*' has been applied to the *allées couvertes* of Japanese megalithic structures.

XI, 13 Duke Chao, who fled from Lu in 517, had used this building as a basis for operations against his enemies, the Chi Family. It is probable, therefore, that the remark of Min Tzu-ch'ien was applauded by Confucius for its loyalist, pro-dynastic tendency.

XI, 24 For the Holy Ground, see additional note to III, 21. The Millet is in early texts always closely associated with the Holy Ground and not treated as the object of a separate cult.[1] It was interpreted as symbolizing the fruits of the soil in general. It was no doubt a sheaf of millet (if grain had been meant another word would have been used) and may have been the Last Sheaf, kept over from the previous harvest. 'Last Sheaf' ceremonies are common in India, Indo-China and Indonesia.

XI, 25, 7 The ritualists describe four rain-ceremonies, one for each season. But there is reason to believe[2] that the ceremony carried out at the end of spring or beginning of summer and traceable throughout Chinese history down to the present day is the only one that has,

1 'The *Chi*, "Millet", is a detail of the *shê*,' as Chêng Hsüan puts it, in commenting on *Chou Li*, XXII.
2 See K. Shiratori, *Tōyō Gakuhō*, XXI, 2, pp. 104 seq.

as a regular institution, had any real existence. During times of drought an emergency ceremony might indeed be performed; but the four ceremonies, each corresponding to a season, a colour, etc., are a pure fantasy of the ritualists.

A constant feature of these ceremonies is, as Professor Shiratori has shown, the participation of boys and young men.

$5 \times 6 + 6 \times 7$ makes 72, a number used in other dances.[1] The performance of lustrations preceded every sacrifice, and there is not the slightest reason to emend the character *yü* 'bathe', on the ground that the season was too cold for bathing (cf. *Lun Hêng*, P'ien 45, fol. 11).

The commentator quoted by the *Lun Hêng* (first century A.D.) is trying to explain this passage in the light of the popular rain-ceremonies held in his own day, and I do not think we can accept his interpretation in all its details.[2] The whole of this very literary passage bears the stamp of belonging to a milieu different from that of the brief colloquial sayings. It is noteworthy that *an* (usual sense 'peaceful') is used as an interrogative particle.[3] This usage does not seem to belong either to the older language (only one very doubtful example occurs in the *Songs*) or to the language of Lu (no other example in the *Lun Yü*; none in *Mencius*). On the other hand, it is extremely common in the (more northerly?) dialect of the *Tso Chuan*, and in third century B.C. writings generally.

XII, 20 *lü i hsia jên*. Cf. *Tso Chuan*, Hsüan Kung 12th

1 e.g. the dance to Hou Chi, the god of agriculture, which was performed by 'capped youths five times six which is thirty, and boys six times seven which is forty-two'. See *Han Ch'iu I*, quoted among the fragments collected in *P'ing Ching Kuan Ts'ung Shu*, Supplement, ch. 2, fol. 6.

2 Cf. M. Granet, *Fétes et Chansons Anciennes de la Chine*, 1929, p. 158.

3 But the text used by Lu Tê-ming seems to have had the usual particle *yen*.

year, 'A people whose prince knows how to defer to others (*nêng i hsia jên*) may be treated as reliable.' *lü* sometimes means 'in general', 'on the whole'. (See Wang Nien-sun, *Tu Shu Tsa Chih* VIII, 4 and Yü Yüeh, H.P. 1392, fol. 7.) I doubt if that is the sense here.

XIII, 3 For *kou* ('chance') see *Han Shih Wai Chuan*, III, fol. 1 and IV, fol. 1 verso. Also *Tso Chuan*, Chao Kung, 18th year. It is used when things are done 'somehow or other', in a 'hit or miss' offhand fashion, when everything is 'left to chance'. In hypothetical clauses it means 'If by any chance', 'If somehow or other'. It applies wherever a result is achieved by mere accident and not as the result of *tê* ('virtue', moral power). Cf. XIII, 8 and Introduction, p. 59.

XIII, 4 Confucius took the traditional view that it is for common people to work with their hands, for gentlemen to work with their *tê*. Fan Ch'ih had evidently been influenced by views similar to those of Hsü Hsing (*Mencius*, III, 1, IV) who held that it was unfair to live by the labour of others and maintained that 'the wise man should plough side by side with the common people'. There is a parallel passage in *Mo Tzu* (Lu Wên, *P'ien*, 49), where 'a low fellow, from the south of Lu, called Wu Lü', reproaches Mo Tzu with preaching justice, while all the time living on the labour of others. Mo Tzu's reply amounts practically to saying that he is promoting justice more by teaching it to others than he would be by practising it himself.

XIII, 15 Wang Su (died A.D. 256), Huang K'an (died A.D. 545) and Hsing P'ing (died A.D. 1010) all accept that *chi* (current interpretation 'expect', 'count upon') means 'near'. Chu Hsi bases his 'expect' on an isolated and very uncertain usage in *Song* 199.

XIII, 22 It seems clear that *hêng* was the name of a ritual. Cf. *Chou Li*, ch. 50: 'If a great calamity befalls the land, then send for *wu* (shamans) and perform the *wu-hêng* (shamanistic *hêng* ceremony).' The explanations given by Chêng Hsüan and other *Chou Li* commentators are forced and unconvincing. *Mo Tzu* (XXXII. Forke's translation, p. 371) quotes from a 'book of the former kings': 'to perform the *hêng* dance in the palace is called yielding to the influence of shamans'. To dance *hêng* 'continually' (which is the usual interpretation) makes poor sense. I would also suggest that the words 'ill, *hêng*, not die' in the *Book of Changes*, section 16, mean 'If anyone is ill, perform the *hêng* rite and he will not die.' The saying of the 'men of the south' (i.e. of Ch'u?) is also quoted in Section 32 of the *Changes*.

XIV, 16 The usual interpretation, 'Wên was crafty and not upright, Huan was upright and not crafty' is, as Wang Nien-sun long ago observed (*Ching I Shu Wên*, on this passage), nonsensical. The story of Wên (Double Ears,[1] as he was called) is known to us chiefly through a heroic legend embodied in *Kuo Yü*, IX and X. The commentators try to discover a lack of ritual correctness in the story of his being visited by the Divine King (T'ien-wang, i.e. the ruler of Chou). But this requires some ingenuity. We only know a legend that praises him; we must suppose Confucius to have known one which denigrated him.

Of Duke Huan's failure in emergencies no convincing example is cited. For this sense of *chüeh*, see Liu Pao-nan's *Lun Yü Chêng I*.

XIV, 33 Usually taken as meaning 'who does not anticipate deceit ... and, yet immediately perceives it

1 Like many heroes, he was noted for strange physical peculiarities; his ribs were all in one piece.

when it occurs'. There are two objections to this rendering: (1) The *i* of *pu hsin, i* . . . usually means 'or', not 'but'; (2) *hsien chüeh* normally means to perceive beforehand, not 'to perceive immediately', and the text says nothing about 'when it has occurred', or the like. Confucius is criticizing a current maxim about the *chün-tzu*. Cf. the *Ta Tai Li Chi* passage quoted below in the textual notes.

XV, 10 The tunes of Chêng and Wei are often referred to as 'new music' or the 'common music of the world'. Towards classical music, the 'music of the former Kings' (*Mencius*, I, 2, I) ordinary as opposed to serious-minded people had the same feelings as they have towards our own classical music to-day. 'How is it', the Prince of Wei asked Tzu-hsia, 'that when I sit listening to old music, dressed in my full ceremonial gear, I am all the time in terror of dropping off asleep; whereas when I listen to the tunes of Chêng and Wei, I never feel the least tired?' (*Li Chi*, XIX, fol. 5).

XV, 25 The current interpretation is 'lent it to others to drive'.[1] This gives a sense totally unconnected with what goes before. Moreover, *chieh jên* occurs elsewhere[2] in the sense 'to avail oneself of the services of others', but never in the sense 'to lend to others'. *Chieh* in the sense 'to lend' is very rare in early texts, while in the sense 'to borrow' it is very common.

XVI, 14 It will be noticed that although the words *jên* (person) and *chün* (prince), here applied to a lady, are not exclusively masculine, they are chiefly and

[1] 'To ride' is an anachronism; for horses were not ridden in the time of Confucius.
[2] *Tso Chuan*, Hsiang Kung, 19th year; and *Kuan Tzu*, P'ien 33, *chieh-jên*, 'set other people to do it for you'.

prevailingly applied to men rather than to women. For example, in VIII, 20, Confucius says that King Wu had not really 'ten *jên*' to help him; for one of them was a woman. *Hsiao T'ung* ('Little boy') means a page-boy, and is an exclusively masculine term. Thus it may be said that the sovereign's wife may not be referred to (either by himself or anyone else) by any term that is feminine in implication and must in referring to herself use a term that is definitely masculine.

This is in obedience to the general principle that a sovereign must be spoken of as though he were free from ordinary human needs and desires.[1] It will also be noted that the sovereign speaks of himself as the 'lonely one'. This he does under all circumstances, and not only in reference to his wife. Thus his city is 'the lonely one's city', etc. In China he was 'lonely' in the sense that his father whose throne he had inherited, was necessarily dead. But a king is often technically motherless as well as fatherless. For at his accession he must either, as in some parts of the world, marry his mother, and so lose her as a mother; or else 'never set eyes on his mother'.[2] Or again, his mother has been ritually sacrificed during the funeral ceremony of his father. It is possible that the expression 'the lonely one' goes back in China to times when the king was technically motherless as well as fatherless.

XX, 1 *T'ien chih li-shu* was no doubt understood in a quasi-abstract sense by the compilers of the *Analects*: 'Heaven's succession', i.e. the succession accorded by Heaven. It is possible, however, that in its original setting, as a formula used in the accession-rites of kings, it had a much more concrete sense: 'The calendar[3] and counting-sticks of Heaven' (i.e. of the Ancestors).

1 Cf. C. G. Seligman, *Egypt and Negro Africa*, a Study in Divine Kingship, 1934, p. 47.　2 *Op cit.*, p. 43.　3 i.e. 'succession' of agricultural tasks.

239

There is a hiatus after 'his charge to Yü'. In other Chinese works (e.g. in the forged portions of the *Shu Ching*, in *Mo tzu* and in the *Kuo Yü*) many of the sentences strung together in this paragraph will be found utilized for a different purpose and interpreted with a different meaning. A discussion of all these parallels belongs rather to the textual criticism of the *Shu Ching* than to a study of the *Analects*, and I shall not attempt it here.

The Ku version treated XX, 2 and 3 as a separate book.

TEXTUAL NOTES

Translator's Preface, p. 21: *Jên*, 仁. *Min*, 民.
p. 27: *Shih*, 士.

I. 1. 不亦, cf. VIII. 7. 2. Sometimes written 不以 (*Mencius*, III, 2, IV, 1). In such phrases *i* seems to mean 'indeed', sometimes with a slight concessive form, like the French *tout de même* in *cela, c'est tout de même trop fort*. It seldom means 'also' in the *Analects*.

I. 1 .2.[1] 有 variant 友 ('friend').

I. 4. For 傳 the Lu version read 專.

I. 7. 易 for 惕. Cf. 111. 4.

I. 12, end. 可 行. The Han stone-engraved text (*apud* Hung K'uo, *Li Shih*) omits 可.

I. 16. Read 樂 道, which is the reading of the Huang K'an text (6th century A.D.). On the T'ang stone-engraved text *tao* was added marginally.

II. 3. 格 is for the obsolete character 徦, which had the meaning 至·

II. 8. For 饌 Chêng Hsüan reads 餕.

II. 19. 錯 for 措.

II. 24. 謟 does not make sense. Surely a mistake for 諂. The same confusion occurs elsewhere; cf. Chu Ch'i-fêng's *Tz'u T'ung* (Shanghai, 1934), p. 1073. In future cited as T.T.

III. 4. 易 for 惕. Cf. I. 7 above.

III. 8. Commentators since Han times have taken 起 in the sense 發明, 'make clear'. It is true that 起 can have

---

1 Where two arabic figures are used, the second refers to the number of the sentence, as marked in the editions of Legge and Soothill.

the sense 發動, 'set in motion', but it is doubtful if it can mean 'make clear'. Moreover, such an interpretation involves the necessity of understanding after 予 an 意 which is not in the text. It is simpler to take 起 in the sense 'keep upright', 'support'; cf. *Kuo Yü*, Chin Yü, IV. 世相起: 'From generation to generation [Chou and Chin] are to support one another.'

III. 11. 示, read *chih*. Phonetic borrowing for 寘, 'put'. Cf. *Hsün Tzu*, 27: 示諸檃栝, 'If you put it (timber) in a vice'.

III. 12. It is quite certain that there is a pun on 在 and 祭. The phonological relationship between these two words was, however, in Chou times a very slender one and I suspect that 祭 has been substituted for the less familiar word 是 (dzieg), which could well be called 'like' 在 (dz'eg). Cf. the alleged use of 在 as a phonetic substitute for 司 and 嗣 (Chu Chün-shêng's phonetic *Shuo Wên*, under 在).

III. 14. 郁郁. For other ways of writing this binome, see T.T. 2258.

III. 21. For 祉 Chêng Hsüan reads 主, which is also the reading of the *Po Hu T'ung*; the *Shuo Wên* character is 宔. The word 主, *chu*, means a stance for spirits. Chinese etymologies should be made with great reserve; but it is worth noting that 主 may be cognate to 住, 'bide'. The pictogram 主 is interpreted as representing a wick. This may be another use of the same root; for a wick is the 'stance' of the flame.

III. 22. The 反 of this phrase here and elsewhere is probably a corruption of 危,, i.e. 岞. Cf. *Êrh Ya*, 岞謂之坫.

IV. 2. 因 for 姻.

IV. 5. 造次 for 躁趒.
顛沛 for 蹎跋.

IV. 6. 蓋 for 盍: 'How not?', i.e. 'they must exist'. Cf. VII. 27 and XIII. 3.

IV. 10. I adopt Chêng Hsüan's 無敵無慕. 之 in the last

242

clause is for 是. Cf. Shu Ching, *Wu I*, 惟 耽 樂 之 從, modernized as 是 從 in Han quotations of the passage: 'It was solely upon abandoned pleasures that they were bent.' The demonstrative 之 is also closely connected with 是; cf. 之 子 in the *Songs* and 之 人, 'this man', in *Chuang Tzu*, I. 4. See also XI. 18 and XIII. 22 below.

IV. 12. 放 is for 倣.

IV. 13. 何 有. Cf. VI. 6; VII. 2; IX. 15; XIII. 13; also *Mencius*, VI. 2, 1. 4 (Legge, p. 299), and many further examples in *Tso Chuan*, etc. The idiom means 'What more is there to be said?', 'That settles the matter', 'On that point at any rate we can be satisfied', and the like.

IV. 18 勞 for 慇.

V. 4. 慇 for 嗑? 合 and 盍 are 'etymologically the same word' (Karlgren, *Analytic Dictionary*, p. 56). Cf. *Lieh Tzu*, IV. 12: 佞 給 而 不 中, 'glibly chattering, but never hitting the mark'.

V. 7. 2. For 賦 the Lu version read 傅.

V. 13. 有 for 又, as constantly in old texts.

V. 17. 節 is a phonetic borrowing for 梲, cognate to 棁 which has the same meaning. 梲; *Êrh Ya* writes this word with the character 棳, which exists here as a variant.

V. 18. 2. For 崔 the Lu version read 高.

V. 21. 裁 for 載. Cf. 裁 使, 'to turn to account', and *Shih Tzu* (尸 子) fragments: 'Heaven and Earth produced the myriad things; the Sages 裁 之, turned them to account.'

V. 25. 2. It is better to omit 輕; omitted at first in T'ang stone-engraved Classics, and added later. For further evidence, see Liu Pao-nan's *Lun Yü Chêng I*.

V. 25. 3. 慕 for 訕.

VI. 3. 1. 庾 for 斞.

VI. 3. 2. 周 for 賙.

VI. 4. 犂 for 駩, 'brown and black'. 騂 is commonly used of cattle as well as horses; but 牸 also exists.

VI. 21. (Additional note) *shou*, 守, 'to secure'.

VI. 24. Read 井 有 仁. The variant 人 is certainly wrong. 逝 is for 折. Cf. 邁 for 萬 in inscriptions.

VI. 26. 厭, abbreviation for 黶, 'exorcize'.

VII. 3. 遘 in sense of 構. The rhyme indicates that 遘 (like 講 and other words in the series) had an alternative reading *kog*.

VII. 4. 燕. Chêng Hsüan reads 宴.

VII. 7. 誨; the Lu reading was 悔.

VII. 8. There is no evidence for the existence of 悱 except as an alternative form of 悲. The word here intended is 咈, 'the sound of spittle', applied to one who is bubbling over with things to say.

憤, 'welling up of emotion', is probably cognate to 噴, 'spurt up', 'spit'.

啟 properly means 'to instruct'; 启, 'to open'.

VII. 10. 馮 is for 淜.

VII. 13. For 爲 樂, some texts read 嬀 樂, 'music of the Kuei'. Kuei was the clan-name (*hsing*) of the T'ien Family who usurped the throne of Ch'i in 386 B.C. Those who follow this reading regard the Master's use of the term Kuei, meaning the rulers of Ch'i, as prophetic; for Confucius had already been dead for 100 years when the T'ien came into power.

VII. 16. The Lu version reads 亦 not 易; Cf. *Lieh Tzu*, II. 16: 二 者 亦 知, 'These two things are easy to know'; variant, 易. There is no evidence that the philosophical interpretation of the *Changes* was adopted by the Confucians till the second half of the 3rd century B.C. The Lu reading is adopted by most modern scholars.

VII. 27. 蓋 for 盍. Cf. IV. 6.

VII. 32. Read 忝 愼. For various ways of writing this binome, see T.T. 1407. There is no evidence that 莫 can mean 'perhaps'.

VII. 33. 正; Lu version 誠.

VII. 36. 蕩; Lu version 湯. Perhaps for 暢. 長 for 悵?

VII. 37. 子, variant 君子. 厲; variant 例 (homophones).

VIII. 12. 至 should be 志. Cf. *Mencius*, VI. 1. xx (Legge, p. 297), where 志 has a variant 至; also *Hsün-Tzu*, VIII, Par. 4, where 志堅 has been corrupted into 至堅, but *Han Shih Wai Chuan* (III, 3 recto) quotes correctly as 志. There are other examples of this confusion which despite the difference in finals (至 with d, 志 with g) must be a phonetic one. Neither the seal nor cursive forms could give rise to confusion.

Comparison with the *Mencius* passage shows that a pun on 鵠, 'target' (keep your mind on the target), and 穀, 'salary', is perhaps intended.

VIII. 20. 亂 in such contexts is a misunderstanding of 嗣, archaic for 司, 'to administrate'. The idea that 亂 could mean both to rebel and to rule led to a theory that 'the ancients' constantly said just the opposite of what they meant.

VIII. 21. There is a chance that the whole passage from 菲 to 洫 is intended as rhyme: 食 with 服, 神 with 冕, 室 with 洫. The last word now has a guttural ending; but 血 (dental ending) must surely be phonetic in 洫. Cf. the transition of 卹 from dental ending (as in the *Songs*) to guttural ending (as in T'ang times).

IX. 2. 絞, 'harsh', ought logically to be written 恔; but this was docketed for another meaning.

IX. 3. For 純 Chêng Hsüan read 紃, old form of 緇. It is easy to see how the unfamiliar 紃 got corrupted into the familiar 純, and Chêng's reading is probably right. The same confusion occurs several times in *Chou Li* and *Li Chi*.

IX. 5. What is supposed to have happened to Confucius in K'uang (as is clear from numerous anecdotes) is that he was surrounded 圍 'by a cordon several men deep' (*Chuang Tzu*, XVII. 3) in the hope of starving him out. Cf. *Shuo Yüan*, XVII: 'They surrounded K'ung Tzu's house.'

畏 does not make sense and it is perhaps a mistake (due to resemblance of sound) for 圍.

IX. 7. Some versions of Chêng Hsüan's text read 悾 悾.

IX. 9. 冕. Chêng Hsüan reads 弁. The Lu version had 絻.

IX. 9. 趨. The Pelliot MS. reads 趍, a reading also current in Sung times. Certainly a corruption.

IX. 12. 沽. The variant 賈 is the correct 'spelling'.

IX. 23. 從 (which does not make sense) is for 聳, 'rouse'; Chêng Hsüan glosses it by 悅.[1]

巽 與 = 選 舉 Cf. *Li Chi*, Li Yün chapter, 選 賢 與 能, 'choose out the superior and promote the competent', where *Ta Tai Li Chi* (Chu Yen[2] chapter, fol. 3) has 舉.

The traditional interpretation of 繹: 'unravel' and so 'carry out', is rather forced. Perhaps 繹 stands for its homophone 易, 'change'.

IX. 30. 偏 for 翩 ('swift flight'). Cf. *Songs*, 268. 1.

X. 1. 便 for 辯, which is the reading in the Life of Confucius (*Shih Chi*, ch. 47).

X. 2. 侃 is here for 衎 (cf. T.T. 1383). Hence the *Chi Chieh*: 和 樂 之 貌. Cf. *Lieh Tzu*, IV. 5, 與 言 衎 衎 然, 'conversed amiably with him'; and also the 侃 侃 of XI. 12, below, which makes better sense if taken in this way.

X. 2. 跔 踏. The idea is 'stepping warily'; cf. 踖 and 疎.

與 constantly interchanges with 豫, and 'relaxed' is the idea here. Cf. *The Book of Songs*, Vol. II, p. 14.

X. 3. 襜 (TIAM) does not involve the idea of 'straight', but merely of hanging down, 'flopping'. Cf. 耽 (TAM), 'pendulous ears'; also 耽, 衻 and 瞻 (TIAM) in the same sense.

1 Pelliot MS.
2 Some versions call the chapter 'Wang Yen'.

X. 3. 翼 如 is simply another way of saying 翼翼, a descriptive compound very common in old texts, with the meaning 'noble', 'majestic'. It has nothing to do with outstretched wings.

X. 4. 鞠躬 is an alliterative compound. The sense is � 弓, 'bent and bowed'.

遲 is for 緹, alternative form of 縰, 'slacken'.

X. 5. For 踖, cf. 蹙 and 縮, 'recoil'. For 循 we should, as Chu Chün-shêng has pointed out in his phonetic *Shuo Wên*, write 遁. 有, as often, has the sense of 或. 'As though he were dragging something' (the usual interpretation) would be 如有所曳, or the like.

X. 6, end. 吉 is a mistake for 告. The confusion is a very frequent one.

X. 10. 儺. The proper character is presumably 魌 which the *Yü P'ien* defines as meaning 'to startle and drive away pestilent spirits'. For 儺 (NA) the Lu version read 獻 (HIAN).

The same saying occurs in the Chiao T'ê Shêng (11th) chapter of the *Li Chi*, with 禓 for 儺, and the note 'for 禓 (SHIANG) some texts read 獻, others 儺'. 禓 is understood to mean 'spirits of those who died in battle', and subsequently turned into noxious spirits.

The meaning of 獻 and its relationship to 儺 are very uncertain. It may simply mean 'offering' and have originally signified the alternative method of dealing with evil influences, i.e. by propitiation instead of by violent expulsion.

X. 13. 拖. Also written 扡, 袘 and 扡.

X. 16. 容. Variant 客 ('guest').

X. 17. The Lu version read 內顧, omitting the negative. This is probably right.

XI. 13. For 仍 the Lu version read 仁.

XI. 17. 辟 for 躄.

Chêng Hsüan defines 唶 as 畔唶, a phrase which is

also written 阪 嗲 and seems to mean careless deportment.

XI. 18. 之 不 欲. 之 is the copulative = 是; cf. IV. 10 above.

XI. 21. 兼人 for 磏仁? Literally, 'is angular in his Goodness'. In *Han Shih Wai Chuan*, I. 11 磏仁 is the lowest of the four kinds of Goodness, and the examples given show that 'fanatical' is the nearest English equivalent of 磏.

Old texts constantly confuse 人 and 仁. Thus the Pelliot MS. from Tun-huang reads 仁 for 人 in both clauses of *Analects*, VIII. 6. All attempts to make sense of 兼人 reading it as it stands have been hopelessly forced. 兼 cannot mean 'wants to excel', nor can 兼人 mean 'does the work of two men', on the analogy of such phrases as 兼任, 'do two jobs at once'.

XI. 25. 1. For 吾以 Chêng Hsüan reads 吾己.

XI. 25. 3. For 居, 'living as private persons', cf. 居士, used in same sense as 處士.

XI. 25. 4. 率, variant 卒.

XI. 25. 5. 歸民 should surely be 民足?

XI. 25. 7. 鏗. The *Yü P'ien* reads 捐.
     撰. Cf. 譔, 'eloquent'.

For 歸 the Lu version and Chêng Hsüan read 饋. This is, I think, merely a phonetic borrowing. The two characters constantly interchange.

XII. 5. 4. 失 for 迭.

XII. 9. 孰與 seems to mean 'how?', rhetorical question implying a negative.

XII. 12. For 折 the Lu version read 制. (Approximately TIAT and TIAD.)

XII. 16. 成 seems to be for 稱. Cf. *Lieh Tzu*, V. 6, 成爲孝子, 'acclaimed as a filial son'.

XII. 21. 其 for 己. Cf. 彼其之子 (frequent in the *Songs*), also written 彼己之子.

XII. 22. 錯 for 措. Cf. II. 19.

XIII. 3. 蓋 for 盍 'How not?', i.e. 'he must'. Cf. IV. 6.

XIII. 8. 苟 in this sense is sometimes written 姑; a cognate but not identical word.

XIII. 11. 勝 for 竣, in *Shih Ching* written 懲. Cf. 凌 also written 勝 (*Shuo Wên*). Original TL initial?

XIII. 18. 躬. Chêng Hsüan read 弓. Despite the frequency with which this Kung is mentioned in early literature, Chu Hsi failed to recognize it as a proper name.

XIII. 20. 硜 硜 is a descriptive binome written phonetically and has nothing to do with 'pebbles' or 'grit'. Cf. 輕 in the senses 'cheap', 'unimportant', etc.

XIII. 21. 狷 (*Mencius*, 獧) is the 懁 'hasty' of *Shuo Wên*; cognate to the 儇 'nimble' of *Song* 265. 狂 and 狷 are complementary not contrasted terms. *Mencius*, in his version of this passage (VII. 2, XXXVII. 2) seems to interpret the word as though it were 涓, 'clean'.

XIII. 22. 之 羞. 之 is for 是. Cf. above, IV. 10. 羞 for 醜 (both words are of the SIOG type), according to Chu Chün-shêng, phonetic *Shuo Wên*.

XIII. 27. I suspect that 木 is a textual mistake for 朴.

XIII. 28. 偲, variant 愢. I suspect that it is cognate to 責, which is used to define it. The relationship according to Karlgren's reconstruction is *siag* and *tsĕk*.

XIV. 6. Ao's name is also written 澆 and 傲.

XIV. 16. 譎, talk 'crookedly'. 遹, 'act crookedly', would be more in place. The usual contrast is between 權 and 正.

XIV. 29. For 而 read 之 (Huang K'an text).

XIV. 31. 方; Chêng Hsüan read 謗.

XIV. 33. Cf. *Ta Tai Li Chi*, chapter *Tsêng Tzu Li Shih*: fol. 3. 君 子 不 先 人 以 惡, 不 疑 (ngjieg; for 逆 ngiag) 人 以 不 信. For 抑, cf. *Mencius*, II. 2, IV. 3.

XIV. 42. Read 斯 己 not 斯 巳.

XIV. 46. 夷 is for 跠.

XV. 5. Some texts read 參 然 for 參.

249

XV. 16. The Lu reading 惠 makes better sense. Cf. *Han Fei Tzu*, 9: 行小惠以取百姓.

XV. 29. *Ku-liang Chuan* (Hsi kung, 22nd year) adds 又之 after 改: 'If one points out a man's mistake and he does not change, to repeat it (i.e. rebuke him again) may, indeed, be called a mistake.'

XVI. 1. 4. 邦, variant 封.

XVI. 1. 10. 寡 and 貧 in lines 1 and 3 of the poem should be transposed. 安 at the end of line 4 should be 和. See Y. Ojima in *Shinagaku*, Vol. II, No. 10, p. 65. Omit 安無傾, which should come at the end of paragraph 11.

XVI. 4. 便辟, also written 盤辟, 'bending at the knee'. 便佞 for 諞佞; so quoted by *Shuo Wên*.

XVI. 6. For 躁 the Lu version read 傲, 'presumptuous'. The saying occurs in several Han texts, always with the reading 傲.

XVII. 1. 1. 歸 is a Lu version reading. The Ku version read 饋.

XVII. 4. 莞爾; for various ways of writing this descriptive, see T.T. 628.

XVII. 8. 蔽 for 弊.

XVII. 8. 2. 居 appears to be an exclamatory particle, demanding attention. Sometimes written 姬. Cf. *Lieh Tzu*, II. 3.

XVII. 12. 窾 means a gap, and does not mean to climb. Cf. *Mencius*, VII, 2; XXXI, 2. 窾 may be merely a phonetic borrowing for 躋, 'climb', 'cross'. See T.T. 357.

XVII. 16. 廉 (LIAM); Lu version 貶 (PIAM). Cf. 律 (LIUET) and 筆 (PIET). The reasons that admit these two words into the same phonetic series are clearly the same as those that give rise to LIAM, variant PIAM. What those reasons are is a matter for phonologists to decide.

XVII. 19. 3. The Lu version read 夫 for 天, apparently in both cases. Possibly the second 天 should be 夫.

XVII. 24. 窒. This is the word that is also written 蛭, 懫 ānd 愼. The Lu version read 室.

For 微 Chêng Hsüan read 絞; the meaning intended is clearly 狡.

XVIII. 4. For 歸 Chêng Hsüan read 饋.

XVIII. 5. The Lu version read 期 斯 巳 矣, and omitted 而after 殆: 'The only thing to do is to choose one's time.'

XVIII. 6. 沼 沼 is an exception to the general rule that descriptive binomes are written phonetically not ideogrammatically in early texts. It is, therefore, not surprising to find that Chêng Hsüan read 悠 悠.

XVIII. 8. *Shih Chi*, 47, reads 行 中 清. For 廢 Chêng Hsüan read 發.

XVIII. 10. 施 for 弛.

XIX. 10. Chêng Hsüan says that 厲 (LIAD) is a phonetic substitute for (? dialectical for) 賴 (LAD); 'throws the burden upon'. This is certainly right; 'oppresses' is too general.

XIX. 12. 孰 for 熟, as constantly; for example, repeatedly in *Li Chi, Hsün Tzu, Chuang Tzu*. If we take it in the sense of 'which', we have to understand some such words as 'one must take into consideration' before the 'which'. Neither the early commentators nor Chu Hsi make any attempt to construe the sentence.

誣 does not fit the context. There is a variant 憮.

XX. 1. 蔽. 斃 would make better sense; but cf. *Mo Tzu*, P'ien, XVI: 有 善 不 敢 蔽, 'The good I dare not keep in obscurity.'

周 親; cf. *Shih Tzu* 尸子 (fragments): 文王曰苟 有 仁 人, 何 必 周 親, 'Wên Wang said, "If I can find good men, I will not confine my appointments to my own Chou kinsmen."' It is certain that 'Chou' is here to be taken in this sense.

XX. 2. 戒 for 誡.

視for 底, synonymous with 致. Cf. 眡 which is the

251

alternative form (*Shuo Wên*) of 視. 'Look at' does not make sense.

客 rhymes with 人, and the passage runs better if we omit 也.

For 出納 Huang K'an (6th century) and Lu Tê-ming (7th century) both read 出內. The reading 納 seems to have begun in Sung times.

INDEX

Ai, duke of Lu 84, 91, 107, 156, 175
An-yang 13
Ao 170
Apastamba Dharma Sūtra 52

Chan Kuo Ts'ê 105, 207
Chang Yü 17
Changes, the Book of 41–2, 118, 176, 237, 244
Chao, duke of Lu 121, 210, 234
Chavannes, E. 68
Ch'ang-chü 207
Ch'ao, prince of Sung 111
Chêng Hsüan 17, 63, 81, 124, 130, 144, 225, 231, 234, 241, 242, 244, 245, 246, 248, 249, 251, 262
Ch'ên Hêng 175
Ch'ên Wên-tzu 22, 104
Ch'êng Hao 65, 68, 104, 281
Ch'êng I 65
Chi Huan-tzu 193, 207
Chi K'ang-tzu 9, 84, 109, 141, 145, 158, 174, 178, 193, 207
Chi Tzu (Marquis of Chi) 23, 206
Chi Tzu-ch'êng 155
Chi Tzu-jan 149
Chi Wên Tzu 104
Chieh-ni 207, 208
Chieh Yü 207
Chien, duke of Ch'i 175
Chih, Chief Musician 127, 210
Ching, duke of Ch'i 157, 196, 206
Ching, grandee of Wei 163
Ching I Shu Wen 68
Chiu, prince of Ch'i 173, 174
Ch'i version 17
Ch'i-tiao K'ai 100
Ch'ih Jên 191

Chou, duke of 11, 40–1, 115, 127, 147, 210
Chou Jên 191
Chou Li 69, 90, 203, 223, 224, 233, 234, 237
Chou Li Chêng I 69
Chou, the tyrant 206, 216
Chou-shêng Lieh 63
Chu Chün-shêng 242, 247, 249
Chu Hsi 39, 64–6, 140, 148, 157, 225, 236, 251
Chu Tzu Ch'üan Shu 65, 225
Chuang Tzu 71
Chuang Tzu 105, 117, 131, 135, 136, 198, 207, 225, 243, 245, 251
Chuang Tzu of P'ien 172
Chung Ni, see Confucius
Chung Shan Fu 230
Chun-shu Yü 175
Chung-yung, see *Doctrine of the Mean*
Ch'ü Po Yü 176, 183
Confucius 7, and passim
Conrady, August 170
Couvreur, S. 68

De Groot, J. J. 232
Dirges 55, 122, 218
Doctrine of the Mean 17, 113, 136

Êrh Ya 242, 243
Erkes, Eduard 170

Fa Yen 135
Fa Yü 135
Fan Ch'ih 47, 81, 112, 159, 160, 162, 166, 236
Fang Chi 16
fêng ('Phoenix') 41

253

Filial Piety, Canon of (*Hsiao Ching*) 32
Frazer, Sir James 51, 53, 232
Fu Tzu 226
Fu Tzu–chien 99

Genkyo, Fukube 64
Granet, Marcel 70, 235
Great Learning, The 17, 94, 157

Haloun, Gustav 122, 226
Han Ch'iu I 235
Han Fei Tzu 30, 165, 184, 207, 250
Han Shih Wai Chuan 17, 114, 157,
183, 236, 245, 248, 259
Ho Ting-Shêng 46
Holy Ground, the (*Shê*) 91, 191,
224–5, 234
Hou Chi 12, 170, 235
Hou Han Shu 125, 203
Hsi Tx'u 156
Hsia dynasty 11, 88
Hsin-hsü 172, 207
Hsin-lun 18
Hsing P'ing 236
Hsü Hsing 236
Hsüan Chü 135
Hsüng Tzu (Confucian philosopher
of the 3rd century BC) 16, 17
Hsün Tzu 89, 118, 134, 147, 168,
171, 176, 188, 194, 201, 242,
245, 251
Hu Shi 119
Hu Shih Wên Ts'un 119
Huai–nan Tzu 51
Huai–nan Tzu 105, 165
Huan, duke of Ch'I 43, 157, 171,
173, 174, 237
Huan T'an 18
Huan T'ui 35, 154
Huang Ch'ing Ching Chieh
(abbreviation H.C.C.C.) 13, 68
Huang Ch'ing Ching Chieh Hsü Pien
(abbreviation H.P.) 68, 225
Huang K'an 64, 147, 211, 225, 236,
241, 249, 252

I Chou Shu 97, 100, 155, 174
I Li 90, 234
I Wên Lei Chü 233
I Yin 160

Jan Ch'iu 9, 14, 22, 47, 87, 100,
107, 109, 110, 117, 144, 146,
147, 149, 150, 152, 163, 164,
172, 191
Jan Kêng 109, 144
Jan Shu 172
Jan Yung 22, 99, 107, 108, 144, 153,
161
Johnston, Sir Reginald 31
Ju Pei 203
Jung (ritual attitude) 48–9

Kao Ch'ai 148, 150
Kao Tsung 180
Kao Yao 11–12, 160, 169
Karlgren, B. 78, 243, 249
Knight, see *Shih*
Knights, Leader of, see *Shih-shih*
Ku Chieh-kang 8
Ku Wên version ('Ku version') 18,
118, 240, 250
Ku-liang Chuan 168, 188, 228, 250
Kuan Chung, see Kuan Tzu
Kuan Tzu 22, 91, 92, 157, 171, 173,
174
Kuan Tzu 121, 205, 238
K'ung Wên Tzu 102, 175
K'ung Yeh Ch'ang 99
Kung-hsi Hua 22, 100, 107, 108,
122, 149, 150, 151, 152
Kung-ming Chia 172
Kung-po Liao 178
Kung-shan Fu–jao 199
Kung-shu Wên-tzu 172, 174
Kung-sun Ch'ao 216
Kung-yung Chuan 77
K'ung An-kuo 63, 140, 213
K'ung-tzu Chia Yü 88, 226
Kuo Yü 15, 33, 94, 157, 179, 237,
240, 242

Lao 9, 131
Lao Tzu 39
Legge, James 14, 17, 34, 39, 45, 68, 231
Li Chi 16, 19, 60, 89, 92, 116, 125, 140, 174, 197, 238, 246, 247
Li I Chih, see Hou Han Shu
Li Shih 243
Lieh Tzu 157, 198, 207, 225, 243, 244, 246, 248, 250
Lies, polite 37
Lin Fang 86
Ling, duke of Wei 113, 117, 174, 182
Liu Pao-nan 115, 144, 205, 237, 243
Liu T'ai-kung 90
Liu-hsia Hui 11, 185, 206, 209, 210
Lods, A. 125
Lu Te-ming 209, 211, 213, 235, 252
Lu version 17, 113, 221, 244, 245, 247, 248, 250, 251
Lun Hêng 17, 189, 235
Lun Yü 14
Lun Yü Chi Chieh 63, 225, 233, 246
Lun Yü Chi Chu 64
Lun Yü Tsa Chieh 66
Lü Pu-wei 16
Lü Shih Ch'un Ch'iu 32, 136, 143, 149, 165

Ma Jung 63
Magic Square 41–2
Mārkandeya Purāna 52
Maspero, Henri 10, 71, 228
Mémoires Historiques 68
Mencius 39, 71
Mencius 9, 11, 16, 30, 44, 81, 82, 94, 110, 113, 122, 128, 131, 134, 142, 144, 148, 151, 153, 158, 167, 168, 178, 179, 180, 189, 195, 197, 198, 202, 204, 221, 226, 236, 238, 241, 243, 245, 249, 250
Mêng Chih-fan 110
Mêng Ching Tzu 125

Mêng Chuang Tzu 215
Mêng Hsien Tzu 215
Mêng I Tzu 81, 99, 107
Mêng Kung Ch'o 172
Mêng Wu Po 81, 100, 125
Mien, music-master 190
Min Tzu-ch'ien 109, 144, 146, 147, 233, 234
Ming 35
Ming T'ang, the 42
Mo Tzu 32, 71, 130, 219, 231, 251
Mo Tzu 115, 165, 236, 240

Nan Jung 99, 145
Nan-kung Kuo 99, 170
Nan-tzu 113
Ning Wu Tzu 104
No (expulsion rite) 140–1, 233
Numbers 13, 41

Oracle bones 85

Pao Hsien 63, 81, 187
Pelliot, Paul 63
Pelliot MS. 124, 130
P'êng Tsu 10, 115
Pi Hsi 200
Pi Kan 23, 206
P'i Ch'ên 170
P'ing, duke of Chin 61
Po I 22, 105, 118, 196, 209
Po Niu 35
Po Yü (Li), son of Confucius 145, 196, 201

Quietists 22, 24, 39

River Chart, the 41

Seligman, C. G. 239
Shang Ti 36
Shao ('succession dance') 61, 92, 117, 184
Shao Hu 173
Shao K'ang 170

Shao–lien 209
Shê, 'duke' of 119, 165
Shên Ch'êng 101
Shen Chu-liang 119
Shêng 11, 22, 227
Shih (Knight) 8
Shih Chi 19, 100, 225, 226, 246, 251
Shih Ching, see *Songs*
Shih Shu 170
Shih Txu 243, 251
Shih Wên 18
Shih-shih ('leader of the knights') 9,
    145, 206, 216
Shiratori, Professor 234
Shu Ching ('Book of History') 15,
    18, 45 seq., 75, 84, 179, 191, 200,
    219, 220, 240, 243
Shu Ch'i 23, 105, 118, 196, 209
Shu-sun Wu-shu 217
Shun 12, 114, 128, 160, 180, 182,
    189, 219
Shuo Wên 242, 247, 249, 250, 251
Shuo Yüan 113, 226, 233
Songs, the Book of 12, 21, 27, 33,
    36, 40, 45, 76, 79, 80, 83, 86,
    87, 91, 116, 120, 125, 126, 127,
    136, 137, 145, 156, 160, 162,
    179, 184, 197, 201, 229, 231,
    233, 235, 236, 243, 245, 246,
    248, 249
Soothill, E. 39, 47, 68
Ssu-ma Ch'ien, see *Shih Chi*
Ssu-ma Niu 154
Stein, Sir Aurel 63
Succession Dance, see *Shao*
Sun I-jang 69
Sun Yat-sen 68
Sung, State of 13

Ta Tai Li Chi 42, 105, 238, 249
Ta Hsüeh, see *Great Learning*
T'ai, Mount 87
T'ai P'ing Yü Lan 122
T'ai Po 124, 209, 230
Tan, king of Chou 124

T'an-t'ai Mieh-ming 110
T'ang 13, 42, 219
Tao Tê Ching 30, 83, 178
T'ien Wên 170
Ting, duke of Lu 90, 164, 165
T'o, priest 111, 175
Transliteration 69
Tsai Yü 91, 101, 113, 144, 203, 204
Tsang Wên Chung 103, 172, 185
Tsang Wu Chung 172, 173
Tsêng Hsi 150, 151
Tsêng Tzu (Master Tsêng) 14, 60,
    75, 77, 81, 97, 124–6, 148, 160,
    176, 215, 216
Tso Ch'iu Ming 105
Tso Chuan 14, 15, 32, 34, 89, 100,
    119, 131, 146, 153, 156, 170,
    171, 172, 173, 175, 182, 185,
    191, 204, 211, 227, 232, 236, 238
Tso-wang 108
Ts'ui Tzu 103
Tu Shu Tsa Chih 68
Tun-huang 18
Twins 211
Tzu Ssu Txu 16
Tzu-chang 14, 83, 85, 103, 147,
    148, 155, 156, 157, 158, 179,
    183, 199, 212, 220, 221
Tzu-ch'an 102, 171
Tzu-ch'in 77, 196, 217
Tzu-fu Ching-po 178, 217
Tzu-hsi 171
Tzu-hsia 14, 76, 81, 87, 110, 144,
    147, 150, 154, 160, 212, 213,
    214, 215
Tzu-kung 14, 79, 82, 90, 99, 101,
    102, 109, 117, 118, 131, 133,
    144, 146, 147, 155, 160, 166,
    167, 174, 177, 182, 184, 186,
    203, 205, 216, 217
Tzu-lu 9, 13–14, 15, 22, 26, 55, 83,
    100, 102, 106, 109, 113, 116,
    122, 132, 136, 143, 144, 146,
    147, 148, 149, 150, 151, 157,
    161, 168, 172, 175, 178, 179,

180, 182, 191, 199, 200, 204,
207–9
Tzu-sang Po-tzu 107
Tzu-wên 22, 102
Tzu-yu 14, 81, 98, 110, 144, 199,
214, 215
Tzu-yü of Chêng 171
Tz'u T'ung (abbreviation T.T.) 142,
241, 244, 250

Umehara, S. 234

Wang Nien-sun 68, 236, 237
Wang Su 63, 236
Wang Yin-chih 68
Wang-sun Chia 89, 175
Way and Its Power, The 11, 15, 21,
26, 36, 49, 98, 206
Wei Tzu (Marquis of Wei) 23, 206
Wei-shêng Kao 105
Wei-shêng Mou 177
Wên, duke of Chin 43, 173, 237
Wên, king of Chou 40, 131, 163,
216
Wilcox, Ella Wheeler 70
Wilhelm, Richard 42, 69

Wu, king of Chou 40, 128, 216,
220, 232
Wu Mêng Tzu 121
Wu-ma Ch'i 121

Yang Fu 216
Yang Huo 18, 120, 193, 198, 232
Yao 12, 114, 180, 189, 219
Yao Sui 229
Yen Hui 9, 13, 35, 82, 101, 106,
107, 108, 109, 110, 116, 126,
132, 134, 135, 144, 145, 146,
149, 153, 184
Yen Tzu (Ch'i statesman) 19, 103
Yen Yu, see Tzu-yu
Yi, the Archer 170
Yu, Master 14, 78, 156
Yu Tso 66, 67
Yu Chung 209
Yü, the Great 11, 128, 129, 170, 219
Yü P'ien 247, 248
Yü, the Recorder 183
Yü Yüeh 68, 225, 236
Yüan Ssu 108, 169
Yüan Yüan 13, 68

Zen 39, 65

ABOUT THE TRANSLATOR

ARTHUR WALEY (1889–1966) established his reputation both as a poet and a translator with *A hundred and seventy Chinese poems* (1918). His many fine translations in both prose and verse (which include *The Tale of Genji* 1925–33) introduced a wide public to Chinese and Japanese literature, and remain as highly regarded in our own day as when they were first published.

ABOUT THE INTRODUCER

SARAH ALLAN formerly taught at the University of London. She is now the Burlington Northern Foundation Professor of Chinese Studies at Dartmouth College. Her books include *The Heir and the Sage: Dynastic Legend in Early China, The Shape of the Turtle: Myth, Art and Cosmos in Early China* and *The Way of Water and Sprouts of Virtue.* She is currently writing a book on time and space in Chinese and Western art.

CHINUA ACHEBE
Things Fall Apart

AESCHYLUS
The Oresteia

THE ARABIAN NIGHTS
(2 vols, tr. Husain Haddawy)

AUGUSTINE
The Confessions

JANE AUSTEN
Emma
Mansfield Park
Northanger Abbey
Persuasion
Pride and Prejudice
Sanditon and Other Stories
Sense and Sensibility

HONORÉ DE BALZAC
Cousin Bette
Eugénie Grandet
Old Goriot

SIMONE DE BEAUVOIR
The Second Sex

SAMUEL BECKETT
Molloy, Malone Dies,
The Unnamable
(US only)

SAUL BELLOW
The Adventures of Augie March

HECTOR BERLIOZ
The Memoirs of Hector Berlioz

WILLIAM BLAKE
Poems and Prophecies

JORGE LUIS BORGES
Ficciones

JAMES BOSWELL
The Life of Samuel Johnson
The Journal of a Tour to
the Hebrides

CHARLOTTE BRONTË
Jane Eyre
Villette

EMILY BRONTË
Wuthering Heights

MIKHAIL BULGAKOV
The Master and Margarita

SAMUEL BUTLER
The Way of all Flesh

JAMES M. CAIN
The Postman Always Rings Twice
Double Indemnity
Mildred Pierce
Selected Stories
(1 vol. US only)

ITALO CALVINO
If on a winter's night a traveler

ALBERT CAMUS
The Outsider (UK)
The Stranger (US)
The Plague, The Fall,
Exile and the Kingdom,
and Selected Essays
(in 1 vol.)

WILLA CATHER
Death Comes for the Archbishop
My Ántonia
(US only)

MIGUEL DE CERVANTES
Don Quixote

RAYMOND CHANDLER
The novels (2 vols)
Collected Stories

GEOFFREY CHAUCER
Canterbury Tales

ANTON CHEKHOV
The Complete Short Novels
My Life and Other Stories
The Steppe and Other Stories

KATE CHOPIN
The Awakening

CARL VON CLAUSEWITZ
On War

S. T. COLERIDGE
Poems

WILKIE COLLINS
The Moonstone
The Woman in White

CONFUCIUS
The Analects

JOSEPH CONRAD
Heart of Darkness
Lord Jim
Nostromo
The Secret Agent
Typhoon and Other Stories
Under Western Eyes
Victory

THOMAS CRANMER
The Book of Common Prayer
(UK only)

DANTE ALIGHIERI
The Divine Comedy

CHARLES DARWIN
The Origin of Species
The Voyage of the Beagle
(in 1 vol.)

DANIEL DEFOE
Moll Flanders
Robinson Crusoe

CHARLES DICKENS
Bleak House
David Copperfield
Dombey and Son
Great Expectations
Hard Times
Little Dorrit
Martin Chuzzlewit
The Mystery of Edwin Drood
Nicholas Nickleby
The Old Curiosity Shop
Oliver Twist
Our Mutual Friend
The Pickwick Papers
A Tale of Two Cities

DENIS DIDEROT
Memoirs of a Nun

JOHN DONNE
The Complete English Poems

FYODOR DOSTOEVSKY
The Adolescent
The Brothers Karamazov
Crime and Punishment
Demons
The Idiot
Notes from Underground

W. E. B. DU BOIS
The Souls of Black Folk
(US only)

GEORGE ELIOT
Adam Bede
Daniel Deronda
Middlemarch
The Mill on the Floss
Silas Marner

WILLIAM FAULKNER
The Sound and the Fury
(UK only)

HENRY FIELDING
Joseph Andrews and Shamela
(UK only)
Tom Jones

F. SCOTT FITZGERALD
The Great Gatsby
This Side of Paradise
(UK only)

PENELOPE FITZGERALD
The Bookshop
The Gate of Angels
The Blue Flower
(in 1 vol.)
Offshore
Human Voices
The Beginning of Spring
(in 1 vol.)

GUSTAVE FLAUBERT
Madame Bovary

FORD MADOX FORD
The Good Soldier
Parade's End

E. M. FORSTER
Howards End
A Passage to India

ELIZABETH GASKELL
Mary Barton

EDWARD GIBBON
The Decline and Fall of the
Roman Empire
Vols 1 to 3: The Western Empire
Vols 4 to 6: The Eastern Empire

J. W. VON GOETHE
Selected Works

NIKOLAI GOGOL
Dead Souls

IVAN GONCHAROV
Oblomov

GÜNTER GRASS
The Tin Drum

GRAHAM GREENE
Brighton Rock
The Human Factor

DASHIELL HAMMETT
The Maltese Falcon
The Thin Man
Red Harvest
(in 1 vol.)

THOMAS HARDY
Far From the Madding Crowd
Jude the Obscure
The Mayor of Casterbridge
The Return of the Native
Tess of the d'Urbervilles
The Woodlanders

JAROSLAV HAŠEK
The Good Soldier Švejk

NATHANIEL HAWTHORNE
The Scarlet Letter

JOSEPH HELLER
Catch-22

ERNEST HEMINGWAY
A Farewell to Arms
The Collected Stories
(UK only)

GEORGE HERBERT
The Complete English Works

HERODOTUS
The Histories

PATRICIA HIGHSMITH
The Talented Mr. Ripley
Ripley Under Ground
Ripley's Game
(in 1 vol.)

HINDU SCRIPTURES
(tr. R. C. Zaehner)

JAMES HOGG
Confessions of a Justified Sinner

HOMER
The Iliad
The Odyssey

VICTOR HUGO
Les Misérables

HENRY JAMES
The Awkward Age
The Bostonians
The Golden Bowl
The Portrait of a Lady
The Princess Casamassima
The Wings of the Dove
Collected Stories (2 vols)

SAMUEL JOHNSON
A Journey to the Western
Islands of Scotland

JAMES JOYCE
Dubliners
A Portrait of the Artist as
a Young Man
Ulysses

FRANZ KAFKA
Collected Stories
The Castle
The Trial

JOHN KEATS
The Poems

SØREN KIERKEGAARD
Fear and Trembling and
The Book on Adler

RUDYARD KIPLING
Collected Stories
Kim

THE KORAN
(tr. Marmaduke Pickthall)

CHODERLOS DE LACLOS
Les Liaisons dangereuses

GIUSEPPE TOMASI DI
LAMPEDUSA
The Leopard

WILLIAM LANGLAND
Piers Plowman
with (anon.) Sir Gawain and the
Green Knight, Pearl, Sir Orfeo
(UK only)

D. H. LAWRENCE
Collected Stories
The Rainbow
Sons and Lovers
Women in Love

MIKHAIL LERMONTOV
A Hero of Our Time

PRIMO LEVI
If This is a Man and The Truce
(UK only)
The Periodic Table

THE MABINOGION

NICCOLÒ MACHIAVELLI
The Prince

NAGUIB MAHFOUZ
The Cairo Trilogy

THOMAS MANN
Buddenbrooks
Collected Stories (UK only)
Death in Venice and Other Stories
(US only)
Doctor Faustus

KATHERINE MANSFIELD
The Garden Party and Other
Stories

MARCUS AURELIUS
Meditations

GABRIEL GARCÍA MÁRQUEZ
The General in His Labyrinth
Love in the Time of Cholera
One Hundred Years of Solitude

ANDREW MARVELL
The Complete Poems

W. SOMERSET MAUGHAM
Collected Stories

CORMAC McCARTHY
The Border Trilogy (US only)

HERMAN MELVILLE
The Complete Shorter Fiction
Moby-Dick

JOHN STUART MILL
On Liberty and Utilitarianism

JOHN MILTON
The Complete English Poems

YUKIO MISHIMA
The Temple of the
Golden Pavilion

MARY WORTLEY MONTAGU
Letters

MICHEL DE MONTAIGNE
The Complete Works

THOMAS MORE
Utopia

TONI MORRISON
Song of Solomon

MURASAKI SHIKIBU
The Tale of Genji

VLADIMIR NABOKOV
Lolita
Pale Fire
Pnin
Speak, Memory

V. S. NAIPAUL
A House for Mr Biswas

THE NEW TESTAMENT
(King James Version)

THE OLD TESTAMENT
(King James Version)

GEORGE ORWELL
Animal Farm
Nineteen Eighty-Four
Essays

THOMAS PAINE
Rights of Man
and Common Sense

BORIS PASTERNAK
Doctor Zhivago

SYLVIA PLATH
The Bell Jar (US only)

PLATO
The Republic
Symposium and Phaedrus

EDGAR ALLAN POE
The Complete Stories

MARCEL PROUST
In Search of Lost Time
(4 vols, UK only)

ALEXANDER PUSHKIN
The Collected Stories

FRANÇOIS RABELAIS
Gargantua and Pantagruel

JOSEPH ROTH
The Radetzky March

JEAN-JACQUES
ROUSSEAU
Confessions
The Social Contract and
the Discourses

SALMAN RUSHDIE
Midnight's Children

WALTER SCOTT
Rob Roy

WILLIAM SHAKESPEARE
Comedies Vols 1 and 2
Histories Vols 1 and 2
Romances
Sonnets and Narrative Poems
Tragedies Vols 1 and 2

MARY SHELLEY
Frankenstein

ADAM SMITH
The Wealth of Nations

ALEXANDER SOLZHENITSYN
One Day in the Life of
Ivan Denisovich

SOPHOCLES
The Theban Plays

MURIEL SPARK
The Prime of Miss Jean Brodie,
The Girls of Slender Means, The
Driver's Seat, The Only Problem
(1 vol.)

CHRISTINA STEAD
The Man Who Loved Children

JOHN STEINBECK
The Grapes of Wrath

STENDHAL
The Charterhouse of Parma
Scarlet and Black

LAURENCE STERNE
Tristram Shandy

ROBERT LOUIS STEVENSON
The Master of Ballantrae and
Weir of Hermiston
Dr Jekyll and Mr Hyde
and Other Stories

HARRIET BEECHER STOWE
Uncle Tom's Cabin

ITALO SVEVO
Zeno's Conscience

JONATHAN SWIFT
Gulliver's Travels

JUNICHIRŌ TANIZAKI
The Makioka Sisters

W. M. THACKERAY
Vanity Fair

HENRY DAVID THOREAU
Walden

ALEXIS DE TOCQUEVILLE
Democracy in America

LEO TOLSTOY
Collected Shorter Fiction (2 vols)
Anna Karenina
Childhood, Boyhood and Youth
The Cossacks
War and Peace

ANTHONY TROLLOPE
Barchester Towers
Can You Forgive Her?
Doctor Thorne
The Eustace Diamonds
Framley Parsonage
The Last Chronicle of Barset
Phineas Finn
The Small House at Allington
The Warden

IVAN TURGENEV
Fathers and Children
First Love and Other Stories
A Sportsman's Notebook

MARK TWAIN
Tom Sawyer
and Huckleberry Finn

JOHN UPDIKE
The Complete Henry Bech
(US only)
Rabbit Angstrom

GIORGIO VASARI
Lives of the Painters, Sculptors
and Architects (2 vols)

VIRGIL
The Aeneid

VOLTAIRE
Candide and Other Stories

EVELYN WAUGH
The Complete Short Stories
Black Mischief, Scoop, The Loved
One, The Ordeal of Gilbert
Pinfold (in 1 vol.)
Brideshead Revisited
Decline and Fall (US)
Decline and Fall, Vile Bodies,
Put Out More Flags (UK)
A Handful of Dust
The Sword of Honour Trilogy
Waugh Abroad: Collected Travel
Writing

EDITH WHARTON
The Age of Innocence
The Custom of the Country
The House of Mirth
The Reef

OSCAR WILDE
Plays, Prose Writings and Poems

MARY WOLLSTONECRAFT
A Vindication of the Rights of
Woman

VIRGINIA WOOLF
To the Lighthouse
Mrs Dalloway

WILLIAM WORDSWORTH
Selected Poems (UK only)

W. B. YEATS
The Poems (UK only)

ÉMILE ZOLA
Germinal

This book is set in BEMBO which was cut
by the punch-cutter Francesco Griffo
for the Venetian printer-publisher
Aldus Manutius in early 1495
and first used in a pamphlet
by a young scholar
named Pietro
Bembo.